Fast Track to FCE

PEARSON
Longman

Alan Stanton
Mary Stephens

Coursebook

Contents map

1 Entertainment

Lead-in

Look at the stills from two different films opposite and discuss these questions. Use expressions from the box.

1 What kind of films do you think they are?
2 Have you seen either of them? Which would you prefer to see? Why?
3 What types of film do you like best? What kinds don't you like?
4 Who is your favourite actor? Describe a film he/she has appeared in.

> thriller / horror film / romantic comedy / documentary / musical
> to look (rather/very) exciting / violent / frightening
> to find (love stories) boring
> to prefer films with a good story/lots of special effects
> to be a (great) fan of (science fiction movies)
> to play the lead role / hero / heroine / villain in ...
> to be about/tell the story of ... / to be set in ...

Reading 1: *multiple matching*

exam file

> In **Paper 1**, **Part 1**, you match headings to parts of a text. Each heading summarises the main point(s) of one paragraph.

1 Look at the title of the text opposite and read the instructions for the exam task. Discuss these questions.

1 What kind of text are you going to read?
2 What do you know about the subject?
3 Think of words that you may come across in the text. Make a list.

2 Skim the text once quite quickly to get a general understanding. Are these statements true or false?

Paragraph:

0 What a film is about is not important.
1 To make a film in Britain, the first thing you need is a good script.
2 A film-maker has to be a good organiser.
3 Most film-makers work for charities.
4 Film-makers can get money from a lot of different organisations.
5 Filming can start as soon as the film-maker has got the money.
6 The cinema audience does not see many of the most important people involved in a film.

> ▶▶ *exam tip!*
> Remember, the first, last or middle sentence of a paragraph usually tells you what it's about.

3 1 Read the first paragraph (Question 0) more carefully. Then look at the example answer (H).

1 Which words in the paragraph express the same idea as the heading H? Underline them.
2 Does the heading use the same words as the text or different ones?

2 Read through the other headings. Then read the next paragraph of the text (Question 1). The key phrase has been underlined.

Which heading summarises the main point of the paragraph? Look for words with a similar meaning.

3 Continue in the same way with the remaining paragraphs. Underline key words. Match these to the heading that expresses the same idea. Use your answers in Exercise 2 to help you.

Over to you

4 Find and underline all the jobs related to film-making which are mentioned in the article.

1 Would any of the jobs appeal to you? Why/Why not?
2 Which of the following do you think would be most important for each job: talent, training, experience?

You are going to read an article about how a film is made. Choose the most suitable heading from the list A–H for each part (1–6) of the article. There is one extra heading that you do not need to use. There is an example at the beginning (0).

A Building a team
B Finding the money
C Achieving success
D It's a business
E The people behind the scenes
F Preparing to film
G The first step
H The message of the film

Making a film

How are films made and where does the money come from? Here's what happens.

| 0 | H |

Whether it is a documentary or a work of fiction, the film-maker must have a clear idea of what the film is trying to say and who the audience might be. In the case of short films by first-time directors, this is almost inevitably a television audience. Film-making is an extremely expensive business. Even a short film of 10–15 minutes can cost £35,000–£80,000 to make. A 'low-budget' feature-length film can cost more than £0.5 million. Therefore, the film-maker must be sure that the theme of the film will attract an audience.

| 1 | |

Unlike the Hollywood system, where a studio or producer commissions the scriptwriter, low-budget <u>films in Britain usually begin with a script</u>, which is like a play written specially for the cinema. Various organisations look at this and consider whether to provide funding. Screenplay writing is an art and there are courses all over Britain for people who want to learn to do it.

| 2 | |

Film-making is a co-operative process that often involves hundreds of people. Unlike a novel or a painting, one person cannot really take the credit for a finished film, although the director and leading actors often get most of the media attention. A film-maker has to show that he or she is able to put together a crew of technicians and actors and find sets and locations.

| 3 | |

Even on a low-budget film, a lot of money is involved and directors usually form their own company. Some people choose to set themselves up as a charity if they are catering for a specialist audience or allowing the local community access to their equipment. The advantage is that they don't have to pay tax to the government.

| 4 | |

There are several organisations which provide financial support for young directors. The British Film Institute gives funding of up to £35, 000 for short films by first-time directors. The *BBC* and *Channel 4* each have over £400,000 to spend on encouraging independent film-making.

The National Lottery also provides finance to cover up to 50% of the total cost and there are various specialist funds that can help financially.

| 5 | |

After the money has been raised, filming does not begin immediately: the film-maker plans the shoot down to the last detail. Storyboards, which are a series of drawings, map out the whole film, scene by scene, as it comes in the story. The scenery has to be built, technicians have to be hired, and actors found for the different roles.

| 6 | |

Many people that you do not see in the film play a vital role. The director, camera operator and sound recordist are obviously important. But so is the continuity person who keeps a detailed note of each scene and checks the clothes and hairstyles of the actors so they are consistent throughout the film. It is another person's job to mark the beginning of each shot by writing the number on a board and snapping it shut as filming begins. Without the unseen experts, no film could reach the screen!

BBC, Channel 4: British television channels

Grammar: *present and future* ▶ p.177–8

grammar file 4

A Present simple
1 I **don't** often **go** to the cinema.
2 I normally **watch** movies on video or satellite.
3 **Do** you **like** horror films?

B Present continuous
1 Please don't disturb me. **I'm watching** TV.
2 They**'re showing** Hitchcock's movies on TV this month.

C always
1 He **always watches** the news on TV. (= every day)
2 He**'s always borrowing** my CDs. (= too often)

D State verbs (*have, know, think,* etc.)
1 They **have** a beautiful home. (= own)
2 They **are having** dinner right now. (= are eating)

grammar file 5

A Predictions: *will/going to*
1 She **will** probably **get** an Oscar for her excellent performance. (= I believe this.)
2 She**'s going to get** an Oscar – the reviews are fantastic. (= I'm sure: I have information now.)

B Plans; arrangements; fixed events/timetables
1 We**'re going to see** that new movie tonight.
2 We**'re meeting** our friends outside the cinema.
3 The film **starts** at eight o'clock.

C Decisions
1 There's a new film on. **I'll phone** for tickets! (= I decided this minute.)
2 **I'm going to phone** for tickets later today. (= I decided earlier.)

D Offers, requests, promises: *will*
1 **I'll get** the tickets, shall I?
2 Don't worry! I **won't be** late.

1 Read the article below and put the verbs in brackets into the present simple or continuous form.

This is a busy week for teenage Hollywood star, Leo Fisher. He's over here to promote his latest film, so he (1) .... (give) lots of interviews and (2) .... (appear) on chat shows.

Although he (3) .... (only/stay) for a few days, he (4) .... (have) a great time! Leo told Star Magazine that he (5) .... (usually/not have) the chance to relax when he's in Hollywood. That's why he (6) .... (make) the most of his time here.

Now he's a millionaire, Leo (7) .... (think) of buying a private plane. But he (8) .... (not/think) his parents will approve. 'They (9) .... (always/complain) about my dangerous hobbies,' he told us.

Leo (10) .... (currently/consider) new film offers. He (11) .... (look at) a script for a thriller just now. It's about a group of intelligent robots that (12) .... (attempt) to take over the world. Sounds exciting!

Leo (13) .... (believe) his success is a matter of luck not talent. We (14) .... (not/agree) and we can't wait for his next movie!

2 **1 Ask a partner questions like this about people you know.**

A: What does Leo Fisher do? (*your cousin/uncle,* etc.)
B: He's an actor.
A: What do you think he's doing right now?
B: He's probably reading a new script.

2 Tell the class about three of your friends'/family's annoying habits.

Example:
My brother is always losing things.

3 **Read the conversation and put the verbs in brackets into the correct form.**

A: (1) .... (you/do) anything tomorrow?
B: I haven't decided yet. Maybe I (2) .... (just/stay) at home. What about you?
A: Oh, I (3) .... (play) football with Ben and some friends if the weather's OK. In the evening we (4) .... (go) to the open-air cinema. They (5) .... (show) Leo Fisher's latest movie.
B: Have you heard the weather forecast? It (6) .... (rain) all day tomorrow.
A: Oh, no! We can't miss the film. Well, we (7) .... (just/have to) take our umbrellas. Anyway, we (8) .... (probably/not notice) the weather. Who cares about the rain if the movie's good?
B: That's true. What time (9) .... (the film/begin)?
A: The doors (10) .... (open) at six o'clock. I (11) .... (meet) Ben at 6.15.
B: It sounds too good to miss. I think I (12) .... (come) too!
A: Why not? We (13) .... (try) to get you a ticket if you like.
B: Great, thanks. I (14) .... (pay) you back when I see you.

4 **Find out about a partner's plans for tomorrow / this weekend / the holidays. Get as many details as possible. Ask questions like this:**

What are you doing this weekend/this summer?
Who are you going with?
Are you going to ...?
Do you think you'll ...?

Use of English 1: *transformations*

exam file

In **Paper 3**, **Part 3**, you rewrite sentences using a given 'key' word. This task tests your knowledge of grammar and vocabulary. Structures tested may include:

- verb tenses
- indirect speech
- comparisons
- conditionals
- passive
- modal verbs
- gerunds and infinitives
- changing from a noun to a verb structure or vice versa

You also need to have a good knowledge of:

- phrasal verbs
- the grammatical patterns of certain words, e.g.: *pay no attention* **to** + noun, *take no notice* **of** + noun, *be interested* **in** *(do***ing***) sth.*

▶▶ *exam strategy*

- Read the prompt (first) sentence carefully.
- Next, read the gapped sentence. Decide what part of the meaning of the prompt sentence is missing.
- Look at the key word. What structure can it be used with?
- Look carefully at the words before and after the gap to help you identify the structure you need.
- Fill in the gap with between two and five words including the key word. (Contractions, e.g. *don't, they've*, count as two words.)

1 **Complete the second sentence so that it has a similar meaning to the first sentence, using the word given. Do not change the word given. You must use between two and five words, including the word given. (In this exercise, the part of the prompt sentence that you need to change has been underlined to help you).**

1 I <u>might decide to record</u> that film on video.
   of
   I .... that film on video.
2 What are <u>your plans for</u> this weekend?
   to
   What .... do this weekend?
3 She told me, 'It's <u>not necessary for you</u> to book in advance.'
   have
   She told me, 'You .... book in advance.'
4 'This camera <u>is not mine</u>,' he said.
   belong
   'This camera ....,' he said.
5 The careers officer <u>advised me not to</u> become an actor.
   you
   'If I .... become an actor,' the careers officer said.

6 I <u>haven't been to</u> the cinema since March.
   last
   The .... to the cinema was March.
7 What <u>is the pronunciation of</u> this word?
   you
   How .... this word?
8 <u>You must follow</u> the instructions exactly.
   be
   The instructions .... exactly.

2 **What structure did each question in Exercise 1 test? Refer to the list in the exam file to help you. You will practise all these structures as you work through this coursebook.**

3 **The answers to the questions below contain common errors made by students. Find and correct the errors. Match the mistakes to these tips.**

a) Don't change the key word.
b) Don't change the words of the prompt sentence unnecessarily.
c) Don't change the meaning of the prompt sentence.
d) Don't write more than five words in the gap.
e) Check for correct grammar and spelling.

1 It's my responsibility to check the tickets.
   for
   I *am responsible for* the tickets.
2 'Do historical novels interest you?' he asked Jenny.
   was
   He asked Jenny *wether or not she was interested* in historical novels.
3 The price of the ticket includes refreshments in the interval.
   are
   Refreshments in the interval *are part of* the price of the ticket.
4 My sister would rather not go to the party with us.
   feel
   My sister *doesn't feel like go* to the party with us.
5 John always puts 100% effort into his work.
   hard
   John always *works as hardly as* he can.

Now check your answers to Exercise 1 again.

▶▶ *study tip!*

Record the grammatical patterns that words are used with in your vocabulary notebook, e.g.:

verb + preposition/particle
*to belong **to** someone*

expressions with gerunds/infinitives
to feel like doing something

Can you add more examples from pages 6 and 7?

Listening: *extracts (multiple choice)*

exam file

In **Paper 4**, **Part 1**, you listen to eight short extracts, and answer one multiple-choice question for each extract. You hear the questions on the recording as well. These focus on the following types of information:

- Who is speaking?   • What are they talking about?
- What feeling / attitude / opinion is being expressed?

1 Look at the exam task opposite.

1 Read Question 1. What do you have to listen for? Underline the key words.

2 Now read the options A–C.

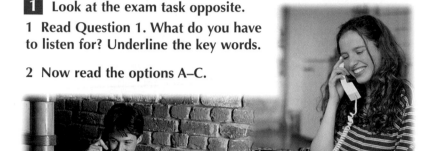

1 What could this conversation be about?
2 Which words in the list below might you hear?

ticket / seat / delay / sold out / ticket agency / timetable / in advance / departure / to cancel / scriptwriter / last night

3 Which words in the list can be used about all of the topics mentioned: train, theatre and flights?
4 Which words in the list can be used for only one or two of them?

3 📼 **Listen to Question 1 on the recording. Choose from options A–C. You will hear the extract twice.**

1 Which phrase(s) told you the right answer?
2 Were the words in the recording the same as the words in the questions or different?

2 📼 **Now listen to the rest of the recording and complete the exam task.**

▶▶ *exam strategy*

- Read and listen to the question and the options. Underline key words in the question and think about what ideas and vocabulary you might hear.
- Listen to the extract carefully. Listen out for key words and phrases and choose the best option.
- As you hear the recording the second time, check your answers.

3 📼 **Compare your answers with the rest of the class. Listen to the recording again. For Questions 2–8, what key phrases gave you the answers?**

You will hear people talking in eight different situations. For questions 1–8, choose the best answer, A, B or C.

1 You hear someone talking to a friend on the telephone. What does the speaker's friend want to do?

A travel by train
B go to the theatre   [1]
C book a flight

2 Listen to this man talking about his work. What was the main problem?

A lack of money
B bad advice   [2]
C poor equipment

3 You hear a man being interviewed on the radio. What is his profession?

A footballer
B writer   [3]
C musician

4 You overhear a woman talking to her friend. Who did she see on the train?

A an old friend
B a politician   [4]
C a film star

5 You hear an advertisement on the radio. What is being advertised?

A a CD
B a video   [5]
C a book

6 A friend of yours phones you on her mobile phone. Where is she?

A at the airport
B at a pop concert   [6]
C at a political demonstration

7 A man describes something to you. What is he describing?

A a recording studio
B a restaurant   [7]
C an expensive shop

8 You overhear a man talking in an office. What is he doing?

A apologising
B agreeing   [8]
C insisting

Speaking: *interview*

exam file

In **Paper 5**, **Part 1**, the examiner asks you to give some basic information about yourself. This part tests social language and lasts about three minutes. You may be asked about:

- your home town
- your family
- your work or studies
- your spare time activities
- your future plans

1 📼 **You are going to hear two candidates, Maria and Carlos, doing Part 1 of the Speaking Test. Listen once and answer these questions.**

1 Which of the topics listed in the exam file does the examiner ask about?
2 What do you learn about the candidates?

▶▶ exam strategy

- DO give answers to the examiner's questions which are complete but not too long.
- DON'T think for a long time before giving an answer.

2 📼 **Listen to the recording again. Which candidate, Maria or Carlos:**

1 gives responses that are complete?
2 gives responses that are too short?

3 **Read the following extract from Part 1. The answers contain common errors made by candidates. They may be grammatically wrong or unsuitable in other ways. Correct the mistakes.**

1 Q: Let's begin with your home town. Where are you from?
   A: I'm coming from Rome. ✗
2 Q: What do you like most about the town where you live?
   A: I like very much the river. ✗
3 Q: And what about your family? Do you have a large family or a small family?
   A: We are four in my family. ✗
4 Q: Can you tell me something about your family?
   A: It is ordinary. ✗
5 Q: And what about you? How important is it for you to learn English?
   A: I need English for to get a good job. ✗
6 Q: How long have you been learning English?
   A: I learn English since five years. ✗
7 Q: Let's move on to what you do in your spare time. What is there to do in the evenings in your home town?
   A: Anything. It's boring. ✗
8 Q: Which do you prefer, watching TV or going to the cinema?
   A: I would rather prefer the cinema. ✗
9 Q: What sort of films do you like to watch?
   A: I like more the action movies. ✗
10 Q: Now, thinking about the future. What kind of job would you like to do in the future?
   A: I'm hope to become engineer. ✗

4 **In groups of three, role-play Part 1.**
1 Practise asking and answering the questions in Exercise 3.

Student 1: You are the examiner. Ask the questions.

Students 2 and 3: You are the candidates. Answer the examiner's questions.

2 Prepare some more questions of your own for each topic, and change roles.

▶▶ exam tip!

Be ready to answer questions about yourself, but DON'T prepare long answers in advance.

1 Pictures at an exhibition

Lead-in

Look at the pictures from an art exhibition and discuss these questions. Use words and expressions from the box.

1 Describe the pictures.
2 What's your opinion of them?
3 Do you think they have anything in common?

> an abstract painting
> a portrait / landscape / still life
> in the foreground / background / middle /
>   on the right/left / to one side we
>   can see ...
> strange / mysterious / fantastic /
>   off-putting / intriguing

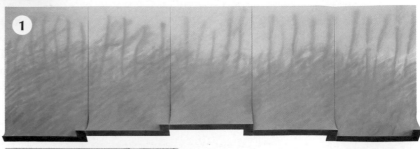

Reading 2: *multiple matching*

> ▶▶ *exam strategy*   Paper 1, Part 1
>
> • Read the title of the text and the instructions to get an idea
>   of the topic.
> • Skim the text once quite quickly for general understanding.
> • Look through the list of headings, then read the text again,
>   paragraph by paragraph.
> • Identify the main point of the paragraph and underline key phrases.
> • Match the key phrases to the appropriate heading.

1 Look at the exam task opposite. What can you predict about the content of the text from the title, sub-heading and instructions? Discuss these questions.

1 Why might a national art gallery invite a group of teenagers
   to organise an exhibition?
2 What are some of the challenges and difficulties that could face
   the teenagers?
3 What benefits could they gain from this experience?

2 Check your answers to the questions in Exercise 1 during your first reading.

3 Here are some clues to help you match each paragraph of the text to the right heading during your second reading.

Question:

1 This paragraph describes the process of selecting works of art
   related to one topic. Which heading summarises this idea?
3 What changed Kerrie's attitude to art?
5 Why did the group choose the painting 'Riverfall'? Did the
   teenagers always agree about their choices?
6 What did the teenagers gain from organising the exhibition?
   What did the gallery gain?

Vocabulary: *using context*

4 Explain the meaning of the words in bold in the text (1–5). Use these clues to help you.

1 Look at the previous sentence.
2 What did the gallery want to do?
   There is a synonym in line 79.
3 Read the whole sentence. Did all the
   teenagers like this painting or only
   some of them?
4 What other words begin with *rem-*?
   Is this really a painting of flowing
   water?
5 There is a near-synonym in the same
   sentence.

Over to you

5 Discuss these questions.

1 How popular is going to art galleries
   and museums in your country?
2 Can you suggest ways of making them
   more attractive to young people?
3 Describe a visit you have made to
   a gallery or museum in the last year.

You are going to read an article about some young people who organised an art exhibition. Choose the most suitable heading A–I for each part (1–7) of the article. There is one extra heading that you do not need to use. There is an example at the beginning (0).

A Determined to get it right
B The most popular choice
C Choosing a theme
D Benefits on both sides
E A big gap remains
F Moving in the right direction
G Unrealistic expectations
H A learning experience
I An unusual challenge

ART: *Not just for old folk!*

Fourteen teenagers were invited to choose works of art for an exhibition at Liverpool's famous Tate Gallery. Lesley Garner investigated.

0 **I**

When teenager Kerrie Bagan joined the Liverpool Tate Gallery's experimental *Young Tate* group, she thought it would be very boring. Then the Tate management offered the group a unique opportunity. They invited these inexperienced teenagers to organise an art exhibition on a subject of their own choice, to be shown to the public the following winter.

1

Only a tenth of the museum's collection of works of art is ever on show at one time. The *Young Tate* group **was given access to**[1] almost the entire collection, with only a few minor restrictions. After months of often heated discussion, the teenagers made their final selection. The result was a show called *Testing the Water*, a collection of paintings and sculpture all related to the topic of adolescence.

2

Visitors to the exhibition found a surprising collection of works of art whose overall effect is thoughtful and mysterious. The Tate management found that their original intention in involving young people – to **draw** more of them **into**[2] the gallery – is going to take a lot more than one exhibition. And the teenagers found that, although they appreciated art better the more they learned about it, there is still a gulf between them and the world of the art gallery.

3

Very few members of the group knew anything about art before they joined *Young Tate*, and it took time for them to become comfortable with the art world. Two of them even kept their involvement in the group a secret from their friends. 'It wasn't until we started on the background of the artists that I got interested, because then I began to understand what they were trying to get across in their paintings,' said Kerrie. 'I wasn't keen on any art until then. I began to find out more.'

4

I went around the exhibition with Stephen Connell, a fan of techno music and one of the few members of the group who did know something about art before they began. What I noticed most was the enormous effort and commitment the teenagers had put into selecting the most appropriate works for their exhibition. 'We wanted a theme that fitted, that we could identify with,' said Stephen. 'We didn't want to be laughed at just because we're teenagers.'

5

Only one painting was chosen **unanimously**[3], on the simple basis that they all loved it: a huge, calm, green abstract, that is **reminiscent of**[4] flowing water, called 'Riverfall'. The picture gives the gallery a calm, **tranquil**[5] atmosphere. It is a very good example of the personal, thoughtful mood of much of the chosen art. Another example of this is a disturbing little painting of a thin girl staring intensely, like someone examining their reflection in a mirror. 'The painting fitted,' explained Kerrie, 'because all adolescents are worried about the way they look.'

6

The Liverpool teenagers learned just how much thought goes into both an individual work of art and the process of showing it to the public. But that doesn't immediately solve the Tate Gallery's problem, which is how to attract more young people. Paul Willis, Professor of Cultural Studies at Wolverhampton University, spells it out: 'The vast majority of this age group don't experience the arts. They get their culture from popular music, television, cinema. Galleries and museums could be braver in mixing items from their collection with popular, everyday items.' But the Tate management now have a better idea of how teenagers think.

7

Naomi Horlock, the Tate's Education Officer and organiser of the *Young Tate* group, is also aware that young people need to feel more welcome. And she knows – from a recent visit to Australia and New Zealand, where visiting galleries is popular with young people – that it is possible. 'We set up *Young Tate* because we wanted to find young people who didn't necessarily know much about art, but who would gradually become more confident and would offer us informal advice. We wanted to get them into the gallery. And we are getting closer to that goal.'

Use of English 2: *lexical cloze*

exam file

Paper 3, **Part 1** is mainly a test of vocabulary. You read a text with 15 gaps and choose one word or phrase from four options to fill each gap. The word must fit the meaning of the text and the grammar of the sentence. You need to be able to choose or recognise:

- the correct word from a set with similar meanings.
- common collocations – words that go together.
- the grammatical patterns that words are used with.
- prepositional phrases and fixed expressions.
- phrasal verbs, e.g. *get up*.
- linking words, e.g. *but, because*.

1 **Words with similar meanings**

1 Read each sentence carefully and fill in the gap with the best word. Use each word once.

viewers / audiences / spectators / onlookers

1 The football match was watched by 50,000 ....
2 Many television .... complained about a particularly violent episode of a popular series.
3 As the actors arrived for the film premiere, there were cheers from the crowd of ....
4 This theatre company puts on a lot of plays for schools and other specialist ....

2 Read this paragraph and underline the best word in each set.

The Minack Theatre in Cornwall is built on a headland and has a marvellous (1) *display / view / sight* of the bay. During performances, you can often (2) *glimpse / look / catch* dolphins out at sea. The Minack was planned and financed by one woman. It took her 20 years to complete the (3) *effort / labour / task*. Plays are performed in summer but visitors are welcome at any season if they pay a small (4) *cost / fare / fee*.

2 **Collocations**

1 Underline the best word in each set in this paragraph.

The British film 'Shakespeare in Love' (1) *tells / speaks / says* the story of Shakespeare's early life. It is (2) *highly / utterly / extremely* funny, and quite different (3) *that / from / as* what you might expect. The director believed (4) *passionately / emotionally / greatly* in the project, but how would audiences receive it? Happily, they loved every minute of it. It became a (5) *large / vast / huge* success at the box office and was nominated for 13 Academy Awards.

2 Now match items 1–5 in Exercise 2.1 to these types of collocation.

a) adjective + noun   d) adjective + preposition
b) verb + noun   e) adverb + adjective
c) verb + adverb

3 **Grammatical patterns**

1 Read the following paragraph and underline the correct words. Check the grammar after the word. This will help you to choose.

A friend (1) *informed / told / mentioned* that he wanted to be an actor. I (2) *suggested / advised / said* him to write to a local film studio. They (3) *allowed / permitted / let* him sit in on a rehearsal. Now he (4) *intends / wants / hopes* auditioning for a part.

2 Now group all the verbs in italics in Exercise 3.1 according to these patterns.

a) verb + *that*   d) verb + object + *that*
b) verb + object + bare infinitive   e) verb + *to*-infinitive
c) verb + object + *to*-infinitive   f) verb + *-ing*

4 **Phrases with prepositions**

Read this paragraph and decide which word, A, B, C or D, best completes each gap. The whole phrase is given in italics to help you.

A well-known director got a phone call telling him that a friend was (1) ..... *trouble*, so he flew home to Hollywood (2) ..... . But when he arrived, he discovered, *to his utter* (3) ....., that it was all a trick. He had actually won an Oscar for his latest film! *For the first* (4) ..... in his life, he broke down and cried in public.

1 A under   B in   C with   D out of
2 A at his own expense   C on his own account
   B to his own cost   D at no expense
3 A understanding   C realisation
   B shock   D amazement
4 A occasion   B event   C time   D period

5 **Phrasal verbs**

1 Underline the correct particle in each set.

I was planning to (1) look *up / round / through* the new arts centre yesterday. I set (2) *up / in / out* bright and early to beat the queues, but when I got there the centre was packed. So I gave (3) *up / in / away* and went home.

2 Give examples to show the meanings of the other verb + particle combinations in Exercise 5.1.

Example:
I use my dictionary to <u>look up</u> new words.

6 Linking words

Read this paragraph and decide which linking expression, A, B, C or D, best fits each space.

When a friend invited me to an art exhibition recently, I decided to go (1) .... the fact that I know very little about art. (2) .... the paintings, there were some very interesting sculptures. I rather enjoyed my visit, (3) .... I didn't like the abstract paintings at all. (4) ...., I have enrolled in an art class so I can learn more about modern art.

1. A in spite of   C apart from
   B even though   D because
2. A As well   C In addition to
   B More than   D Apart
3. A although   C even
   B otherwise   D despite
4. A Because of   C As well as
   B Due to   D As a result

7 Now try the exam task opposite. Work with a partner and use your dictionary to help you.

▶▶ *exam strategy*

- Read the title and the whole text, ignoring the gaps.
- Go back to the beginning. Read the sentences with gaps very carefully. The word you need must fit the grammar **and** meaning of the sentence.
- When you have finished, read the whole text again and check that your answers make sense.

Read the text below and decide which answer A, B, C or D best fits each space. There is an example at the beginning (0).

0   A forms   B means   C roles   D shapes

VIDEO GAMES

Video games are one of the most influential (0) *A* of entertainment in modern society. But do they (1) ..... a good influence or a bad influence, particularly when we consider how popular they are with children? (2) ..... both users and video companies claim that there is no (3) ..... between violence on the screen and real-life behaviour, a (4) ..... number of people are beginning to (5) ..... that this may not be true.

What cannot be (6) ....., of course, is that some of the most successful video games are also the most violent and it would seem that they owe much of their popularity to their violent character. (7) ....., the plain fact is, non-violent video games just do not (8) ..... commercially, whereas their more violent counterparts do.

Most video games originate in the USA, a country where children are encouraged to be very competitive. Some people there seem to (9) ..... video games because they (10) ..... this competitive spirit in a very basic (11) ..... – man versus man or man versus nature. But ironically, if you ask any English teacher, they'll (12) ..... you that these two conflicts are the ones most commonly found in great works of literature. It is possible, therefore, that parents, and other people who are (13) ..... of the influence video games may have on the young, really just (14) ..... to understand them and the part they (15) ....., in our culture.

1	A result	B respond	C relate	D represent
2	A Still	B Moreover	C However	D Although
3	A joint	B knot	C link	D tie
4	A climbing	B growing	C rising	D spreading
5	A suppose	B distrust	C doubt	D suspect
6	A denied	B disagreed	C replied	D refused
7	A Even though	B As regards	C In case	D What's more
8	A catch up	B get off	C pick up	D take off
9	A disgust	B disapprove	C dislike	D displease
10	A call	B carry	C show	D give
11	A kind	B way	C type	D sort
12	A state	B tell	C say	D speak
13	A afraid	B alarmed	C anxious	D worried
14	A avoid	B lack	C fail	D miss
15	A make	B play	C act	D serve

Writing: *formal letter of application*

In **Paper 2**, **Part 2**, you have 1 hour 30 minutes to complete **two** writing tasks. You have to write between 120–180 words in an appropriate style for each of the tasks.

The task in Part 1 is compulsory. In Part 2, you choose one from four options. One option may be a formal letter of application.

▶▶ *exam strategy*

Make sure you:

- cover **all** the relevant points in the advertisement.
- relate your skills and personal qualities to the job advertised.
- sound positive. You want the job. If you talk about your weaknesses, you are unlikely to succeed!
- use the appropriate style and format for a formal letter. Don't use informal words or phrases. Be consistent.
- use a new paragraph for each main topic.

1 **Read the writing task below.**

1 Underline the points you need to keep in mind when you write your letter. The first point has been underlined for you.

You have just seen this advertisement in a local paper.

Culture International

Wanted: young people for crowd scenes in the musical show 'The Lion King'. Dates: June 4 – June 18. (You must be available for at least one week). Previous experience not necessary as training will be given. This is an international production so you must be able to communicate in English.

To apply, give a full description of yourself, explain why you would like the job and tell us exactly when you would be available.

Write your **letter of application**. Do not write any postal addresses. Write your answer in **120–180** words in an appropriate style.

2 **Which of the following points should you include in your letter? Cross out any that are not relevant or suitable.**

a) the reason(s) why you would like the job
b) who you are and what you are doing currently
c) what kind of person you are
d) any relevant skills
e) one or two of your bad points/weaknesses
f) your knowledge of English
g) a description of your favourite musical shows
h) any useful experience that makes you suitable for the job
i) when and how long you are available

2 **Read what one student wrote and answer these questions.**

1 Which piece of information did he forget to include? Check with your list in Exercise 1.2.
2 Does the writer sound as if he wants this job? If so, what parts of the letter tell you this?

Dear Sir or Madam,

I have just read your advertisement for people to appear in the 'The Lion King'. I would very much like to be in your show.

I am a 17-year-old student. At present, I am attending school but I'm off to university next September. As far as my character is concerned, I am reliable and hardworking but also quite an extrovert. I really enjoy meeting new people and being the centre of attention. I love drama and have acted in a lot of school productions. Last year we made a video film for our class project, and guess what – I was the star performer! I am also a great dancer.

My family has spent a lot of time living abroad, mainly in Australia. So you can see why my English is excellent, can't you?

I would like to be involved in your show because I think it would be a fascinating experience. I have always wanted to appear in a big show. In fact, I have been dreaming of an opportunity like this for years.

I look forward to hearing from you.

Yours faithfully,

John Simpson

John Simpson

Focus on style and register

3 **1 Formal letters usually contain a number of set phrases or expressions. Look at the letter in Exercise 2 again. Underline the words and phrases the writer uses to:**

a) address the person he is writing to.
b) give his reason for writing.
c) say why he wants the job.
d) close the letter politely.
e) sign off formally.

Are there any other expressions you could use in this letter for a)–e)?

2 Underline three phrases or expressions in the sample letter that are much too informal. How could you rewrite these to make them more appropriate?

Focus on grammar ▶ *p.179*

4 **1 Underline all the examples of the present perfect and past simple tenses in the letter in Exercise 2.**

2 Explain why each tense is used.

grammar file 8

A Present perfect

● **for completed past actions connected to now**
1 *I've seen a lot of musicals.* (**when** is not important)
2 **Have** you **ever read** *a Shakespeare play* (= in your life)? *No,* **never.**
3 *I've* **already seen** *that show. I don't want to go again.*
4 *We've* **been** *to three movies* **this month.** (= unfinished time period)

● **for activities/states that are still continuing/true**
5 *I've attended/been attending drama school for two years.*
6 *The teacher* **has known** *me since I was a child.*

B Present perfect simple or continuous?
1 *I've* **been learning** *some new dance steps.* (focus on activity)
2 *I've* **learned** *some new dance steps.* (focus on result)

C Present perfect or past simple?
1 *He* **has starred** *in several films.* (time unknown)
2 **Last year** *he* **starred** *in a film about a man who ...* (time stated)

3 Read the following sentences. Find and correct the mistakes in the use of present perfect and past simple. (There are two examples of correct tense use.)

1 I ~~just saw~~ *have just seen* your advertisement for contestants for a talent show in the newspaper.
2 My friends and I play music together since we are 12.
3 Our band is well known locally because we gave several concerts.
4 We first performed in public two years ago.
5 Since then we appeared on stage at least six times.
6 We have recorded a song at a recording studio last winter but not many people have heard it yet.
7 None of us ever took part in a talent show before.
8 This could be our big break. We are trying to get on television for years.
9 I've always been wanting to be famous but so far it hasn't happened.
10 This is the first time we have the chance to perform for a really big audience.

Over to you

5 **1 Write your answer to the following task in 120–180 words in an appropriate style. Follow the advice in the exam strategy box.**

You have seen this advertisement in a magazine.

TALENTED PEOPLE NEEDED

Can you sing, dance, play an instrument, tell jokes?

We are looking for young people to take part in our international TV talent shows this September. Individuals or groups. Dates: Friday 2nd and Saturday 3rd December.

To apply, write and tell us about yourself/your group and your experience. Indicate which date you prefer and explain why you want to be in the show.

Write your letter of application. Do not write any postal addresses.

2 Check your work carefully, or ask another student to check it. Refer back to the points in the exam strategy box.

2 Challenges

Lead-in

Look at the pictures and read the paragraph opposite. Answer these questions.

1 Who was Ernest Shackleton?
2 What did he hope to do?
3 What do you think happened to his ship and his crew?

In 1915, Anglo-Irish explorer Ernest Shackleton (1874–1922) lost his ship and his dream of crossing Antarctica on foot. What began as a journey of exploration became a 20-month battle to stay alive, demanding ingenuity, courage and leadership. All these Shackleton held in full measure.

Reading 1:
multiple-choice questions

exam file

In **Paper 1**, **Part 2**, you answer seven or eight multiple-choice questions on a text. You have to choose the best option, **A**, **B**, **C** or **D**.

The questions are in the same order as the information in the text. They mainly test details, but there may be a question on vocabulary, pronoun reference and global understanding of the text.

1   Look at the exam task opposite. Read the text once quite quickly. Then answer these questions to check your general understanding.

1 What happened to Shackleton's ship?
2 How did the crew try to survive?
3 How did Shackleton save the lives of his crew?
4 Why did the writer choose to write about Shackleton?

2   1   Read the questions that follow the text. (You will read the options later.)

2   Underline the key words in each question and decide what information you need to look for in the text.

3   Find the parts of the text that give you the answers, using the words you underlined to guide you. Mark these parts.

Example:

Question 1: What makes Shackleton's story so special for the writer?
Text, line 5: This is no ordinary adventure story … it has the power to move people deeply.

You are going to read an article about the famous polar explorer Ernest Shackleton. For each of the questions, choose the answer (**A, B, C** or **D**) which you think fits best according to the text.

AN EPIC OF
SURVIVAL

The story of Ernest Shackleton's unsuccessful expedition to Antarctica in 1914 is one of the greatest in the history of exploration. Shackleton saved his men from almost certain death when their ship was crushed by ice in the frozen sea off Antarctica. But this is no ordinary adventure story. The strength of Shackleton's determination and leadership is so great, and the story itself is so incredibly thrilling, that it has the power to move people deeply.

One evening, I was standing at a bus stop with *South*, Shackleton's written account of his adventure, tucked under my arm. A man turned to me with pure admiration in his eyes. 'Shackleton', he said quietly, knowing that if I had read even half of the book, I would share his respect for this wonderful man and what he achieved.

On the expedition, Shackleton planned to cross Antarctica from one side to the other, something never achieved before. But his ship, the *Endurance*, became trapped in the ice when the sea froze just 100 miles from the coast of Antarctica. Shackleton realised that the crossing would have to be abandoned. The only thing he and his men could do was wait in the hope that, when the ice melted, the ship would survive intact. In the event, the ship remained stuck in the ice for ten months and eventually sank.

Shackleton also realised that he would have to keep the 27 members of his crew fit and in good spirits if they were going to survive. For this was 1915, and they had no radio or other means of contacting the outside world. He organised games of

3 Now read the questions <u>and</u> the options on page 199.
Decide which option best matches the text. Look for words and phrases that are similar in meaning to the words in the option. This will help you to confirm that you have got the right answer. Use these clues to help you with the task.

Question:

1 All the statements **A–D** are relevant to the text, but the question asks about the writer's opinion. In the last sentence of paragraph 1, which phrase is similar in meaning to one of the options?

2 All of these things were problems, but what worried Shackleton most? Look for repeated phrases that refer to the same idea.

3 Which option can you find evidence for in the text, even if it is not actually stated?

6 'It' is the subject of the sentence, but which are the two main verbs? Which option **A–D** 'involved' sailing?

 exam tip!
Use context clues to work out the meaning of unfamiliar words (see Unit 1, page 10).

Over to you

4 1 Look at the adjectives in the box below. Which adjectives are positive and which are negative? Which can be both depending on the context or situation?

> courageous romantic reckless admirable sensible inflexible irresponsible strong-willed ambitious unconventional selfish

2 Which adjectives best describe adventurers like Shackleton and his crew?

football on the ice to keep the men occupied. Despite the extremely cold conditions, and with only wild
30 birds to eat, Shackleton remained confident and optimistic. He paid great attention to the psychological condition of his men and responded immediately to any signs of depression or despair.
This was just as well because things were going to
35 get worse. As the ice began to melt, it crushed the ship to pieces instead of freeing it. The situation seemed hopeless, but Shackleton had a plan. They would walk across the floating ice, **dragging** three small boats saved from the *Endurance* behind them,
40 until they reached the open sea; then they would sail to Elephant Island, the nearest piece of dry land. The difficult trek took weeks, but the sea crossing was even worse. For seven sleepless, nightmarish days and nights, the men endured storms and cold that
45 froze their clothing into solid ice. But somehow they reached the island. They had not stepped on land since leaving England 497 days before. They were exhausted, but almost hysterical with joy.
But they were still in danger. Elephant Island was
50 uninhabited and no ships ever visited it. The winds blew at 150 kph; they were cold, wet, hungry and suffering from frostbite. But Shackleton had another plan. Taking one boat and five men, he decided to set sail for the island of South Georgia, where there was
55 a whaling station. **It** was their last chance of rescue, but involved sailing 1,200 km across a sea well known for its 80-metre high waves. If the navigator made a mistake and they missed the narrow island, the nearest
60 land was Africa, 4,000 miles away.
One day, I went to see the little boat they sailed in on display at Shackleton's old school in London. I stood in front of the boat, thinking about that terrible journey.
65 The boat seemed so small, so fragile, and what they had achieved seemed so wonderful, that I was overcome by emotion and I wept.
For Shackleton and his men did
70 reach the island, only to spend another three days crossing a mountain range on foot before they reached the whaling station. They had survived the most unimaginable hardships to save their
75 shipmates, all of whom were later rescued. The survival of every member of the crew is a tribute to Shackleton's leadership skills, because here was a man who knew how to motivate and inspire
80 others; something his story is still doing today.

1 What makes Shackleton's story so special for the writer?

2 What did Shackleton see as the greatest threat to his crew on the ice?

3 What does the word 'dragging' in line 38 tell us about the small boats?

4 How did the men feel when they reached Elephant Island?

5 Why did Shackleton decide to leave Elephant Island?

6 What does 'It' in line 55 refer to?

7 How did the writer feel when she saw the small boat in London?

8 Which phrase best summarises the writer's opinion of Shackleton?

Grammar: *the past* ▶ pp.178–9

grammar files 6, 8

A	**Past continuous** for an action in progress in the past	1	**In the 1760s**, the British Royal Navy **was planning** an expedition to the Pacific.
B	**Past simple** for single completed key events	2	They **chose** Captain James Cook to lead it.
C	**Past perfect** for an action which happened before another action or time in the past	3	**By the age of 27**, Cook **had** already **proved** he was a skilful sailor.
	The **past perfect continuous** focuses on duration	4	**Before** he **joined** the Navy, he **had been sailing** cargo ships up and down the coast of England.
D	**Past continuous + past simple** for interrupted actions	5	**While** he **was leading** his first expedition, Cook **discovered** Australia.
		6	He and his crew **were sailing** up the coast of Australia **when** the ship **hit** the Great Barrier Reef.
E	**Present perfect** to relate past events to the present	7	Cook **died** in 1779 but his achievements **have** never **been forgotten**.

1 Read the sentence halves 1–10 in the left-hand column and underline the verb tenses and time expressions. Use these as clues to help you match them to a)–j) and make true sentences.

1 Human beings <u>have dreamed</u> of travelling to the moon

2 <u>By the time</u> the Americans <u>won</u> the race to put a man on the moon,

3 Space travel was full of risk; in 1967 a spacecraft caught fire

4 On 16th July 1969, the crowds who had been gathering on the beaches of Florida

5 As soon as the 'Saturn' had got to a distance of 60 km from the moon,

6 The astronauts crawled into the lunar module 'The Eagle'

7 While technicians on Earth were monitoring the landing,

8 When they checked, however,

9 After the astronauts had landed on the moon,

10 It is amazing to think that the rocket had travelled 386,160 km

a) they were alarmed to hear a warning bell ring.

b) held their breath as the 'Saturn' rocket took off.

c) by the time it reached the moon.

d) ever since they first looked into the heavens.

e) it went into orbit around it.

f) and it descended gently towards the surface of the moon.

g) as it was getting ready for take-off, and three astronauts died.

h) they found there was no major problem.

i) they had <u>already</u> spent millions of dollars on space exploration.

j) they came down a ladder from the module and started collecting samples to take back to Earth.

2 Read the following text and put the verbs in brackets into the right tense. Sometimes more than one tense is possible.

WORLD'S FIRST ALL-WOMAN EXPEDITION REACHES THE NORTH POLE

The adventure started in 1995, as Victoria Riches (1) .... (make) her way to work by Underground. She was bored because she (2) .... (do) the same thing every day for a year. Then, something (3) .... (happen) to change her life.

She (4) .... (read) the paper on the train, when she (5) .... (see) an unusual article. A group of women (6) .... (look) for adventurers to join their all-woman team. They (7) .... (plan) to walk to the North Pole, something that no woman (8) .... (ever/achieve) before!

Victoria wasn't sure why she (9) .... (be) keen to join the expedition. Before reading the article, she (10) .... (never/want) to pull a sledge over sea ice or endure temperatures of minus 40 degrees Celsius! So why (11) .... (she/wish) to do it now?

That evening she (12) .... (ring) her mother and (13) .... (tell) her that she (14) .... (think) of applying to go to the North Pole. She (15) .... (imagine) her mother would be shocked. But after she (16) .... (hear) all about it, her mother (17) .... (decide) she wanted to go too!

There was a large number of applicants and they all (18) .... (have to) take a selection test. When Victoria and her mother (19) .... (finally/hear) that they (20) .... (pass) the test, they (21) .... (feel) excited but terrified! Their real-life adventure (22) .... (just/begin)!

Over to you

3 Discuss.

If you saw an advertisement inviting you to join an expedition as an explorer or an astronaut, would you apply? Why/Why not?

Use of English 1: *structural cloze*

exam file

In **Paper 3**, **Part 2**, you read a short text with 15 gaps, and write one word in each gap. The task tests your knowledge of grammar **and** vocabulary – although the missing words are mainly grammatical words, they may be part of a phrase or expression. Correct spelling is required. The missing words may include:

- articles, e.g. *a, the*
- determiners, e.g. *this, such*
- quantifiers, e.g. *few, some*
- comparatives and superlatives, e.g. *more, most*
- pronouns, e.g. *who, which*
- prepositions, e.g. *at, by, in*
- auxiliary verbs, e.g. *is, has*
- linking words, e.g. *because, if*
- parts of phrasal verbs, e.g. *(run) away, (get) up*

1 Look at the exam task below. Read the title and the whole text to get an idea of the content. Use these questions to help you summarise the main points of the story.

1 Who were Gerow and Griffiths?
2 Why had they taken the plane up?
3 What happened to Griffiths?
4 What did Gerow do?
5 Why did Griffiths manage to survive?

> ➤➤ *exam tip!*
> Don't try to complete the gaps on the first reading. It is much easier to fill them in when you have understood what the text is about. ◀◀

2 Read the text again, sentence by sentence. Look at the words before and after each gap and decide what type of word is missing. Note down the word class. Use the clues provided to help you.

3 Now fill in the gaps. Put only <u>one</u> word in each gap.

4 Read the text again from the beginning. Use these questions to help you check your answers.

1 Does the completed text make sense?
2 Have you spelled all the words correctly?

Read the text below and think of the word which best fits each space. Use only **one** word in each space. There is an example at the beginning (0).

AN AMAZING ESCAPE IN THE AIR

In December 1942, an aircraft took (0) ..*off*.. from an airfield in Minnesota, USA. On board were the pilot, Sid Gerow, and the engineer, Harry Griffiths. The plane (1) .... just left the factory and this was its first flight. The two men were responsible (2) .... checking that everything was (3) .... working order.

Griffiths had (4) .... carry out inspections (5) .... the doors and windows, making sure they were securely closed. He was checking a door near the pilot's seat (6) .... suddenly it gave way and he fell (7) .... of the aircraft. Fortunately, he managed to hold onto the door although he knew that he would soon lose (8) .... grip. The air temperature was minus 13 degrees Celsius and strong winds (9) .... blowing him about.

Gerow realised exactly (10) .... had happened because he felt the cold air and heard Griffiths' shouts, but he had to stay in his seat to control the aircraft. He decided not to land because this would be very dangerous for Griffiths. Suddenly, he had a brilliant idea. Below him he (11) .... see a frozen lake. He took the plane down as low as possible and reduced speed. A few metres (12) .... the ice, at a speed of 160 kph, Griffiths let go. He hit the ice (13) .... slid for one kilometre. Circling round, Gerow (14) .... relieved to see his colleague get up and walk (15) .... the shore of the lake. His plan had worked!

CLUES

Question:

1 *left* is a past participle, so the missing word must be an auxiliary verb.
2 *responsible* is an adjective and *checking* is a verb in the *-ing* form. The missing word must be a ... .
3 The phrase ... *working order* needs a ... to complete it.
4 The verb *had* must be followed by an infinitive with ... .
5 What kind of word can link the two nouns here?
6 What kind of word do you need to link these two clauses?
8 Who is this sentence about? You need a word that indicates possession.
11 What kind of verb can come in front of a bare infinitive?

Listening: *sentence completion*

1 **Before you listen, read the instructions and the exam task below to get an idea of the content. Then answer these questions about the content of the listening.**

1 What is Paul's occupation?
2 What questions does the interviewer ask Paul?

Example:
How did you first find out about mountaineering?

2 **Think about what kind of information is missing. Use these clues to help you.**

Question:

1 In what ways could Paul have found out about mountaineering – for example, from a friend?
2 What kind of trip could Paul be referring to?
3 What part of the body can you injure when you fall?
4 Where might Paul hang the rope?
5 What kind of information is missing?
6 What sort of things can you 'make' in this context?
7 What kind of information is missing?
8 Will Paul mention a positive or negative characteristic of climbers?
9 What kinds of books can you think of?
10 What kind of information is missing?

3 **Read the answers to the first two questions below, which were written by a student. They express the right idea but don't fit grammatically. Can you correct them?**

Paul first found out about mountaineering from a [*in a magazine.* **1**]

Paul remembers going to Switzerland on a [*skiing holiday* **2**] trip.

4 **1** 🔲 **Now complete the exam task. Listen to the recording once and answer the questions using up to three words only.**

2 🔲 **Listen to the recording a second time and check your answers. Do they make sense? Do they fit grammatically?**

You will hear an interview with a mountaineer. For questions 1–10, complete the sentences.

Paul first found out about mountaineering from a [**1**]

Paul remembers going to Switzerland on a [**2**] trip.

Paul's worst experience was when he fell and injured his [**3**]

Paul now has the rope which saved his life hanging above his [**4**]

After his accident, Paul was unable to walk back to his [**5**] before dark.

Paul thinks that people who travel together should begin by making a [**6**]

Paul says his worst travelling companion was a man who worked as a [**7**]

Paul describes many climbers as both too ambitious and [**8**]

To relax, Paul listens to music and reads [**9**] books.

Paul says that he enjoys spending time in [**10**] when he's in Argentina.

Speaking: *individual long turn*

exam file

In **Paper 5**, **Part 2**, you talk on your own for a minute. You have to:

- compare and contrast two photographs on a similar theme, **and**
- comment and give a personal reaction to them.

The examiner also invites you to make a very brief comment on the other candidate's photographs.

▶▶ *exam strategy*

- DO listen carefully to the task which the examiner gives you.
- DON'T give separate descriptions of each photo, or describe them in detail.
- DO keep talking for the full minute. If the examiner interrupts you, this indicates you have completed this part.

1 🎞 **Look at the photos opposite, and listen to the examiner's instructions on the recording. Answer these questions.**

1 What is the theme of the photos, according to the examiner?
2 What task does the examiner give Candidate A, Georgia?

2 **Work in pairs.**

Student 1: Compare and contrast photos 1 and 2. Say what is similar in both. Say what is different.
Student 2: Speculate. Complete the examiner's task.

Use expressions from the box below and the functions files 1 and 2 on page 200.

an icy landscape   snow and ice   freezing cold
desert   sand   extreme heat

It must be difficult (to keep warm).
You'd need (warm clothes/protection from the sun).
You'd have to (carry enough supplies).
You might/could (run out of water / get lost / lose your way).
If you had an accident, (it would be difficult to get help).

3 🎞 **Listen to Candidate A, Georgia, doing the same task. Then answer these questions.**

1 Were her ideas similar to yours?
2 Did she describe the photos in too much detail?
3 Did she fully complete the examiner's task?
4 Did she keep speaking without a lot of pauses?
5 What word didn't she know? How did she paraphrase it?

4 🎞 **Listen to Candidate B commenting on the photos.**

1 What question does the examiner ask Candidate B, Iannis?
2 Do you agree with Iannis's response? Why/Why not? What reason would you give?

5 **Turn to the photos on page 202. Work in pairs.**

1 🎞 **Listen to the examiner's instructions to Candidate B, Iannis.**
Student 1: Do the task. Use phrases from the box on page 202 and the functions files 1, 2 and 3 on page 200.

2 🎞 **Now listen to the question which the examiner asks Candidate A, Georgia.**
Student 2: Respond to the examiner's question.

Lead-in

You are going to read a text about some people who went on an activity weekend.

1 Look at the photos in the text and discuss these questions.

1 What are the people in the photos doing?
2 What equipment are they using?

2 Scan the text and find the names of: a) the sports they did. b) the equipment they used.

3 Discuss.

1 Which of the activities do you think is most/least dangerous? What are the risks?
2 What kind of person do you need to be for each sport?
3 Which activity would you find most/least enjoyable? Why?

You are going to read an article about a weekend of adventure. For each of the questions 1–8, choose the answer (A, B, C or D) which you think fits best according to the text.

Reading 2: *multiple-choice questions*

▶▶ exam strategy — Paper 1, Part 2

- Read the whole text once quite quickly for general understanding.
- Read the questions and underline key words. DON'T read the options **A–D** yet.
- Find the parts of the text that you think answer the questions or complete the sentences, and underline key words there.
- Read the options and choose the one that best matches the ideas in the text. Look for words and phrases with similar meanings in the options and the text.

1 Read the sub-heading and the first paragraph of the text only. Answer these questions. (Note down your answers to Questions 2 and 3.)

1 What kinds of jobs did members of the group do?
2 Which activities do you think each of them found easiest? most frightening? most challenging?
3 How do you think they felt at the end of the weekend?

A Weekend with the Wild Ones

They were just ordinary people – including a social worker, an engineer, an aromatherapist and a student. But for one weekend they became intrepid adventurers, tasting the thrills of caving, abseiling and archery.

We met on Friday night: an ordinary bunch of people seeking an escape from our everyday life. Justin and James, our good-looking, fit and patient
5 instructors laid out what they had in store for us. The menu included: an assault course, caving, canoeing, orienteering, archery, rock-climbing and even abseiling off a 30-metre viaduct.
10 Andy, an engineer, was ready for everything, while Neil, a student, was quietly confident as he admitted he'd done a bit of climbing before, and some hillwalking. Meanwhile, Vicki and Sarah,
15 who both worked for a design agency, declared that they had 'never done anything like this before' and were wondering what they had let themselves in for. Kate, an aromatherapist, was very
20 keen to get started.
Saturday began with a gentle stroll up a hill and we learned the basics of map-reading. We were only out for about

three hours but some of the uphill bits
25 were hard work and Justin had to urge us on with helpful comments such as 'Nearly there!' and 'Stopping only makes it more difficult to keep going!' Sarah amazed herself by getting to the top of
30 the hill without fainting.
'I never knew water could taste this good!' she said, taking a swig from my bottle before collapsing onto the grass to enjoy the view.

35 Next was caving, something I'd always wanted to try but never got round to. A short drive in the minibus and we were at the cave entrance. We were given helmets with torches before we squeezed through
40 the narrow gap in the rock into the cave. I had imagined we would be wading through deep pools of muddy water. It turned out to be less messy than I had expected although just as exciting. Having
45 learned basic caving techniques and safety rules, we eventually emerged from the cave, sweaty and muddy but completely elated by the experience.
We took archery very seriously. We
50 divided into two teams, according to age. I found myself in the older group. Andy hit the target a few times but the rest of our performance was embarrassingly bad. We had a great time though, and in different
55 wind conditions, it might have been a different story. That's my excuse, anyhow!

2 Read the rest of the text quite quickly. Were your answers to Questions 2 and 3 in Exercise 1 correct?

3 Now use the exam strategy to answer the questions. Be prepared to justify your answers to the class.

Vocabulary: *idiomatic expressions*

4 **1 Find words and expressions in the text that mean the same as:**

1 a group (para. 1)
2 to drink something quickly, taking a large amount of liquid in your mouth (para. 4)
3 manage to do (para. 5)
4 enjoy yourself very much (para. 6)
5 to try, to make an attempt (para. 11)
6 to start shaking because you are nervous (para. 12)
7 you think someone must be joking (para. 14)
8 to talk about something excitedly because you enjoyed it very much (para. 16)

2 Now discuss these questions.

1 Is the text: **a)** formal or informal? **b)** personal or impersonal? **c)** serious or humorous?
2 What kind of publication and reader do you think it was written for?

Sunday morning was abseiling, probably the most frightening experience of the weekend, but incredibly thrilling.
60 One look at the 30-metre drop was enough to convince Vicki: there was no way she was doing it. Justin gently urged her, but wasn't going to force anyone.

As I clambered over the edge of
65 the viaduct, my harness firmly tightened, I tried to think of something nice, such as the delicious buffet that would be our evening meal. Would I live to enjoy it? I soon discovered the truth:
70 once you get used to dangling in space 30 metres above rushing water, abseiling is addictive.

'I love these downhill activities!' said Sarah as she glided down gracefully.

75 Just when we thought things couldn't get any more challenging, we moved on to rock-climbing. We approached the 20-metre rock face. There was a tiny crack in it, but to climb it looked impossible.
80 Despite her fear of heights, Vicki decided to have a go, got almost to the top, then came down on the safety-rope. It was only then that she realised: 'I've abseiled!'

My turn next. I had got a third of the
85 way up before I lost my nerve and my knees turned to jelly.

'I can't do it!' I whimpered down to Justin. But Justin was clearly used to hearing this. He calmly called up
90 instructions.

'There's a tiny ledge to your left!' And there was. 'Now stick your right foot in the crack.' He had to be kidding, but he wasn't.

'Don't use your knees!' Bit by bit, I
95 forced myself to get to the top. I felt elated. I'd just climbed a 20-metre cliff!

Sadly, our weekend had come to an end and we collapsed into the minibus. Our bodies were still pumping adrenaline as
100 we chatted incessantly and raved about our achievements, already planning our return trip. That is, except Sarah. She was fast asleep.

1 Why did the participants choose to spend the weekend in this way?
   A They wanted to learn new skills.
   B They are very adventurous people.
   C They wanted to make new friends.
   D They wanted a change from routine.

2 How did they find their first activity?
   A It was quite tiring.
   B It was very useful.
   C It made one person very ill.
   D It made them all thirsty.

3 What does 'It' in line 42 refer to?
   A the water
   B the cave
   C the experience
   D the weekend

4 The writer claims he would have achieved more at archery if
   A the teams had been organised differently.
   B the weather had been different.
   C they had taken it more seriously.
   D they hadn't spent so much time talking.

5 What happened when they first tried abseiling?
   A The instructor, Justin, had to persuade them it was safe.
   B They nearly got extremely wet.
   C Not everybody took part in the activity.
   D They rewarded themselves with a meal afterwards.

6 What was the most demanding activity?
   A archery
   B caving
   C abseiling
   D rock-climbing

7 What happened during the rock-climbing lesson?
   A Somebody refused to start.
   B Somebody became very anxious.
   C Somebody fell.
   D The instructor, Justin, had to climb up himself.

8 At the end of the weekend, what was their strongest feeling?
   A great excitement
   B sadness
   C physical exhaustion
   D sleepiness

Vocabulary

1 **Read the information in the box below and do the exercises that follow. They will help you to become aware of typical noun and adjective endings, and negative forms.**

Word formation

You can change words in the following ways in English:

1 Add a suffix to the end of a word, e.g.:
work (verb/noun) → *work**er*** (noun)
Sometimes you need to make a change to the stem, e.g.:
patient (adjective) → *patie**nce*** (noun)

2 Add a prefix to the beginning of a word, e.g.:
courage (noun) → ***en**courage*,
***dis**courage* (verb)

3 Make an internal change, e.g.:
choose (verb) → *ch**oi**ce* (noun)
strong (adjective) → *str**e**ngth* (noun),
*str**e**ngth**en*** (verb)

---

2 **Nouns from verbs**

Sometimes you can form more than one noun from a verb. Make a noun from each of these verbs by adding a suffix. Make sure they fit the collocations.

decide / explore / enter / equip

1 oil/polar ....
2 make a .... /an important ....
3 .... fee/examination
4 camping/special ....

3 **Names of jobs**

Make nouns that are names of jobs by adding a suffix to these words. Say what each job involves.

1 navigate ....
2 engine ....
3 history ....
4 therapy ....

Think of some more jobs that have the same endings.

4 **Adjectives from nouns**

Make adjectives to describe people by adding a suffix to these nouns.

1 courage ....   3 ambition ....
2 romance ....   4 sense .... /..........

Which adjective best describes you?

5 **Nouns from adjectives**

Make nouns from these adjectives. What do you notice?

1 active ....   3 ingenious ....
2 able ....   4 real ....

6 **Negative prefixes**

Make these adjectives negative by adding a prefix. Put them under the right heading.

responsible / patient / honest / inhabited / fortunate / credible / agreeable / hospitable

un-	dis-	im-	ir-	in-
....	....	....	....	....
....	....			....

7 **-ed/-ing adjectives**

Complete this paragraph using the words in brackets in the correct form.

Many people feel (1) .... (BORE) by their jobs, and don't find everyday hobbies (2) .... (STIMULATE) enough. Nowadays, they can make their lives more (3) .... (INTEREST) by going on an adventure holiday, and taking part in a range of (4) .... (CHALLENGE) activities. Personally, I would feel (5) .... (TERRIFY) if I had to abseil off a cliff, or go down a cave. But some people don't feel at all (6) .... (FRIGHTEN) by this kind of thing.

8 **Now complete these lists to help you revise.**

Typical noun endings: -ion, ...
Typical adjective endings: -ive, ...
Negative prefixes: un-, ...

! spelling

Correct spelling is required in the exam. What is wrong with the spelling in these answers?

1 I found his *explaination* difficult to understand.   **EXPLAIN**
2 There was a good *attendence* at the meeting.   **ATTEND**

Use of English 2: *word formation*

1 **Look at the exam task below. Read the whole text for general understanding.**

1 Where do you think the text is from?
2 What is it advertising?

2 **Read each line again. Before you fill in the gap, ask yourself:**

1 What type of word do I need for the gap? (noun, verb, etc.)
2 Does the context need a positive or a negative word?
3 Does the context need a singular or a plural word?

3 **When you have finished, read the whole text again to check that the words make sense. Remember to check your spelling.**

4 **Which answers required:**

a) a suffix?   b) a negative prefix?   c) a plural form?   d) two changes to the stem?

▶▶ *study tip!* ◀◀

To help you prepare for this question, it's a good idea to record all the different forms of a word in your vocabulary notebook. Pay careful attention to spelling changes. Include the plural forms of nouns.

Read the text below. Use the word given in capitals at the end of each line to form a word that fits in the space in the same line. There is an example at the beginning **(0)**.

LEARN NEW SKILLS!

Our new multi-activity holidays offer a wide **(0)** *variety* of	VARY
courses, ranging from **(1)** ..... to cookery. And they are so	MOUNTAIN
(2) ..... that everyone can afford them. Supervision at all times	EXPENSE
by our experienced, **(3)** ..... staff is included in the price of the	QUALIFY
holiday. If you are **(4)** ..... in trying out an adventure course,	INTEREST
don't worry if you are **(5)** ..... – we understand that not everyone	FIT
is a super-athlete. Our helpful **(6)** ..... will take your level of	INSTRUCT
(7) ..... into account, and design the course accordingly. You don't	ABLE
have to be physically **(8)** ..... to enjoy one of our holidays.	ACT
There are different courses for computer fans, **(9)** ..... and artists.	MUSIC
Everyone has a lot of fun and you will never feel **(10)**	COURAGE
So write or telephone now for an application form and join in the fun.	

Writing: *transactional letter*

exam file

Part 1 of **Paper 2** is compulsory. You are given information in the form of short texts and notes. There may also be illustrations or diagrams. You always have to write **a letter** of 120–180 words based on this information. You may need to give and/or request information. The letter may be **formal** or **informal**.

▶▶ exam strategy

Make sure you:
- read the question very carefully.
- include **all** the points you are asked to write about. If you omit any relevant points, you won't pass Part 1.
- make a plan **before** you write to help you organise the points logically.
- avoid copying whole phrases or sentences from the input.
- use an appropriate style. Your letter must have a positive effect on the reader if he/she is to take the action you require.

1 Read the writing task below.

1 Who is going to read your letter? Should the style of your letter be formal or informal?

2 Most of the information you need to include in your letter is given to you. Underline the points you must cover in your reply.

> You have written to an Activity Centre inquiring about breaks and requesting a brochure. Today you received a letter and a brochure from the Centre Manager. You have some queries and have made notes on the brochure.
>
> Read the letter from the Centre, together with the brochure and your notes. Write a letter in reply, giving the information requested and also covering the notes you wrote on the brochure.

> Thank you for your letter. I enclose the brochure you requested. Please let me know which type of break you are interested in and the date you wish to come (see the enclosed brochure).
>
> Please let us know if you need any more information. We look forward to receiving your booking.
>
> Yours sincerely
>
> *Mark Kelly*
>
> (Mr) Mark Kelly
> Centre Manager

HIGHLAND ACTIVITY CENTRE

someone to meet me at the station?

Located in the beautiful mountains of Northern Scotland.
(Nearest mainline station: Inverness.)

FACILITIES: The centre has excellent facilities including a games room and swimming pool.

SLEEPING ACCOMMODATION: Bunk beds in most rooms. — *any single rooms?*

ACTIVITIES: These include abseiling, canoeing, caving, rock-climbing. We cater for all ages. — *beginners too?*

STAFF: All our instructors are experienced and qualified.

KIT: Please bring suitable clothing. Specialist equipment is provided free (e.g. helmets, ropes). *???*

FOOD: Cooked breakfasts and dinners at the Centre. Packed lunches provided every day.

TYPES OF BREAK:

Adventure	16+ years	Dates: 28/4, 12/6, 1/9
Teen Action	13–15 years	Dates: 13/6, 18/9, 21/10
Fun 9–12 years	9–12 years	Dates: 23/6, 14/9

Write a letter of between **120** and **180** words in an appropriate style. Do not write any postal addresses.

Focus on planning and organisation

2 **1 Look at this checklist of points to include in the letter. Compare them with the points you underlined in Exercise 1.2. Two items are missing. What are they? Add them to this list in note form.**

- *type of break I want*
- *any single rooms?*
- *suitable clothing? (What, exactly?)*
- *will someone meet me at the station?*

2 Put each of the points listed in Exercise 2.1 under one of these headings.

Information to supply: *Questions to ask:*

3 Decide which points are similar and can go together in one paragraph. Copy and complete this plan with a summary of each paragraph in the order you are going to follow. Add more boxes if you need to.

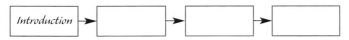

3 **Read the first part of a sample answer below.**

1 Answer these questions about content and organisation.

1 How many points has the writer covered in this part of the letter? Cross them off the checklist you completed in Exercise 2.1.
2 Has the writer copied whole phrases word for word from the input material in the task?
3 The second section of the letter should have two paragraphs. Mark where the break should come.
4 The writer has dealt with the points in a logical order. Is it the same as the order you chose in Exercise 2? Is your order equally appropriate?

Dear Mr Kelly,

Thanks a million for your letter and brochure, which arrived today. I am very interested in taking an Adventure Break at your Centre.

I would like to come on 12th June and the train arrives in Inverness at 7 p.m. I wonder whether someone could possibly meet me at the station. I have some queries about sleeping arrangements and clothes. First, could you tell me if there are any single rooms? I am a light sleeper so I would prefer my own room. I wonder if you could also tell me what sort of clothes to bring. Will I need walking boots, for example, or will they be provided?

Turning to the activities, I wonder

2 Answer these questions about style.

1 Has the writer used an appropriate style? Does anything need changing?
2 What is the correct ending for a formal letter when you know the name of the person you are writing to?

Focus on grammar ▼ *p.181*

4 **1 Find three examples of indirect questions in the sample letter.**

1 Why does the writer use them?
2 What expressions are used to introduce them?
3 What do you notice about word order and punctuation?

grammar file 14

Indirect questions use the same word order as a statement.

Direct questions	**Indirect questions**
1 Are the instructors qualified? →	**I'd like to know** if/whether **the instructors are** qualified.
2 Will we have any free time? →	**Could you tell me** if/whether **we will** have any free time?
3 What time do we have to get up every morning? →	**I wonder if you could tell me** what time **we have to** get up every morning.

2 Make the following into indirect questions, as in the example.

Example:
Can beginners take part in all the activities or only some?
Would you let me know whether beginners can …

1 Is it possible to go caving without any previous experience? *I was wondering* ……………..………......... .
2 What's the maximum number of people in each activity group? *I'd be grateful if you could tell me*
..……………………………………………… .
3 Is there a fitness room in the activity centre?
..……………………………………………… .
4 Can I hire walking boots at the centre or do I have to bring my own?
..……………………………………………… .
5 Do you offer discounts for groups?
..……………………………………………… .

Over to you

5 **Read the writing task in Exercise 1 again and write your own letter of reply. Follow the advice in the exam strategy box. Remember to:**

- use the plan you made in Exercise 2.
- use the correct greeting and ending for a formal letter.
- use formal style and form questions politely.
- check your writing for errors when you have finished.

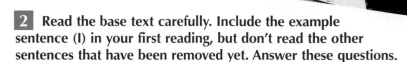

3 Education

Lead-in

Look at the list of school subjects in the box and discuss these questions.

1 Which ones are/were available at your school? Can you add any more subjects to the list?

Geography	History	Physics	Maths
Chemistry	Biology	Music	Latin
Information Technology	English	Art
Design Technology	Religious Studies
Technical Drawing	Physical Education

2 Put the school subjects you are studying/have studied in order:
- from easiest to most difficult (easiest = number 1).
- from most enjoyable to least enjoyable.
- from most useful for your future career to least useful.

Compare your lists with other students and give reasons for your answers.

Reading 1:
gapped text (sentences)

1 Read the title, the sub-heading and the first paragraph of the text opposite. Answer these questions.

1 What is the text about?
2 What do these words mean?
   a) supermodel
   b) catwalk
   c) a six-figure contract

2 Read the base text carefully. Include the example sentence (I) in your first reading, but don't read the other sentences that have been removed yet. Answer these questions.

1 When was Susan Jackson 'discovered'?
2 What has been more important to her, school or modelling?
3 How can modelling help her to achieve her career ambition?
4 Which paragraphs in the text refer to the past, which refer to the present, and which to the future?

3 Now read the sentences in the box.

1 Look at the underlined words in each sentence. What kind of words are they?
2 Which sentences are in the past tense, which are in the present tense, and which in the future tense?

2 Look at the first gap (Question 0). Answer these questions.

1 What information do you need to fill the gap?
2 Read the example answer (I). Who does the word *She* refer back to?
3 Read the sentence after the gap. Why does the sentence say *The agent* and not *an agent*?

4 Now identify the sentences that go in gaps 1–7, using language links to help you. Remember, there is one extra sentence in the box that you won't need.

5 Read through the complete text to check that it makes sense. Then compare your answers with a partner.

Vocabulary: *phrasal verbs*

6 1 Which particle or preposition is used with these verbs? What do the verbs mean in the text?

1 to sign someone ....
2 to whisk someone ....
3 to insist .... doing something
4 to catch .... something
5 to get .... something
6 to turn something ....

2 Add the verbs that are new to your vocabulary notebook. Remember, it's a good idea to list phrasal verbs under the particle or preposition.

Over to you

7 Discuss.

Susan is determined to become an architect. What career have <u>you</u> set your sights on? What qualifications do you need?

You are going to read a magazine article about a young model. Eight sentences have been removed from the article. Choose from the sentences A–I the one which fits each gap (1–7). There is one extra sentence which you do not need to use. There is an example at the beginning (0).

A model student

Our reporter investigates one schoolgirl's high-earning holiday job.

Britain's newest supermodel is resisting the bright lights of New York's catwalks to study for her school-leaving exams, despite the offer of a six-figure contract with a cosmetics company.

Susan Jackson was first discovered at the age of 14. **0** **I** The agent signed her up immediately, but for the first two years, Susan was too busy working towards her GCSE exams at school to devote much time to her new career.

Two days after finishing her last exam paper, however, she was whisked off to Paris for a month to work for the Ford model agency. Her first week in Paris was extremely tiring and confusing. She also met many girls who'd been there for a month and hadn't been given any work at all. **1** After a few days, she was selected to do the Chanel catwalk show, and she was well on the way to becoming a celebrity. An invitation to do a show in New York followed.

2 Working in her half-term break from school in October, she managed to earn £6,500 a day. But that was not all. At the show, she was spotted by scouts from the cosmetics company, Cover Girl. A Cover Girl contract is a coveted step on the route to supermodel status. Previous models who have worked for the company include Helena

Christensen and Rachel Hunter.

After seeing her in action, Cover Girl's talent scouts invited Susan back to the States for a job interview. But Susan didn't want to take any more time off school, where she had already started her two-year

Advanced Level courses. **3**

Susan insists on staying on at school to complete her A-levels in Maths, Physics and Design Technology. **4** Although most of this is in the US, it can generally be fitted into school holidays and breaks.

5 But she is the person who is strictest about catching up on any coursework that she may miss as a result. 'I want to get good qualifications,' she explains. 'I enjoy school and being with my friends. It helps me to feel normal.' Susan realises that if she modelled full-time, every day, she'd be spending a lot of time with people she doesn't know. 'It just isn't for me,' she says.

Susan admits that sometimes things can get a bit difficult. There have been times when she's had a pile of homework to get through, and the phone hasn't stopped ringing all day. **6**

7 She's set her sights on a degree in Design but not, as it happens, in fashion. She's keen to follow her father in the field of architectural design and technical drawing. So she's continuing to do just enough modelling work to keep that money coming in, without spoiling her chances of getting into university.

GCSE: *General Certificate of Secondary Education. These are exams which school students in Britain take at age 15/16.*

A It was <u>there</u> that Susan, now aged 16, really caught the attention of the fashion world.

B <u>But she</u> knows her own mind and prefers to turn some work down rather than put her long-term plans at risk.

C <u>So</u> she did a screen test for <u>them</u> in London <u>instead</u>, but still got <u>the</u> job.

D <u>Until then</u>, Susan had been accompanied by one of her parents, or by her brother, a university student.

E <u>On the other hand</u>, Susan <u>also</u> realises that she is in a position to earn enough to pay her way through university.

F <u>She</u> was just beginning to think that the life of a model was not for her, when she got her lucky break.

G Fortunately, <u>the</u> new cosmetics contract will only involve her in 15 days' work.

H Where <u>this</u> is not possible, the school has given Susan time off to fulfil her modelling engagements.

I <u>She</u> was spotted at a local cricket match by <u>an</u> agent for a London-based modelling agency.

Grammar: -ing *forms and infinitives* ▼ *pp.179–80*

A We use -*ing* forms:
- **after certain verbs**
1 Sarah **enjoys going** to school.
2 I'm **considering going** to college.

- **after prepositions**
3 He's looking forward **to going** to university.
4 Is there any point **in studying** literature?

- **in certain expressions**
5 It's **no good/use waiting**.
6 It's **not worth waiting**.
7 It's **a waste of time asking**.
8 I'm **having difficulty/problems concentrating**.
9 We **spend** a lot of **time revising**.

B We use *to*-infinitive:
- **after certain verbs**
1 I **want to study** medicine.
2 My friends **taught me to swim**.

- **after certain adjectives or nouns**
3 It's **hard to learn** a language well.
4 It's **my ambition to be** a doctor.

C We use bare infinitive:
- **after *make/let***
1 The teacher **let me go** home.

- **after certain expressions**
2 I'**d rather** not **go**.
3 You'**d better do** your homework.

D -*ing* form or infinitive?
1 I **like to play/playing** tennis on Saturdays. (= no change of meaning here)
2 a) I **remember starting** primary school. (= memory of a past event)
   b) I must **remember to do** my homework tonight. (= I mustn't forget.)
3 a) I **heard** my friend **shout**. (= completed action)
   b) I **heard** my friend **shouting**. (= action in progress)

1 **1 Read the first part of a story and underline the correct form of the verb in each pair.**

Ask my brother, Tom, what he wants (1) *doing/to do* when he leaves school and he'll tell you his ambition is (2) *being/to be* a scientist. Personally, I find it difficult (3) *believing/to believe* that anyone can enjoy (4) *spending/to spend* time in a laboratory. I loathe (5) *doing/to do* Science. I can't bear (6) *memorising/to memorise* boring formulae. In my opinion, nobody should be forced (7) *studying/to study* Chemistry, least of all me! Tom is different …

2 Discuss these questions.
1 How is Tom different from the writer?
2 What do you think the next part of the story will be about?

2 **1 Read the rest of the story. Were your predictions right?**

2 Put the verbs in brackets into the correct form.

Tom adores (8) .... (study) Chemistry and Physics and is always keen on (9) .... (discover) more. Even as a child, I remember him (10) .... (do) experiments in the kitchen. I was always trying (11) .... (prevent) him from (12) .... (make) a mess and (13) .... (blow up) the building. At school, the teachers encouraged him (14) .... (specialise) in Science and never minded him (15) .... (ask) questions in class until two years ago!

This is what happened. Tom persuaded his teacher (16) .... (let) him (17) .... (demonstrate) one of his experiments in class. His teacher made the mistake of (18) .... (permit) him (19) .... (use) a strong-smelling chemical. If he had stopped (20) .... (think), he would have realised this was not a good idea. Of course, the experiment went wrong. Tom forgot (21) .... (put) the lid back on the bottle and the chemical spilt on the floor.

The terrible smell invaded the whole school. The teachers in the nearest classrooms had to stop (22) .... (teach). In the end, the headmaster closed the school and let everyone (23) .... (go) home. They made Tom (24) .... (stay) behind and (25) .... (scrub) the laboratory floor for hours until the smell went.

3 Can you remember anything like this happening at your school?

Over to you

3 **Put the verbs in brackets into the correct form. Then ask and answer the questions in pairs.**

1 Do/Did you enjoy .... (go) to school? Is there anything you hate .... (do) at school?
2 Do you like .... (play) sports? Have you ever tried .... (canoe or abseil)?
3 What games do you remember .... (play) in primary school? What else do you remember .... (do)?
4 How long ago did you start .... (learn) English? Do you find it easy .... (learn)? What aspects of English do you find most difficult .... (cope with)?
5 Are you looking forward to .... (leave) school? What do you want .... (do) as a career?
6 Do you mind .... (get) a lot of homework? Did you remember .... (do) your homework for this lesson?

Use of English 1: *transformations*

▶▶ *exam strategy* Paper 3, Part 3

- Compare the prompt sentence and the gapped sentence. Decide what part of the meaning of the prompt sentence needs to go in the gap.
- Look carefully at the **key word** and at the words before and after the gap, and try to identify what structure is being tested.

1 Use the exam strategy to do the exam task opposite.

2 Compare your answers with a partner. How many different structures were tested in this task?

Complete the second sentence so that it has a similar meaning to the first sentence, using the word given. **Do not change the word given. You must use between two and five words, including the word given. There is an example at the beginning (0).**

Example:

0 What subject did you like best at school?
favourite
What *was your favourite subject at* .... school?

1 How much did that copy of the World Atlas cost you?
price
What .... your copy of the World Atlas?

2 Paul likes to do his homework in bed.
enjoys
Paul .... in bed.

3 You are not allowed to use mobile phones in school.
prohibited
The use .... in school.

4 Tanya has repeatedly borrowed Phil's book without asking.
keeps
Tanya .... book without asking.

5 Sally remembers the first time she went to school very clearly.
going
Sally clearly remembers .... first time.

6 Melanie doesn't often hand her homework in on time.
rarely
Melanie .... on time.

7 Learning poetry by heart seems pointless to me.
point
I can't .... learning poetry by heart.

8 Graham hasn't looked at his old schoolbooks for years.
since
It's .... at his old schoolbooks.

9 I decided not to revise for my exam now, but to do it the night before.
put
I decided .... my exam until the night before.

10 Angela found her Chemistry lessons difficult to understand.
difficulty
Angela .... her Chemistry lessons.

11 Tom did not study hard at school and now he regrets it.
not
Tom .... at school.

Listening: *multiple matching*

exam file

In **Paper 4**, **Part 3**, you listen to five different speakers talking separately about different aspects of the same topic. You hear all five once, then all five again. You have to match each speaker with one of the options **A–F** given.

There will be similarities between the extracts. Sometimes a word in one of the options may occur in more than one extract. You need to listen for the **differences** between the speakers.

1 Before you listen, carefully read the instructions for the exam task below. What topic will the speakers talk about?

> You will hear five people talking about the playwright, Shakespeare. For questions **1–5**, choose from the list **A–F** who is speaking. Use the letters only once. There is one extra letter which you do not need to use.
>
> | | | | |
> |---|---|---|---|
> | A | bookseller | Speaker 1 | 1 |
> | B | teacher | Speaker 2 | 2 |
> | C | student | Speaker 3 | 3 |
> | D | tourist | | |
> | E | film-maker | Speaker 4 | 4 |
> | F | police officer | Speaker 5 | 5 |

2 How much do you know about the topic? Can you answer the questions in this quiz?

QUIZ

1 Where was Shakespeare born?

  a in London, England

  b in Stratford-upon Avon, England

2 In which century was he born?

  a the sixteenth century

  b the seventeenth century

3 Which of these plays did he not write?

  a Hamlet

  b Julius Caesar

  c The Importance of Being Earnest

4 What happened to Hamlet?

  a He was killed in an act of revenge.

  b He became King of Denmark.

3 Now read the options A–F in the exam task. These may give you some ideas about what you will hear.

What do you think each of the speakers might want to say about Shakespeare?

4 🔊 **1** Listen to the recording once all the way through. As you listen, note down what you think each speaker's main message is.

2 Now answer these questions.

1 What makes people like Speaker 1 want to read Shakespeare's plays?

2 What places does Speaker 2 mention and why?

3 How does Speaker 3 feel about Shakespeare's plays and why?

4 Speaker 4 keeps referring to *them* and *they*. Who do you think *they* could be?

5 Why does Speaker 5 mention the different versions of Shakespeare's plays that are available?

3 Which of the jobs listed A–F do you think best matches the main message of each speaker?

5 🔊 Listen to the recording again. Listen out for this information to help you confirm your answers.

- Is Speaker 1 young or old? Where does she read Shakespeare's plays?
- Speakers 3 and 5 both mention *video*. But are they film-makers? Listen for the key words that tell you what their jobs must be.
- There are two words that tell you what Speaker 4's job must be.

Over to you

WHAT'S YOUR OPINION?
Studying classic authors at school is:

a) more likely to put young people off them.

b) a good introduction to great literature.

Speaking: *collaborative task*

exam file

In **Paper 5**, **Part 3**, the examiner gives you and the other candidate a task to do together, based on visual stimulus such as photographs, drawings or diagrams. You have to do **two** things:

● respond to the visual prompts, **and**
● work **together** to reach a decision or conclusion. You don't have to agree: you can agree to differ.

You have three minutes for this.

1 Look at the photos and discuss these questions. Use expressions from the box.

1 What learning situation does each photo illustrate?
2 Which one is most similar to your present or previous school?
3 What are the advantages and disadvantages of each approach?

> a traditional classroom   to work in small groups
> rows of desks   to use up-to-date technology
> to use a library   to do research/project work
> a competitive/relaxed atmosphere
> to express your own opinion   to learn from others
> to learn/work at your own pace   to gain confidence
> to learn facts by heart   to learn practical skills
> to work on your own   self-study
> to be able to ask any questions you like

2 **1** 🔲 **You are going to hear two candidates doing Part 3 of the test. Listen to the examiner's instructions on the recording.**

1 What task does he set the candidates? How many parts does it have?
2 How does one of the candidates ask for clarification?

2 🔲 **Now listen to the candidates doing the task.**

1 What conclusion did they come to?
2 Do you agree with their ideas or not?

3 🔲 **Look at the functions files 4, 5, 7, 9 and 10 on pages 200 and 201 and listen again.**

1 Tick (✓) the expressions the candidates use.

2 Discuss.

1 Did each candidate express his/her opinions clearly?
2 Did the candidates listen to and develop each other's ideas?

▼ ▼ *exam strategy*

● DO listen carefully to the examiner's instructions.
● DON'T come to a decision too quickly.
● DO make sure you both take an equal part in the conversation.

4 Now do the task yourselves. Work in pairs or groups of three. When you have finished, compare your conclusion with other groups.

3 Young entrepreneurs

Lead-in

1 How much do you know about the World Wide Web, or Internet? Read the following statements and decide which <u>one</u> is not true.

1 The Internet was originally designed for military purposes.
2 The first Internet café in Europe was London's 'Cyberia'.
3 You can access the Internet via a mobile phone.
4 Anybody can have their own webpage.
5 You have to be over 16 to use the Internet.
6 Parents can restrict what their children look at on the Internet.
7 You can set up a business on the Internet from your own home.
8 You could meet your future husband or wife over the Internet.

2 Discuss.

1 Do you use the Internet? How much? What for?
2 How far do you think it has changed or will change our lives?

Reading 2: *gapped text (sentences)*

> ►► **exam strategy**　　　　Paper 1, Part 3
> - Read the whole of the base text plus the example sentence carefully.
> - Read the text around each gap carefully and try to predict the missing information.
> - Read the sentences that have been removed and look for one that fits the meaning.
> - Check for language and topic links before and after the sentence.
> - When you have finished, read the whole text again. Does it make sense?

1 Read the title and sub-heading of the text opposite and look at the instructions for the exam task.

1 What is the article about? Who has written it?
2 How many gaps do you have to fill?

2 Read the base text and the example answer. Then answer these questions to check your understanding.

1 What games did Tom like to play as a young child? What did they indicate about him?
2 How did Tom feel about going to school? Why do you think that was?
3 When and how did he begin to show a talent for business?
4 What is 'Soccernet' and how did it develop?
5 What alternative career options are open to Tom?
6 How do his parents and teachers feel about his attitude to school?

3 1 Look at the first gap (Question 0) and the example answer (I).

1 What do the underlined words refer back to in the first paragraph?
2 What do the words in *italics* relate to?

2 Read the next three paragraphs. Use these clues to help you choose the right sentence for each gap.
Question:

1 What information do you expect in the gap?
   a) why Tom didn't settle in the local playgroup
   b) what he did instead
   The sentence after the gap mentions *pastimes*. Which missing sentence contains an associated idea?
2 After the gap the paragraph talks about a *solution* to a *problem*. Which missing sentence refers to a solution that isn't a solution? Underline the words used.
3 The sentence after the gap mentions how Tom *preferred to invest* his money. Which missing sentence describes something else he could have done with his money?

4 Continue with the rest of the text. Pay attention to language links and associated words and ideas to help you.

Over to you

5 Discuss.

Tom has several choices for the future. Which career path would you advise him to follow?

- *I would advise him to ...*
- *I don't think he ought to ...*
- *His best choice would be to ...*
- *I wouldn't recommend ...-ing.*

You are going to read a newspaper article about a schoolboy who set up a successful Internet business. Eight sentences have been removed from the article. Choose from the sentences A–I the one which fits each gap (1–7). There is one extra sentence which you do not need to use. There is an example at the beginning (0).

My son's a computer genius

Tom Hadfield created a £15m Internet business by the age of 16. His father describes life with a child prodigy.

Tom was always advanced for his age. He learned to walk and talk early, and was fascinated by words and numbers. He was only two when he got his first computer. In fact, it was bought for his older sister. Even before his aptitude for mathematics became apparent, Tom was teaching himself to play chess on it. **0 I**

Although Tom's sister attended the local primary school, Tom never quite settled in at the neighbourhood playgroup. **1** Early pastimes included shuffling and memorising the order of two packs of playing cards, or working out how many seconds there are in a day, a week, a year.

We hoped that school would keep him occupied, but although he enjoyed the many friends he made, he soon grew bored with lessons. It wasn't the teachers' fault. **2** What about his friends? What would happen when he was in the top year? The proposed solution raised more problems than it tried to solve.

By the time he was seven or eight, Tom was playing football regularly for his school and for a team organised by supporters of the local football club. His skills as a businessman had begun to show through as well. He washed our car, and those of the neighbours, for 50p each. **3** He preferred to invest it in a bucket, sponge and bottle of car shampoo.

Secondary school began and Tom soon discovered the World Wide Web. For his twelfth birthday, we got him 'wired up', largely because this was the only way to get him home from the house of a friend who already had Internet access. **4** We learned later that Tom was already planning then to postpone serious studying until the year he took his final exams at 16.

Tom says that he drew up the business plan for Soccernet, now the world's most popular football website, while he was daydreaming in a lesson. Since then, its success has provided his father with full-time employment, generated millions of pounds in advertising, and now attracts more than seven million readers a year. The site is now valued at £15m. **5** He has also had the chance of leaving school to pursue a football career as a goalkeeper with Brighton F.C. or stay at school and follow a business career.

6 One is, 'Aren't you worried about Tom spending so long at a computer?' And the other: 'Isn't it a problem that he misses so much school because of his business commitments?' The answer to both is no. Tom spends anything up to twelve hours a day at the keyboard, but he still manages to go around town with his friends and play football two or three times a week. He rarely watches television.

As for missing school, the teachers who understand Tom recognise the benefits he enjoys from being active in the 'real' world. **7** If anything, the past four years have been like an extended business studies project, an experiment in personal and social education. After sixth-form college, Tom hopes to go to Oxford University to study Politics, Philosophy and Economics. Throughout, he intends to enjoy himself doing all the things normal adolescents do, while building up his own business.

So it may not be long before he is sitting at his computer in his room at university, running a global business in his spare time.

A His other interests haven't harmed his education; they have added to it, made it more meaningful.

B They suggested the possibility of moving him up a year but that was no answer.

C There are two questions friends most frequently ask.

D From that day, school began to recede further and further into the background.

E We all hoped secondary school might prove more challenging.

F As a result, Tom has been offered employment around the globe, frequently by corporations that did not realise that he is still a schoolboy.

G Instead he preferred to play by himself at home.

H But he didn't want to spend the money on sweets.

I By the age of three, <u>he</u> had learned how to break into *the program* and change sides every time <u>the computer</u> was about to *declare checkmate*.

Vocabulary

1 Choosing the right word

Underline the correct word in each pair. Then answer the questions truthfully.

1 Are the *teachers/professors* at your school very strict?
2 Are you good at *sensible/practical* 'hands-on' subjects like Design Technology?
3 Which *subjects/titles* should you do well at in your next exams?
4 Did you get good *notes/marks* in your last test?
5 I got an A *grade/mark* for English in my last exams. What about you?
6 How many exams are you *taking/passing* this year?
7 In your country, can you apply for a *grant/fee* if you want to go to university?
8 Would you be interested in a *career/profession* in computing?

2 Words followed by prepositions

Certain verbs, adjectives and nouns are followed by a preposition + gerund.

Examples:
*The teacher insisted **on** us do**ing** a test.*
*I'm hopeless **at** learn**ing** dates.*

The *Longman Active Study Dictionary* can help you to find the right preposition to use. Look at these extracts and answer the questions.

1 Which prepositions follow each of the words?
2 Make your own example sentence with each word.

> **accuse** /əˈkjuːz/ *v* [T] to say that someone has done something wrong or illegal: **accuse sb of doing sth** *Are you accusing me of stealing?* – **accuser** *n* [C]

> **fond** /fɒnd/ *adj* **1 be fond of** to like someone or something very much: *Mrs Winters is very fond of her grandchildren.* **2 be fond of doing sth** to enjoy doing something often: *They're fond of using legal jargon.* **3 fond memories of**

3 Verbs + prepositions

Complete these sentences by adding an appropriate preposition and putting the verb in brackets into the gerund.

1 My brother is preventing me .... (pass) my exams.
2 He insists .... (play) his music really loudly when I'm trying to revise.
3 I'm thinking .... (go) to stay with my neighbours if he doesn't stop.
4 You can't blame me .... (be) angry.
5 I'm really looking forward .... (start) university and he's going to spoil it all.
6 He won't listen though. He says he objects .... me .... (tell) him what to do.

4 Adjectives + prepositions

1 Make true sentences about yourself by completing the following sentences with an appropriate preposition and an -ing form.

1 At school, I'm really good ....
2 I'm completely hopeless ....
3 Sometimes I get tired ....
4 I'm interested .... when I leave school.
5 In my free time, I'm very keen ....
6 At the moment, I'm a bit worried ....
7 So far in my life, I'm proudest ....
8 I think I'm capable ....

2 Work in pairs. Try to guess what your partner has written about him/herself. Ask questions like this:

You're really good at solving Maths problems, aren't you?
Are you hopeless at spelling, like me?

5 Collocations: *do* or *make?*

1 We use *do* or *make* with certain nouns to form fixed phrases. Put the words below into the correct column.

a test / a mess / an attempt / a noise / some work / an effort / an experiment / friends / progress / your homework / some research / a mistake / your best / a course (in something)

Do	Make

2 Now fill in the gaps in these sentences with a preposition + *make* or *do* in the correct form.

1 The teacher is always telling me off .... too many mistakes!
2 I'm really fed up .... tests.
3 The headmaster has warned us twice .... too much noise during English lessons.
4 My friend insists .... her homework before we go out in the evening.
5 My mother was angry with me .... a mess in the bathroom.
6 My little sister is having no difficulty .... friends at her new school.
7 The boys in the class don't believe .... much effort in subjects like Cookery.
8 I've been praised .... so much progress this term!

Use of English 2: *lexical cloze*

►► *exam strategy*

Paper 3, Part 1 ► p.13

1 **1 Read the text opposite and answer these questions to check your understanding.**

1 What skills will students learn for the 'Diploma of Practical Achievement'?

2 Why is the Diploma being introduced? Find two reasons.

2 Discuss.

Do you think the Diploma is a good idea? Why/Why not?

►► *exam tip!*

If you understand what the text is about, you will find it easier to choose the right word for each gap.

◄◄

2 **Now do the exam task. Remember that the word you choose must fit the meaning and the grammar of the gap. Use these clues to help you.**

Question:

2 Only one of the verbs goes with *course*.

3 Which verb is followed by the preposition *with*?

4 Which adjective is followed by *to*?

5 Only one verb goes with *presentation*.

6 Which linking expression makes sense here?

8 This is a fixed phrase.

11 Which word means the same as *hands-on*?

12 This is another fixed phrase.

15 Pay attention to the preposition that follows.

Read the text below and decide which answer A, B, C or D best fits each space. There is an example at the beginning (0).

0   A compulsory   B required   C necessary   D key

ESSENTIAL SKILLS FOR LIFE

From next year, every student in their final year at our school will study for a (0) *A* Diploma of Practical Achievement. This will be in addition to the (1) .... examinations. Up to now, the course has been optional, but from now on every student must (2) .... it.

The aim is to (3) .... students with 'life skills', which the Diploma divides into eight categories. These cover a range of things (4) .... to life beyond school, from sending an e-mail to (5) .... presentations to an audience. Under the heading 'survival', (6) ...., students can learn car maintenance, first aid and cooking. We have discovered that many students cannot do simple things such as (7) .... a puncture or boil an egg. At the other (8) ...., the Diploma includes such things as how to design a webpage and how to (9) .... if someone has a heart attack. It has been called a 'Diploma in Common Sense'.

On the course, students will not be taught in the traditional (10) ...., but rather will be guided and encouraged to do things for themselves. This is above all a (11) ...., 'hands-on' course. To a greater or lesser (12) ...., good schools have always tried to (13) .... these skills. Unfortunately, students have not always (14) .... much interest because such skills are not directly related to passing exams for higher education. We hope this will change now that we have a proper course that will (15) .... to a recognised diploma.

1	A normal	B everyday	C set	D typical
2	A pick	B make	C adopt	D take
3	A give	B equip	C offer	D donate
4	A relevant	B associated	C linked	D concerned
5	A having	B giving	C speaking	D expressing
6	A as a result	B therefore	C for example	D otherwise
7	A service	B maintain	C do up	D mend
8	A extreme	B end	C limit	D point
9	A handle	B guide	C cope	D direct
10	A means	B way	C route	D approach
11	A theoretical	B technical	C practising	D practical
12	A amount	B method	C extent	D depth
13	A grow	B develop	C make	D do
14	A shown	B given	C placed	D proved
15	A move	B result	C take	D lead

Writing: *transactional letter*

exam file

In **Paper 2**, **Part 1**, the instructions for the task will specify who the target reader is, and the context. Based on this information, you have to decide if the letter should be **formal** or **informal**.

1 **Read the writing task below.**

1 Underline or tick the points you must deal with in your reply.

2 Who are you going to write your letter to?

1 Should the letter be formal and polite or informal and friendly?

2 What greetings and endings could you use? (See Writing file p.187.)

You are studying English at a language school in Britain. A friend of yours in another country is coming to study at the same college and has asked you to send some information and advice. Read the information sheet supplied by the school and the notes below. Use the information to write a letter to your friend telling him/her about next term.

Samson Language School
IMPORTANT INFORMATION FOR THE NEXT COURSE

Thursday 18th Apr.,
Friday 19th Apr., 9.00–17.30: Registration for the new course
Friday 19th Apr., 10.00: School bookshop opens
Monday 22nd Apr., 9.00: New classes start
Tuesday 23rd: Welcome Dance from 19.00 in the School Hall.

Register as early as poss. Long queues later, if not!
Get books by Mon.! Cost = £60.00 approx. NB buy
mine for half price?
First lesson – 9.00. Arrive early to get good seat –
and impress teacher!
Dance great fun, worth going!

Write a **letter** of between **120** and **180** words in an appropriate style. Do not write any postal addresses.

▶▶ *exam strategy*

Make sure you:

- know who is going to read your letter and use an appropriate style.
- use key words from the input to make notes before you write.
- expand your notes into sentences. Make sure your sentences are accurate and well-constructed.
- make good use of linking words to connect your sentences.

▶▶ *exam tip!*

Only add a piece of information, a suggestion or request of your own if it is relevant to the task. You will lose marks if you introduce irrelevant ideas.

Focus on expanding notes

2 **1 Look at these notes which a student wrote for a letter of advice to a friend about a different language school. Build the notes into complete sentences. Pay attention to articles and prepositions.**

Example:

Send application in early or not get place

You should send your application in early or you may not get a place. OR *If I were you, I'd send your application in early or you may not get a place.*

1 *Test on 1st day at 10.00 – come prepared!*

2 *Need good dictionary. V. expensive to buy from school – bookshop cheaper.*

3 *Welcome Party 7 p.m. Fri. Recommend going – great fun!*

4 *Tour of city Wed 3 p.m. Very helpful – take notes! N.B. Buy map – easy to get lost!*

5 *Join sports club in school! Excellent volleyball trainer.*

2 Work in pairs. Compare the way you expanded the sentences with your partner. How many alternative ways can you think of?

▶▶ *exam tip!*

Use key words correctly. You can build on key words from the task but you **must not** copy whole segments of text.

3 Read the letter opposite, which one student wrote in answer to the writing task. Answer these questions.

Content

1 Has the writer missed out any points in the task? If so, what are they?
2 The writer has added a piece of advice of his own. Find it and underline it. Is it relevant to the task?
3 Has the writer divided the points into paragraphs logically?

Style/register

4 Is the style appropriate for an informal letter?

Accuracy

5 The writer has made a few mistakes in expanding his notes. Underline and correct the parts of the letter where he has missed out articles, prepositions or other phrases.

Focus on grammar ▶ pp.182–3

4 Find all the examples of conditional sentences in the letter in Exercise 3. Match them to the uses described in the grammar file.

grammar files 18, 19

A Real and likely conditions

To talk about events that are true now or likely to happen in the present or future, we use:

● **If + present + present / modal + bare infinitive/ imperative**
1 If you **know** one language, it **is** easier to learn another one.
2 If you **want** more advice, just **let** me know.

● **If + present + will / modal + bare infinitive**
3 If you **study** at this school, you**'ll** really **enjoy** it.
4 If you **don't book** soon/Unless you **book** soon, you **won't get** on a course.
5 You **will learn** a lot provided/as long as you **work** hard.

B Unlikely conditions

To give strong advice or to talk about doubtful/ hypothetical situations in the present or future, we use:

● **If + past simple + would / modal + bare infinitive**
1 I **wouldn't go** to that school if I **were** you!
2 If you **went** to a smaller language school, it **would/might be** cheaper.
3 If I **didn't like** it here, I**'d leave**.

Dear Laura,

Thank you for your letter of 23rd March. I was really pleased to hear you're coming here to study. If I didn't have exams, I'd stay for another term myself!

Course begins Monday 22nd April but you have to register on the previous Thursday or Friday. I'd advise you to get to school by 9.00, whichever day you choose. If you go early, you'll miss the long queues.

Bookshop opens 10.00 Friday 19th. If you buy your books there, they'll cost about £60 but I've got a better idea. Buy mine. Half price.

First lesson on Monday 9.00. If I were you, I'd get there early, say 8.45, and impress the teacher! Don't be late unless you want to get into trouble. The school is very strict about punctuality.

Finally, there's Welcome Dance on Tuesday 23rd. It's in the College Hall and starts 7 p.m. I recommend going to this, as it's always great fun.

Well that's all for now. Let me know if you want to buy my books.

Best wishes,

Antonio

5 Read the following sentences and put the verbs into the appropriate conditional form.

1 I .... (not/like) to go to a foreign country if I .... (not/speak) the language perfectly.
2 Please visit me soon! If you .... (come) and stay with me, I .... (show) you all the sights.
3 If I .... (can) drive, I .... (take) you all round the area, but I'm afraid I can't!
4 You .... (really/enjoy) meeting my friends as long as you .... (not/mind) being teased.
5 Have you booked a flight? You .... (not/get) one unless you .... (book) soon.
6 It's a promise! I .... (meet) you at the airport – provided your flight .... (arrive) at a reasonable time.
7 If I .... (be) you, I .... (bring) an umbrella in case it .... (rain).

Over to you

6 Read the writing task in Exercise 1 again and write your own answer. Follow the advice in the exam strategy box. **Remember to:**

● make a plan before you start to write.
● use key words from the input to make notes.
● divide your letter into clear paragraphs.
● check your writing for errors when you have finished.

4 Places

Lead-in

Look at the photographs of New York. Use phrases from the box to compare and contrast the photos.

1 What is similar in the photos? What is different?
2 Say what you think it's like to live in this city and why.
3 Would you like to live there?

> skyscrapers   crowds of people   to hurry along
> to be in a rush   to enjoy yourself
> to have a good time   to relax
> (a/an) exciting / stimulating / frightening /
>   stressful (place to live)
> (too much) pollution / noise / traffic
> lots to do/plenty going on

Reading 1: *multiple matching*

1 **Look at the exam task opposite. Read the instructions, then look quickly at the title and the headings in the text. Answer these questions.**

1 What kind of text are you going to read?
2 How many sections does it have?
3 Can you predict what each of the people **A–D** might say about the topic?

2 **1 Look at the example (Question 0).**

1 What are the key words in the question? Underline them.
2 Think of other ways to express the ideas in the question.
   – What examples of necessities can you think of?
   – Can you think of a word that means the opposite of *necessities*?
3 Scan section A to find the relevant part of the text. Look for expressions like the ones you thought of above.

2 Now find the answer to Question 1.

3 Check you are right.

1 Section A also mentions something that is *free*. Find this part.
2 Does it refer to things that someone *needs*? What does it refer to?

3 **Now use the same strategy to answer the rest of the questions.**

Over to you

4 **Discuss these questions.**

1 List five good aspects and five bad aspects of life in New York, according to the text.
2 Which of the negative aspects mentioned in the text would worry you the most?
3 Which of the positive aspects would you find most attractive?

You are going to read an article about living in New York. Answer the questions by choosing from the people A–D. The people may be chosen more than once. There is an example at the beginning (0).

Which of the people

has just enough money to buy necessities?	0 **A**	mentions several sources of income?	7
is able to get things he/she needs without paying?	1	thinks New York is now a safer place than before?	8
has thought about leaving New York?	2	likes the variety of people in New York?	9
enjoys a spare-time activity that is free?	3	works to finance another activity?	10
spends a lot of money for the benefit of others?	4	would like more space?	11
says that prices in New York are rising?	5	thinks other New Yorkers don't always behave well?	12
is disturbed by the noise of the city?	6	sees no reason to complain about his/her situation?	13

Living in the Big Apple

To most people, **New York** seems an incredibly exciting place to live. What do New Yorkers think of their city?

A THE SINGLE GIRL – Sherrin Bernstein

Living in Manhattan is one big financial struggle for Sherrin Bernstein, a trainee beauty therapist. She earns enough to pay the bills, but there is little left for luxuries. 'I can't afford to do expensive things,' she says. But she can have a lot of fun in New York on a budget. A good meal in a restaurant costs little, and her favourite hobby is rollerblading in Central Park, which costs nothing. Apart from a short break in Spain last year, Sherrin has not had a holiday in ten years. She is paying her way through college and earns money by working as a skating instructor. Despite the financial drawbacks, she loves New York. 'The energy in this city is incredible.' The worst aspect, according to Sherrin, is pollution and noise. 'Car alarms go off through the night, police sirens too. It's hard to get a good night's sleep.' The aggressive nature of New Yorkers also makes her uncomfortable. 'People push you out of the way on the subway or in the street. Sometimes I long for a more peaceful way of life.'

B THE FAMILY – Mr and Mrs Miles and their daughters

Seymour Miles, his wife, Jan, and their two daughters live in a three-bedroom apartment, which is large by New York standards. Mr Miles runs his own business and Jan is vice-president at a bank. The Miles say they are fortunate they can afford to send their daughters to a private school. 'The school has an excellent academic reputation, every child has a computer. Things like that influenced our decision to invest so much in their education.' Bringing children up in New York has its benefits and drawbacks. A big advantage is access to New York's rich cultural life. The girls go regularly to museums and art galleries and see all the latest films. 'In New York, they are exposed to the diversity of people, they see other cultures and are enriched by that,' says Mr Miles. The disadvantage is they do not have the freedom to go out in the street and play. 'Everything has to be supervised and arranged in advance.' The Miles say New York is becoming more and more expensive to live in, so many people are leaving and moving out to the suburbs.

C THE COUPLE – Mr and Mrs Rochford

A few years ago, Jeff Rochford considered moving out of New York, where he's lived in all his life. 'Crime was out of control, the economy was in a mess. It was becoming a dangerous place to live. But the clampdown on crime has improved the city tremendously.' Mr Rochford and his wife, Verda, live in a tiny one-bedroom apartment. Although it is expensive to live in Manhattan, Mr Rochford says he feeds off the city's energy and would not live anywhere else. 'Here we've got everything at our fingertips. Anything you want is available 24 hours a day.' Mrs Rochford, however, who grew up on a farm in the country, says she has a 'love-hate' relationship with New York. 'I hate that feeling of being closed in. We're trying to save up for a bigger home,' she says.

D THE HOMELESS PERSON – Gerry Brown

Begging for coins on Fifth Avenue, Gerry Brown doesn't display an ounce of self-pity. 'A lot of wealthy people live here and good luck to them. I know a lot of them and they give me money because they like me.' Gerry, 44, has been

unemployed for five years. He stays at a friend's house and comes into the city centre every day. 'I do odd jobs.' He gets financial support and food stamps each month from the State. The rest of the time he earns money by going through rubbish bins and picking out cans and bottles for recycling. 'I find stuff, like televisions and radios and sell them,' he says. He is experienced enough to know how to look after himself. 'I know where to get a free shower. I know where to get food – the supermarkets, the restaurants – they all give it away.'

Grammar: *comparisons* ▶ *p.177*

grammar file 3

A Comparatives and superlatives
- **one-syllable adjectives, two-syllable adjectives ending in -y**
1 *The countryside is (a lot/much) green**er than** the town.*
2 *I think New York is (by far) **the** livel**iest** city **in** the world.*
- **two- and three-syllable adjectives, most adverbs**
3 *The country is (far/a great deal) **less polluted than** the city.*
4 *This is **the most/the least exciting** city I have ever visited.*
5 *The south is **more/less** densely **populated than** the north.*
- **irregular adjectives/adverbs**
6 *Transport in a big city is **better than** in the country.*

B Comparing similar things
- **(not) as ... as**
1 *City life is/is **not** (nearly) **as** relaxing **as** life in the country.*
- **like or as?**
2 ***Like** all cities, New York is very noisy. (= a comparison)*
3 ***As** a teenager, I find city life really exciting. (= a function/ position)*

C Adding emphasis
- **adding *far / much / a lot*, etc.**
  See examples in A and B.
- **repeating comparatives**
1 *Cities are getting **bigger and bigger**. (= a trend)*
2 ***The bigger** cities get, **the noisier** they become.*

D *too, enough*
1 *Do we have **enough money to** go to the cinema?*
2 *I'm **not old enough to** buy my own flat.*
3 *The city is getting **too dangerous for** us **to** stay in.*

---

1 **There is one mistake in each sentence of this text (10 in total). Read and correct the mistakes.**

I was born in New York, one of most dangerous cities in the world. But now I live in Dublin, the friendliest city I ever went to. The longer I live here, the more I feel happy. Dublin is as most cities: it's noisy and dirty but very exciting. Of course, it has its problems: life in Dublin is getting more and more stressfuller. People don't have as much time to stop and talk than they did in the past. And the busier the city becomes, the more bad the traffic problem gets. This means that the air is much polluted than it used to be. But I don't agree with people who say that the countryside is just as exciting than the city. I love Dublin and I think living in the country must be the worse thing in the world!

---

2 **Read this text and put the words in brackets into the correct form.**

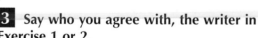

My village is in one of (1) .... (quiet) areas of the country. Living in the city isn't (2) .... (nearly/peaceful) .... living here. The countryside is (3) .... (much/ beautiful) .... any city could be. I think this is (4) .... (beautiful) place in the world. The pace of life is (5) .... (slow) and people are (6) .... (far/friendly) .... they are in the city. There's less crime so it's (7) .... (a lot/safe), too.

The countryside has some disadvantages, of course. It's true that work is scarce here. Jobs are (8) .... (a great deal/ easy) to find in the city. And public transport is often (9) .... (far/bad) in the countryside than in urban areas. My village probably has (10) .... (bad) public transport in the world! People often leave the countryside because it's not (11) .... (lively/enough) for them. However, the (12) .... (long) I live in my village, ... (good) I like it.

---

3 **Say who you agree with, the writer in Exercise 1 or 2.**

Over to you

4 **Work in pairs or groups. Decide which of the following factors you consider are most/least important for a good quality of life. Put them in order (number 1 = most important).**

Examples:

I think a low crime rate is much more important than ...
In my opinion, by far the most important factor is work and jobs. It's more important than anything else because ...
Of course, it's good to have green spaces, but they're not as important as ...

- clean streets with no litter
- low crime rate
- work and jobs
- no traffic congestion
- good public transport system
- good range of leisure and entertainment facilities

- good housing
- green spaces
- good schools
- clean air

Use of English 1: *error correction*

exam file

exam file

In **Paper 3**, **Part 4**, you read a text of about 200 words with 15 numbered lines. You have to decide if a line contains an extra word that should not be there. Between two and five lines will be correct. The unnecessary words are grammatical and may include:

- pronouns (especially after relative pronouns)
- particles
- prepositions
- articles *a* or *the*
- comparatives
- quantifiers
- auxiliary verbs
- linking words

1 **Read the instructions for the exam task below.**

1 What do you have to do?
2 How do you record your answers?

2 **Read the text all the way through to get an idea of what it's about. Don't mark anything during your first reading. Answer these questions.**

1 Where did the writer grow up?
2 How did he feel about it?
3 What disadvantages does he mention?
4 What did he gain personally?

3 **Read the text again, looking at each whole sentence, not just the numbered line. Use these clues to help you with the task.**

Line:

1 Is it a preposition or a verb particle that is unnecessary here?
3 Read the complete sentence, not just the numbered line.
9 Remember to read the whole sentence. Look at the form of the verb on the next line.
14 Ordinary verbs need an *-ing* form or a *to*-infinitive after them.

 **exam tip!**

If you think there is an extra word, underline it. Read the sentence again without the word you underlined. Does it make sense?

4 **Read the whole text again from the beginning to check your answers.**

! *used to / would / use*

What's the meaning of the verbs in bold?

1 My father **used to** take me on long walks.
2 I **would** invent imaginary friends.
3 I like to **use** my imagination.

Read the text below and look carefully at each line. Some of the lines are correct, and some have a word which should not be there. If a line is correct, put a tick (✓) in the space by the number. If a line has a word which should not be there, write the word in the space. There are two examples at the beginning (0 and 00).

COUNTRY LIFE

0	✓	I was born in the countryside and spent my early years there.
00	*as*	Our house was not even in a village, so we were even more as isolated
1	......	than most of country people. People who were brought up in towns
2	......	think that such a life must be boring for a child. They think there is
3	......	not enough to do in the country and that town life is better, but I am
4	......	don't agree. My father used to take me on long walks and I remember
5	......	learning the names of them all the plants and birds. Of course, it was
6	......	sometimes lonely living so far away from other young than people.
7	......	I probably spent too much time on alone in the garden behind the
8	......	house. But this kind of life made me into a much more imaginative
9	......	person. I would invent imaginary friends and together we were used to
10	......	act out fantastic stories the which I had made up in my head. And
11	......	when it rained, I used to read. I remember in looking at the illustrations
12	......	in books and thinking that, although they were supposed for to be related
13	......	to the story, they weren't as good as if the pictures I had in my head
14	......	as I read. Even now, I prefer go the countryside to the town, and I'd
15	......	much rather read books than watch TV because I like to use my imagination.

Listening: *multiple-choice questions*

exam file

In **Paper 4**, **Part 4**, there are always two or three speakers and seven questions. The questions follow the order of information in the discussion. Most of them ask about the speakers' feelings, ideas and opinions. The task format may be three-option multiple-choice questions.

1 **Before you listen, read the instructions for the exam task opposite.**

1 How many people will you hear?

2 What do you think they are talking about?

3 What does the task ask you to do?

2 **Now read Questions 1 and 2.**

1 Underline the key words that tell you what to listen for.

2 ▣ **Listen for the answer to Question 1 on the recording. Which of the following phrases answered the question?**

a) more people

b) buildings ... new ones

c) the biggest change ... is that it is physically much, much larger

Mark the option, A, B or C, that is closest.

3 ▣ **Now listen for the answer to Question 2. Note down which phrase(s) seem to give the answer. Then choose the closest option, A, B or C.**

▶▶ *exam tip!*

The words in the options will be different from the words you hear in the recording. Choose the answer that expresses the same **meaning** as the recording.

◀◀

3 ▣ **Now listen to the rest of the recording and complete the exam task.**

4 ▣ **Listen again. Check and complete your answers.**

You will hear part of a recorded interview between a student and a local historian, Peter Newnham. For each of the questions, choose the best answer, A, B or C.

1 According to Peter, what has changed most in the town?

A the people

B the size   1

C the buildings

2 How does Peter feel about the appearance of the town today?

A He would like to demolish the new buildings.

B He wants more new buildings.   2

C He accepts things the way they are.

3 Peter thinks that the strongest influence on life in the town is from

A the USA.

B foreign countries in general.   3

C Europe and Asia.

4 Peter very much likes the changes which have affected

A sport.

B the weather.   4

C food.

5 Traffic problems

A are not getting worse.

B are the biggest problem.   5

C have been solved.

6 One problem the town has is

A people dropping litter.

B pollution from factories.   6

C keeping the river clean.

7 Nowadays you can find crowds of people

A in the central square.

B at the leisure centre.   7

C by the river.

Over to you

5 **Look at the questionnaire below. Ask and answer the questions in pairs.**

1 How do you think your town has changed in the last two years?

☐ significantly improved

☐ improved

☐ not changed

☐ got worse

2 If you could choose three things to improve the environment of your town, what would they be?

☐ sweep streets more often

☐ impose fines on people who drop litter

☐ reduce amount of traffic

☐ improve public transport

☐ improve parks

☐ provide more sports facilities

☐ other

3 What's the best thing about living in your town?

4 What's the worst thing about living in your town?

Speaking: *three-way discussion*

1 🎧 **Listen to the first part of the recording, in which the examiner gives the instructions for Part 3.**

1 What do you have to do?
2 How many parts are there to the task?

▶▶ exam tip!

The instructions will ask you to do two things. Make sure your discussion covers both these things. Remember to ask if you are not quite sure what to do.

◀◀

exam file

In **Paper 5**, **Part 4**, the last part of the Speaking Test, the examiner joins in and asks questions which are intended to develop the discussion in Part 3. This part lasts about four minutes.

▶▶ exam strategy

Part 4 is a **three-way** discussion.
● DON'T just answer the examiner's questions.
● DO take the opportunity to initiate discussion and express your opinions.

3 **Read the questions that the examiner might ask in Part 4 of the test:**

1 What did you decide?
2 What objections might people have to some of these amenities?
3 Would any of them cause problems such as pollution or excessive noise?
4 What amenities are absolutely essential in every town, in your opinion?

2 **Work in groups of three to do the Part 3 task.**

Students 1 and 2: Follow the instructions and do the task. Remember, you don't have to agree with each other, but you must take turns to talk.

▶ **Functions file 5, 6 and 8 p.200**

Student 3: You are the examiner. Listen to Students 1 and 2 and stop them after three minutes.

4 **1** 🎧 **Now listen to two candidates, Ewa and Rajmund, doing Part 4. Answer these questions.**

1 Which of the questions in Exercise 3 did the examiner ask?
2 Were the candidates' conclusions similar to yours?

2 🎧 **Look at the functions files 7 and 13 on pages 200 and 201 and listen again.**

1 What expressions did they use to summarise the task? Tick (✔) them.
2 Rajmund was rather quiet. What expressions did Ewa use to involve him in the discussion? Tick (✔) them.

5 **Work in groups of three.**

Student 3: You are the examiner. Ask Students 1 and 2 the questions in Exercise 3. Stop the discussion after four minutes.

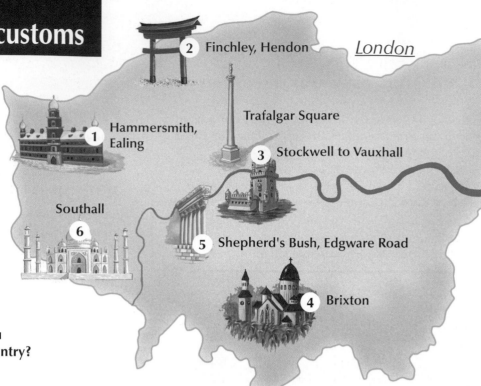

Lead-in

1 You are going to read an article about the different ethnic communities that have settled in London. Look at the map of the city. Match the countries a)–f) to the places on the map, using the pictures of buildings to help you.

a) Japan   d) Lebanon
b) Portugal   e) India
c) Caribbean   f) Poland

2 What famous building do you consider best represents <u>your</u> country?

Reading 2: *multiple matching*

▶▶ exam strategy
- Read the questions and underline key words.
- Scan the text to find the information you need. Look for words and phrases that express the same ideas as the questions, not for identical words.
- When you find the relevant part of the text, read it carefully to make sure it answers the question.

1 Look at the exam task opposite.
1 Read the instructions carefully. This task is slightly different from the one you did on page 41.

1 How many sections does the text have?

2 How many questions have more than one answer?

2 Look quickly at the title and the sub-heading. What kind of information do you think the article will give you?

2 Follow the recommended exam strategy to do the task. Use these clues to help you.
Question:

2 You may not know the name of the national dress, but look for a reference to what people wear.

6 Look for references to dates.

12 Look for another way of expressing *size*.

13 Look for another way of expressing *expensive*.

▶▶ exam tip!
If you can't find the answer to a question, leave it and come back to it later.

Over to you

3 Discuss.

1 What have you learned about each community described in the text? Talk about:

- food   - activities/free time   - clothes   - traditions

2 What <u>three</u> things would you miss most if you had to move away from your town or country?

You are going to read a magazine article about ethnic communities living in London. Answer the questions by choosing from the communities A–F. The communities may be chosen more than once. When more than one answer is required, these may be given in any order. There is an example at the beginning (0).

Which community

is associated with a specific means of arrival?	0 C	is more temporary than the others?	9
is not from the main part of the country of origin?	1	is compared in size with another community?	10
can regularly be seen in national dress?	2	can easily find things to read in their own language?	11
does not live in a particular named district?	3	is said to be increasing in size?	12
is enthusiastic about a particular sport?	4 5	lives in an increasingly expensive area?	13
arrived at four separate times?	6	has to try harder than others to maintain its original culture?	14
is associated with an annual social event?	7 8	lives and works in a different area?	15

Gateway to the Global Village

Britain's capital is a treasure trove of foreign culture. People from all over the world live in London and the result is a thrilling multiculturalism: cafés, restaurants, shops and markets offer you the world on your doorstep. Come and meet people who are …

A   Indian

After the Irish, the Indian community is the second largest in London. The first Indians arrived in 1597 and more came after the founding of the East India trading company in the seventeenth century. Numbers increased when India became independent in 1947 but the community really took off in the 1950s and 1960s with employment opportunities around Heathrow airport.

Although 'Little Indias' exist all over London, the most striking is the district of Southall in West London, not far from the airport. Here Indian foodstalls and video shops are everywhere, spicy aromas fill the air, and women stroll around wearing the typical colourful sari, just as in India. In McDonald's, the piped music is refreshingly Indian.

B   Portuguese

The supermarkets and shops in Lambeth and Stockwell Roads are the most obvious indication that you are in 'Little Portugal', but there is much more to this community than that. Over 20,000 Portuguese live south of the River Thames. The majority have come from the island of Madeira rather than from the mainland of Portugal. This close-knit community is mad about football and folk-dancing and holds its own carnival every February. It's a community that is determined to hold on to its traditions and it's a great place to experience Madeiran culture.

C   Caribbean

When the ship *Emperor Windrush* docked in 1948 with its 500 immigrants, it marked the start of the main period of Caribbean immigration, stimulated by British economic expansion. Since then, over 300,000 have established vibrant communities all around London. The greatest Caribbean celebration is the Notting Hill Carnival, now Europe's largest street party, which takes place every August. However, Brixton, in South London, is the hub of the community. As you step out of the Underground station into Brixton Market, your senses are stimulated by the noise, the bright colours and the rhythmic sound of Caribbean music. This is one of the best places to shop for food in London. However, the area has become a very popular place to live and prices are rising.

D   Japanese

Finchley and Hendon in North London are the principal centres for Japanese people. The national affection for golf has had a noticeable effect on these areas – if you drive up Finchley Road, you have an almost unlimited choice of golf shops and courses. Other than this, there is little evidence of a community. Although there are restaurants and foodstores here, most socialising takes place at home. It isn't as permanent as other communities, either – many Japanese arrive on five-year contracts in the banking and technology sectors and then return home afterwards. The best restaurants tend to be in central London, where most of the community works.

E   Polish

The Polish community isn't as distinct as some other ethnic communities in London. Andrzej Morawicz, President of a well-known Polish club, puts this down to integration. 'When you are a large enough community, it's easy to hold on to your culture and customs. In comparison, the Polish community has become part of British society to a large extent, so keeping up traditions isn't so easy.' All the same, you can hear Polish conversations along King Street in Hammersmith, West London, where newsagents' windows are full of advertisements in Polish for the benefit of the local community. There are also plenty of clubs, restaurants and food shops that help to keep traditions alive. There is even a daily Polish-language newspaper, *Dziennik Polski*.

F   Lebanese

The first Lebanese who came to London were almost all businesspeople, but over the last twenty years people from all walks of life have settled here. Jocelyn, a history graduate from Lebanon, now runs a delicatessen and is very enthusiastic about London life. 'The community is getting stronger and bigger,' she explains. 'When I first came here, I never heard anyone speak Arabic. Now I can hear my language everywhere.' Although there isn't a geographically defined 'Little Lebanon' there are many shops and restaurants in West London and along the Edgware Road.

Vocabulary

1 Word formation: compound nouns

Match a word in column A with a word in column B to form compound nouns. Use each word once only. Tick (✓) the items you can find in your town.

A			B			
1 department	7 shopping		a) station		g) jam	
2 leisure	8 apartment		b) mall		h) office	
3 pedestrian	9 ring		c) transport		i) precinct	
4 tourist	10 public		d) block		j) rink	
5 industrial	11 traffic		e) centre		k) road	
6 skating	12 bus		f) estate		l) store	

study tip!

Keep a section of your vocabulary notebook for compound words and add to it on a regular basis.

2 Phrasal verbs

Fill in the gaps in the sentences below with an appropriate phrasal verb from the box, making any necessary changes.

do up	get away from	give in	pull down
move in	put up	get run over	settle in	wear off

1 My parents wanted to .... the city so the whole family had to move to the country.

2 However, their enthusiasm for country life soon ....

3 My brother and I begged to go back to the city and in the end my parents ....

4 We've managed to buy a new apartment in the city. We .... last month.

5 It felt strange at first but I've .... now.

6 The city has changed. They've .... a lot of old buildings in the centre and .... smart new office blocks in their place.

7 They're .... the old quarter and giving the buildings a fresh coat of paint.

8 They've turned the shopping area into a pedestrian precinct, so nobody .... while crossing the roads these days, thank goodness!

3 Adjectives for places

1 Look at the adjectives in the box that are marked *. Which are positive? Tick (✓) them. Which are negative? Put a cross (✗) next to them.

historic	shabby*	bustling	quaint	unspoiled*
hectic	welcoming*	slow and unhurried	polluted*
up-to-date	peaceful*	ugly*	unattractive*	reserved
stunning*	well looked-after*	overdeveloped*

My city is very old. It is full of (1) .... buildings. The castle, for example, was built in the fourteenth century. It overlooks the sea and the views from the ramparts are really (2) ...., which is why it often appears on postcards. The old quarter is really picturesque; it is full of (3) .... little houses with tiny windows and sloping roofs. Sadly, they've ruined the city centre with so much new development but the old quarter is quite (4) .... They haven't changed it at all. The market here is always (5) .... with life and full of colour.

On the other hand, the pace of life in my city can get really (6) .... and stressful. The air is often terribly (7) .... because of all the factories in the suburbs. Some of the buildings in the city centre have paint peeling off them and are rather (8) .... People can be rather (9) ...., so strangers may sometimes feel lonely.

Despite its problems, my city is well worth a visit, especially at carnival time in February.

2 Choose appropriate adjectives from the box in Exercise 3.1 to complete the description above.

3 Use words from the box in Exercise 3.1 to make sentences about your own town. Comment on the following areas as in the examples:

- the city centre (the buildings, the surroundings, the air)
- the old quarter
- the market
- the residential areas
- the parks and gardens

Examples:
The centre of my city is well looked-after.
There are lots of quaint little streets with small shops.
Unfortunately, the air is badly polluted.

4 Word formation: verbs

1 We form some verbs by adding a prefix or a suffix to a noun or adjective. Look at the table below. What changes may be made to the stem of the word?

Prefix: *en-*	Suffix: *-en, -ify, -ise*
en- + danger (noun) = to **en**danger	*length* (noun) + *-en* = to *length***en**
en- + courage (noun) = to **en**courage	*terror* (noun) + *-ify* = to *terr***ify**
	modern (adj.) + *-ise* = to *modern***ise**

2 The *Longman Active Study Dictionary* can help you to find related words. Find the entry for the noun or adjective, then search up and down that page in the dictionary to find the corresponding verb. Look at these extracts. What verb can we form from *mystery*?

mystery /ˈmɪstəri/ *n* mysteries **1** [C] something which cannot be explained or understood: *Her death is a mystery.* **2** [U] a strange secret quality: *stories full of mystery*

mystic /ˈmɪstɪk/ *n* a person who practises mysticism

mystify /ˈmɪstɪfaɪ/ *v* mystified, mystifying [T] to make someone confused and unable to understand things: *I'm completely mystified about what happened.* /*Physics mystifies me.*

3 Fill in the gaps in the sentences, using the correct form of the word in brackets.

1 Carnivals are usually held in February or March, when the days are beginning to .... (LONG)
2 Some people .... them and say they're a waste of time and money because no one works during carnival time. (CRITIC)
3 Foreigners are often .... when they hear our village carnival lasts a whole week. (HORROR)
4 But I think carnivals .... up our lives. (BRIGHT)
5 Making the costumes .... us to use our imagination and creativity. (ABLE)
6 Carnival also .... our sense of tradition. (STRONG)

Use of English 2: *word formation*

▶▶ *exam strategy*   Paper 3, Part 5
- Read the whole text for general understanding.
- Read each line again and decide:
  – what kind of word is needed to fill the gap (noun, adjective, verb, etc.).
  – whether the word is positive or negative, singular or plural.
- When you have finished, read the whole text again to check it makes sense.

▶▶ *exam tip!*
Look at the whole sentence, not just the line with the gap. You need to understand the whole context to get the right answer. ◀◀

1 Follow the exam strategy to do the task below.

Read the text below. Use the word given in capitals underneath to form a word that fits in the space in the text. There is an example at the beginning (0).

FUN DAYS IN NEW YORK

New York is always an (0) *exciting* place to visit because there is such a wide (1) ..... of things to see and do there. In terms of daytime (2) ....., it is often worth planning your visit to coincide with one of the city's many (3) ..... and parades. The city takes these very (4) ..... indeed, and there are annual (5) ..... organised by almost every ethnic group in the city.

Although these events are often (6) ..... or religious in origin, these days they are (7) ..... little more than an excuse for food, music, dancing and other forms of (8) ..... . There is a (9) ..... for the events to take place in the Spring months and many of them use Fifth Avenue as their principal (10) ..... place. Participating in one of these events will guarantee the trip of a lifetime.

(0)	EXCITE	(4)	SERIOUS	(8)	ENJOY
(1)	VARY	(5)	CELEBRATE	(9)	TEND
(2)	ATTRACT	(6)	POLITICS	(10)	MEET
(3)	FESTIVE	(7)	GENERAL		

2 Describe a festival, big or small, that takes place in your town.

1 What kind of preparations are made for it?
2 What aspects of it would be especially attractive to visitors?

Writing: *article*

exam file

In **Paper 2**, **Part 2**, you may be asked to write an **article** for a student newsletter or college magazine. You may have to include a description or an anecdote. You may also be asked to include an opinion or comment.

▶▶ **exam strategy**

Make sure you:
- know where your article will appear (e.g. in a newsletter, or a college magazine) and who will read it (e.g. your fellow students, strangers). Then choose an appropriate style (formal or fairly informal).
- give your article a suitable, eye-catching title to get the attention of the reader.
- write an interesting introduction to make your reader want to read on, and a well-developed conclusion to complete your article.
- write in a lively way that will interest the reader.
- use a good range of descriptive and opinion language where appropriate.

▶▶ **exam tip!**

DON'T start and end your article in the same way as a letter. ◀◀

1 Read the writing task below.

1 Underline all the points you must cover in your article.

2 Who will read your article? What style should you use?

> You have agreed to write an article describing your town and the people who live there for an international student magazine. Say what you like or don't like about the town.
>
> Write your article in 120–180 words in an appropriate style.

The City that Never Sleeps

I love my city!

My city consists of quite different areas. The centre is full of tall offices, which means it's a bit like a concrete jungle! Other areas are nicer, though. In the old quarter there are shops and restaurants that open 24 hours a day. There's always something going on, so people can go out whenever they want. It's a fascinating place!

The north of the city is really lively. This is the area where the students live. The street cafés that you pass are always full of people chatting and playing music. You can do anything you like here – it's great! People are very broad-minded.

The south of the city, which I don't often go to, is much quieter. It's the district where the wealthy people live. There are expensive houses, many of which have swimming pools and big gardens. It is an elegant area, but the people who live here are much less friendly than elsewhere.

My city is very exciting. Don't you agree?

2 Read the article above that one student wrote and answer these questions.

Content

1 Has the student answered the exam question correctly and given the information required?
2 She has written an eye-catching title. Does it fit the article?

Organisation

3 How many paragraphs has she written?
4 Does each of the paragraphs have a separate topic? What is it?
5 Is the topic of the paragraph stated in a sentence? Underline the topic sentence (the sentence that summarises what the paragraph is about).
6 What's wrong with the first paragraph and the final paragraph?

Focus on introductions and conclusions

3 1 Avoid one-sentence introductions. The first paragraph of your article must be interesting or your reader will give up! Develop and expand your ideas. Which of these would make a better introduction to the article above?

1 *I would like to tell you about my city.*

2 *My city may not be the most beautiful in the world but it is exciting! It's a city that never sleeps. Let me tell you why.*

3 *Do you want to know the best places to go in my city? Let me tell you.*

2 Avoid one-sentence conclusions. Your final paragraph should be well developed and make the article feel 'finished'. Which of these would make a better conclusion to the article you read in Exercise 2?

1 *Come and see my city for yourself. You'll love it!*

2 *Readers will enjoy a trip here, I think. It's worth visiting for many reasons.*

3 *My city is restless and colourful. It may not be the most historic or the most beautiful place in the world, but it is definitely one of the most exciting!*

Focus on grammar ▶ p.184

4 **1 Underline all the examples of relative clauses you can find in the sample article in Exercise 2.**

2 Now read the information in the grammar file opposite. Which relative clauses in the sample article are defining and which are non-defining?

3 Complete the following sentences with a relative clause using the information in the box below. Remember to put commas round non-essential information.

1 We thoroughly enjoyed our trip to the museum, *which took place last week* .
2 The museum .... is open five days a week.
3 Did I show you the guidebook .... ?
4 The curator .... showed us round.
5 The worksheets .... were very useful.
6 There were some exhibits in the museum ....
7 The collection of mummies .... was the highlight of the visit.
8 People .... buried their dead in the form of mummies.
9 I spoke to some people ....
10 We saw a reconstruction of the tomb ....
11 A small boy .... got lost in the gardens.
12 The shop .... was full of interesting things to buy.

One of the Egyptian pharaohs was buried there.	They had been to the special exhibition three times that week.
His school was also visiting the museum.	He is an expert on Egyptian history.
The teacher gave us the worksheets to fill in.	I bought it as a souvenir.
~~It took place last week.~~	It is in the centre of the city.
We were allowed to spend a few minutes shopping in it.	They lived in Ancient Egypt.
They are 9,000 years old.	The collection of mummies occupied one whole room.

grammar file 23

A Use defining relative clauses to identify people and things and give essential information.

● with *which/that, who, whose, where*
1 *The exhibition **which/that** is on at the museum is fascinating.* (= things)
2 *The man **who** showed us round is very knowledgeable.* (= people)
3 *The experts (**who/that**) I talked to were fascinating.* (You can omit *who / which / that* when they are the object of the verb.)
4 *He's the man **whose article** appeared in the newspaper.* (= possession)
5 *The museum is a place **where** you can learn about history.* (= places)

● after *someone/something, anyone/anything*
6 *Is there **anything** special (**that**) you'd like to see?*

B Use non-defining clauses, between or after commas, to give extra information.

● with *who* or *which* (but not *that*)
1 *The old quarter, **which** is near the centre, is very interesting.*

● after quantifiers *some of, all of,* etc.
2 *There are many old buildings, **some of which** are beautiful.*

● referring to the whole previous clause
3 *It's Saturday tomorrow, **which means no school**!*

C Prepositions in relative clauses
1 *I visited the castle **about which** I had read.* (= formal)
2 *Jim, **who** we visited the castle **with**, is an expert.* (= informal)

Over to you

5 **Write your answer to the following task in 120–180 words in an appropriate style.**

You have agreed to write an article about a museum for your college magazine. You have just returned from a visit to the museum. Describe the museum, say what you liked or didn't like about it, and why it could be of interest to your readers.

Write your article.

Follow the advice in the exam strategy box. Remember to:
● make a plan before you start to write.
● divide your article into paragraphs and begin each paragraph with a topic sentence.
● check your writing for errors when you have finished.

Progress test 1

1 Structural cloze

For questions 1–15, read the text below and think of the word which best fits each space. Use only **one** word in each space. There is an example at the beginning (0).

THE HI-TECH HOME

These days it is not always easy to tell the difference (0) *between* a piece of everyday household equipment and a computer. And experts predict that this distinction (1) .... become even harder to make as a whole range of new electronic household appliances comes (2) .... the market.

Imagine, for example, a refrigerator that knows when you are out (3) .... eggs and orders them for you from the supermarket. Or how (4) .... you like to have a television (5) .... is able to search the channels for the type of programmes you like, and then record (6) .... for you to watch at your leisure? And how (7) .... a heating system that listens to the weather forecast and adjusts itself (8) .... preparation for whatever changes are on (9) .... way?

This is probably not the first time that you have heard predictions (10) .... these. Futurists have (11) .... telling us for decades that technology is about to eliminate all kinds of household chores. But (12) .... many improvements in individual areas, 'whole-house control', whereby one integrated electronic system controls all aspects of domestic life, (13) .... not really taken off. Two things promise (14) .... change all that, however. One is the introduction of very powerful microchips and the (15) .... is the spread of information about what is available, thanks to the Internet.

2 Key word transformations

For questions 1–10, complete the second sentence so that it has a similar meaning to the first sentence, using the word given. **Do not change the word given.** You must use between two and five words, including the word given. There is an example at the beginning (0).

Example:

0 You must do exactly what your teacher tells you.
carry
You must *carry out your teacher's* instructions exactly.

1 It's more than a year since I joined the video club.
member
I have .... video club for more than a year.

2 Darren couldn't complete the trip to the Pole because he wasn't well enough.
too
Darren .... the trip to the Pole.

3 At the end of the book, the heroine marries the hero, Jack.
name
At the end of the book, the heroine marries the hero, ... Jack.

4 Which part of the course interested you most?
the
Which .... of your course?

5 You should wait for an invitation before visiting your teacher's house.
without
You shouldn't visit your teacher's house .... invited.

6 The guide gave us permission to take photos in the museum.
let
The guide .... in the museum.

7 Graham's bedroom is much bigger than his brother's.
nearly
Graham's brother's bedroom .... as Graham's.

8 Jane was still singing the song when the lights went out.
finished
Jane .... when the lights went out.

9 It's pointless to wait any longer.
use
It's .... any longer.

10 This is the most beautiful house I have ever seen.
more
I have .... beautiful house than this one.

3 Error correction

For questions 1–15, read the text below and look carefully at each line. Some of the lines are correct, and some have a word which should not be there. If a line is correct, put a tick (✓) in the space by the number. If a line has a word which should not be there, write the word in the space. There are two examples at the beginning (0 and 00).

A SUCCESS STORY

0 ✓ My name is Alicia Parkin and I work as a singer and dancer.
00 *of* After of leaving school, I did a year's foundation course in
1 .... Performing Arts at a college in Cambridge, before are going on
2 .... to do a three-year diploma in the London. After my graduation,
3 .... I spent a year touring the Caribbean on such a cruise ship, which
4 .... was a great experience. I did it a lot of singing and dancing and
5 .... when I came back to England, I was lucky enough for to get a
6 .... part in a touring production of a musical for six months. It was on
7 .... that tour that I was discovered in by an agent who was working for
8 .... one of the big record companies. He has invited me to join a new
9 .... pop group that was being formed. I stayed in that group for nearly
10 .... four years time and, although we didn't really have any big hits,
11 .... I did two world tours, made four albums and a number of pop
12 .... videos. My really big break came across when a film director
13 .... who saw me in one of those videos and invited me to audition
14 .... for a part in his new musical film. It's not a big yet part, but I
15 .... think it could be the start of a too big new career for me.

4 Word formation

For questions 1–10, read the text below. Use the word given in capitals at the end of each line to form a word that fits in the space in the same line. There is an example at the beginning (0).

SURVIVING EXTREME CLIMATES

How is it that humans manage to survive in both the (0) *extremely*	EXTREME
hot desert areas of the world and in the (1) ..... wastes of the Arctic?	FREEZE
The simple (2) ..... is that our bodies are actually designed to be	EXPLAIN
very (3) ..... and this is because, as a race, we have been changing	ADAPT
to meet the needs of different (4) ..... conditions ever since the	CLIMATE
(5) ..... of time. It is, however, true that people can adapt to a hot	BEGIN
climate much more (6) ..... than they can to a cold one. It is only	EASY
possible to live at the poles with the right food, clothing and (7)	EQUIP
But why should this be so?	
Fossils found in Africa show that humans (8) ..... in areas which,	ORIGIN
even then, had some of the (9) ..... temperatures. This meant that	HIGH
our ancestors could cope (10) ..... with the heat, an ability they took	NATURE
with them when they migrated to cooler parts of the world.	

5 Lifestyles

Lead-in

You are going to read an article about the latest trend in shopping: 'supershops'. Look at the photos and discuss these questions.

1 What products do you think the 'supershops' in the photos sell?
2 What other attractions do they offer? (Scan the text opposite to find out.)
3 What are the benefits of these features to the customers?

Reading 1:
multiple matching

1 Skim the text opposite. Then answer these questions to check your general understanding.

Paragraph:

0 What is special about the Levi's store?
1 What company opened the first supershop?
2 What can you do as well as shop in Waterstone's and Levi's?
3 What has been a big problem for shoppers in the past?
4 What in-store entertainment does TopShop offer?
5 How does Nike Town cater for its customers' interests?
6 In what way is Nike Town like a shopping mall?
7 What sort of people can you meet in the new supershops?

2 **1** Read the first paragraph more carefully, then look up and try to summarise what it is about <u>in your own words</u>.

2 Now look at the example answer (I).
1 How similar was your summary sentence?
2 What words in the paragraph are paraphrased in the summary sentence?

3 Continue in the same way with the remaining paragraphs. Use your answers to Exercise 1 to help you.

Vocabulary: *prepositional phrases*

4 **1** Read the text again and find which preposition is used in these phrases. What does each phrase mean?

1 .... stock
2 .... one roof
3 .... offer
4 .... display
5 face .... face

2 Add the phrases to your vocabulary notebook. Write an example sentence for each one.

Over to you

5 Work in pairs. Think of three suggestions for improving your favourite shop.

Example:

What I think they should do first of all is put in a coffee bar. Then customers wouldn't have to go somewhere else for a coffee. My second suggestion would be to …
And finally, I'd suggest …

You are going to read a magazine article about new kinds of shops. Choose from the list A–I the sentence which best summarises each part (1–7) of the article. There is one extra sentence which you do not need to use. There is an example at the beginning (0).

A Supershops solve the problems associated with traditional shopping.
B Enthusiasts will find lots of information and ideas in this supershop.
C The fashion for supershops in Britain was started by one company.
D Supershops offer customers and celebrities the chance to meet.
E The new supershops offer much more than just shopping.
F There's so much else to do that there's no need to buy the products.
G You can buy anything you want under one roof.
H Supershops are offering tough competition to other forms of shopping.
I This shop changes into a high-tech club at night.

Is it a shop?

The latest shops have cafés, catwalks and even clubs.

0 I

The newest and most fashionable place to be seen is 'Coming of Age', the free under-18s Sunday Club at the Levi's Store in London. By day the shop is the place to buy your jeans, but after closing time it's transformed into a state-of-the-art entertainment venue. It can hold 500 people and boasts a £100,000 booth for the disc jockey that's suspended from the ceiling.

1

Levi's is just the latest company to follow the trend set in the late 1990s by leading British booksellers, Waterstone's. Waterstone's opened the first supershop in Scotland in 1997. Fashion giant TopShop and sporting goods specialists Nike Town quickly followed their lead and developed their own supershops, designed to draw you in – and keep you there.

2

Now Waterstone's flagship store in central London is the largest bookshop in Europe. There's more than a million and a half books in stock and it also has a restaurant, juice bar, news café, Internet stations, a gift shop, a personal shopping suite, events arena, exhibition space and private meeting and dining rooms. There's more to do at the Levi's store than buy jeans too. Since it opened, visitors have taken control of the computer consoles, watched the latest videos on huge screens, bought the latest popular hits and looked around the gallery exhibiting young artists' work.

3

For many people, shopping is a nightmare: the crowds, the queues, having to walk from shop to shop just for something that matches your new outfit or for a special

birthday present. But supershops have changed all that. As Waterstone's Marketing and Public Relations Manager says, 'Nobody likes buying one item at one store and another from the next and then trying to find a café where they can sit down for a drink. Being able to do it all under one roof means that people will actually venture out for a day's shopping. In fact, you probably need more than a day to appreciate what's on offer.'

4

The clothes in TopShop, for instance, are just the beginning. Once inside, you can spend time in the 120-seater café or have your hair done in the beauty salon – all while listening to the TopShop radio station which blasts out the latest tunes, plus customer fashion and bargain tips. There's even a specially-built catwalk for fashion shows and a stage where bands perform. So it's no surprise that this is the world's

largest fashion store. 'My friends and I come here every Saturday,' says 15-year-old Lindsay Matthews. 'We stay here all day. Sometimes we don't even look at the clothes. We just hang out at the fashion shows and in the café, or look at the make-up styles on display.'

5

Nike Town, too, encourages customers to do more than just shop. 'Visitors can find out where to play sport in their area, join a running club, pop into the sports clinic, meet athletes and see great images of people playing and enjoying sport,' says Nike's Debbie Cox. 'It's a place to come for sporting inspiration and opportunities.'

6

Like many of the supershops, Nike Town has come from America. Over there, these supershops now rival traditional shopping malls in many states. Nike Town's London store covers 70,000 square feet and has three floors made up of separate buildings – or 'pavilions' – devoted to different sports. Just like any town – or shopping mall – it has its own streets, maps and street signs. Its central point is the three-storey-high projection equipment that displays visuals of sports around the world.

7

At Nike Town customers can see sporting idols face to face and collect autographs. Famous footballers turn up there regularly. Similarly, Waterstone's bookshop invites regular guest authors to give talks and question-and-answer sessions. Well-known and popular authors read their work for audiences packed onto the space-age-style sofas in between the bright tropical fish aquariums. It's just another way that the supershops are transforming shopping into the ultimate pastime.

Grammar: *modals* ▶ *p.182*

A Ability and permission: *can / be able to / may / be allowed to*

1 *In the past, we* **couldn't/weren't able to buy** *everything under one roof.*
2 *Now we* **can/are able to buy** *things without going from shop to shop.*
3 *In the future,* **we will be able to buy** *everything via the Internet.*
4 *Customers* **may/are allowed to use** *the car park free of charge.*
5 *You* **can't/may not/aren't allowed to park** *here unless you are a customer.*

B Advice / obligation / necessity: *should / must / have to / need*

1 *You* **should/ought to stop** *spending so much money on clothes.*
2 *You* **must/will have to pay** *for any goods you break in my shop.* (= I'm the person in authority.)
3 *You* **mustn't shoplift**. (= It is forbidden.)
4 *You* **have (got) to/need to be** *16 before you can buy a car.* (= an obligation imposed by someone else)
5 *We* **had to wait** *20 minutes to be served.* (= past time)

C Lack of obligation/ necessity

1 *You* **don't have to / don't need to / needn't go shopping** *now. We've got everything.* (= It isn't necessary.)
2 *I* **didn't need to queue** *because the fitting room was empty.* (= It wasn't necessary.)
3 *I* **needn't have bought** *paper. We had some already.* (= It wasn't necessary but I did it.)

! *could/was able to*

- Use *could* and *was able to* for general ability in the past.
- Use *was able to* for a particular situation in the past which was completed successfully.
- Use *couldn't* for both general and specific situations.
- You can use *managed to* to suggest a degree of difficulty.

Underline the correct verbs.

1 As a millionaire, he *was able to / could / managed to* spend what he liked.
2 We *managed to/could* find the video we wanted after searching all day.

1 Underline the correct modal verb in these sentences.

1 I didn't have enough money to buy the sweater, but I *was able to/could* borrow some money from my brother.
2 You *don't have to/mustn't* take anything from the shop without paying.
3 I *didn't need to spend/needn't have spent* so much on that sweater. I've just seen the same one for less.
4 You *must/need* be a member of the club to get in free.
5 My great-grandmother was very rich so she *managed to/could* afford anything she liked.
6 You *don't have to/mustn't* pay for that. It's a free sample.
7 You *are allowed/may* to pay by cheque.
8 I think you *have/must* to be 16 before you can have a credit card.
9 I didn't *must/need* to pay the whole amount – I left a deposit.
10 In the future, we *can/will be able to* get everything we want without using cash.

2 Read this letter to the advice column of a magazine.

1 Fill in the gaps with the correct form of an appropriate modal verb.

My friend Clare has a big problem. She's a shopaholic and spends all her free time shopping. She's always buying things she really (1) .... afford at all. Whenever she goes out, her poor mother warns her: 'Listen to me, Clare! You (2) .... go near any shops today! You (3) .... be more careful with your money! Remember, you (4) .... go on holiday next summer if you have no money.'

But Clare just (5) .... stop herself spending! Last week, for example, we went swimming. On the way to the pool, we passed a shop window and Clare saw a swimming costume. She (6) .... to buy another costume as she already has a really nice one, but she bought it anyway. I (7) .... stop her. She (8) .... use all her pocket money to buy it, of course. When she got home, she was really embarrassed. She (9) .... bring herself to tell her mother what she had done.

Now she's old enough, Clare (10) .... wait to get her own credit card. The reason is this: if you have a credit card, you (11) .... wait until you have enough cash to buy something. But I'm worried. If Clare (12) .... control her spending now, how (13) .... to control it when she has a credit card?

2 What advice can you give Clare? Use expressions like these:

- If I were you, I would/wouldn't ...
- I think you should/ought to ...
- You really shouldn't/mustn't ...
- I don't think it's a good idea (for you) to ...
- Have you tried ... ?

Use of English 1: *structural cloze*

1 **Look at the exam task opposite. Read the text to find out:**

1 What is meant by 'e-retailing' in the title?
2 What products can you buy online?
3 What are the pros and cons of shopping via the Web?

2 **Use these clues to help you fill in the gaps.**

Question:

2 What kind of word do you need to link the nouns either side of the gap?
3 What kind of verb can come in front of a bare infinitive?
4 *pop* … is a phrasal verb.
5 You need a word that introduces a question.
9 You need a … to complete the phrase … *offer.*
13 What kind of word can link the noun *people* and the verb *hate*?

▶▶ *exam tip!*

Fill in the gaps you are sure about first. If a gap is difficult, move on to the next one. It will be easier to deal with the gaps you weren't sure about when you have finished the rest.

◀◀

Read the text below and think of the word which best fits each space. Use only one word in each space. There is an example at the beginning **(0)**.

A BRIGHT FUTURE FOR E-RETAILING

Four volunteers recently took part **(0)** ...*in*... an unusual experiment. They spent five days locked in their rooms in a London youth hostel with nothing **(1)** .... a credit card and access **(2)** .... the Internet. They wanted to find out how long they **(3)** .... survive without having to pop **(4)** .... to their local supermarket or department store.

There has been an enormous increase in **(5)** .... is called 'e-commerce' since the late 1990s. You can now buy almost **(6)** .... via the Internet, from pizzas to leading designer labels. What's **(7)** ...., the Internet gives you great choice. If you need a new outfit, for example, you **(8)** .... travel the world to see what's **(9)** .... offer in clothing stores from London to Los Angeles for no more **(10)** .... the cost of a phone call.

Web shops are open 24 hours a day, which **(11)** .... you to choose the goods you want and pay instantly. Of course, you then **(12)** .... to wait for delivery – and that's where the problems can start. Buying groceries on the Internet seems to be the perfect solution for people **(13)** .... hate supermarket shopping. But **(14)** .... it comes to that designer outfit you ordered for next week's party, be prepared for the fact that it **(15)** .... not reach you in time. Delivery times can be up to four weeks.

Listening: *true or false?*

exam file

Another task in **Paper 4**, **Part 4** asks you to decide if statements are true or false. The ideas in each statement will be mentioned in the recording, but you need to decide if the statement accurately summarises what is said.

1 Do these tasks before you listen.

1 Read the instructions for the exam task opposite.

1 How many people will you hear?
2 What are they talking about?
3 What words are you likely to hear?

2 Read through the statements 1–7 and underline key words as in Question 1. What do you need to listen for?

Example:

Question 1: Dan says his mother is being unreasonable. You need to find out: Does Mel agree with this or not? What expressions can we use to say we agree or disagree?

2 1 🔲 **Listen once and do the exam task. If you are not sure what the answer is first time, don't worry. Go on to the next question.**

2 🔲 **Listen again and check your answers. Use these clues to help you if necessary.**

Question:

3 Does *sound like* refer to tone of voice here or something else?
5 Dan uses the expression *be straight with someone*. Does this mean the same as or the opposite of *mislead someone*?
6 Does *object to* mean the same as *couldn't care less about*?

3 Which person sounds most like you:

Mel, Dan, Dan's mother, Mel's sister or Dan's brother?

Explain your answer.

You will hear two friends talking about buying clothes. Decide which of the statements 1–7 are TRUE and which are FALSE. Write **T** for **True** or **F** for **False** in the boxes provided.

1 Mel agrees that Dan's mother is being unreasonable. ☐ 1

2 Mel thinks her sister should spend more on clothes. ☐ 2

3 Mel thinks that she and Dan have similar attitudes towards shopping. ☐ 3

4 Mel often regrets her choice of clothes. ☐ 4

5 Dan agrees that his friends may mislead him. ☐ 5

6 Dan's brother objects to wearing designer clothes. ☐ 6

7 Mel and Dan are both concerned about what other people think of them. ☐ 7

Over to you

4 Work in pairs to complete the questionnaire.

WHAT KIND OF SHOPPER ARE YOU?

Do you: YES/NO

1 rush off to the shops as soon as you have any money to spend? ☐ ☐

2 find shopping a nightmare because you can never find what you want? ☐ ☐

3 find it impossible to resist buying things? ☐ ☐

4 enjoy window-shopping and looking at the latest fashions and gadgets? ☐ ☐

5 prefer spending time on other things rather than shopping? ☐ ☐

6 compare prices before buying something? ☐ ☐

7 only go shopping when you absolutely have to? ☐ ☐

Speaking: *individual long turn*

1 Look at the photographs below, which show people wearing different styles of clothing.

1 Describe what they are wearing, using the words and expressions in the box.

2 Say why you think they have chosen to wear these clothes.

baggy / tight trousers   trainers   tracksuit   jeans
sweatshirt   T-shirt   sweater   shirt   (stretch) top
mini-skirt   long-/short-sleeved
smart / scruffy / trendy / sporty / sophisticated / casual
to take care over the way you look   to feel comfortable
to be fashion conscious   to keep up with the latest fashions
to buy/choose designer labels/clothing   to achieve an image
to be choosy/fussy about what you wear
to pride yourself on your appearance

2 Read the recommended strategy for comparing and contrasting photos.

▶▶ *exam strategy*   Paper 5, Part 2

During the individual long turn:
• DO speak clearly so the examiner can hear you.
• DO avoid frequent pauses and hesitations while you are speaking for one minute.
• DON'T interrupt while the other candidate is speaking. Listen so that you can comment when they have finished.
• DON'T take more than about 20 seconds to comment on your partner's photographs.

3 **1** Work in groups of three.

Student 1: You are the examiner. Give the candidates the instructions on page 203. Time each candidate. If necessary, interrupt Candidate A after one minute. Don't give Candidate B more than about 20 seconds to comment.

Student 2: You are Candidate A. Compare and contrast the two photos on this page, according to the examiner's instructions.

▶ **Functions files 1 and 6 p.200**

Student 3: You are Candidate B. The examiner will ask you to comment on the two photos briefly after Candidate A has finished. You should take about 20 seconds for this.

2 When you have finished, look at the exam strategy box again. How well did each candidate follow the strategy?

▶▶ *exam tip!*

Get used to speaking for one minute before you do the exam so you get a sense of how long a minute is. Don't look at your watch during the Speaking Test – the examiner will time you.

4 Turn to the photos on page 203. Work in groups of three as in Exercise 3. The examiner should give the instructions on page 207.

▶ **Functions files 1 and 8 p.200**

5 Making choices

Lead-in

1 Look at the photographs, which show two very different rooms. Which adjectives and expressions in the box below best describe each room?

bare   cluttered   personal   spacious
cosy   comfortable   plain and simple
sparse   airy   homely   functional
orderly   impersonal   stylish
contemporary   inviting
the basic necessities   to look lived-in

2 Now compare and contrast the rooms, and say which kind of room you would prefer to live in and why.

▶ Functions files 1, 5 and 6 p.200

Reading 2: *multiple matching*

▶▶ *exam strategy*   Paper 1, Part 4 ▶ p.46

1 Look at the exam task opposite.

1 Read the instructions and look at the title and sub-heading of the article.

What is the text about? What do you have to do?

2 Decide what strategy you will use to do the multiple-matching task. Will you:

1 a) read the whole text first? OR
   b) read the questions first and underline key words?
2 a) read all the sections in the sequence? OR
   b) scan the sections to find the information you need?
3 a) read the whole text in detail? OR
   b) read only parts of it in detail to check you have found the right answer?
4 a) make sure you understand every word? OR
   b) ignore new words unless you need to understand them for the task?

3 Look at Unit 4, page 46 to check your answers.

2 Now do the exam task. The key words in question 0 and section A have been underlined to show you how the question paraphrases and summarises ideas in the text.

Use these clues to help you.

Question:

1 Look for other ways of referring to *popular ideas*.
2 How do we know that a piece of clothing was made by a particular designer? Look for this word.
3 Look for another expression that means *spend a lot of time doing*.
4 Look for another way of saying *get rid of*.
7 Look for a reference to <u>when</u> the person buys things.
9 Look for a contrast between what the person <u>used to do</u> in the past but no longer does now.
10 Look for another word for *material* – what clothes are made of.
14/15 Think about the advantages of buying more expensive things. Look for references to these advantages.

Over to you

3 Which of the following statements reflect your own opinions? If you don't agree with them, say what your own view is.

1 'I take ages making choices because I like things to be just right.'
2 'I don't like to have a lot of possessions.'
3 'I know what kind of clothes suit me, so I don't make many mistakes.'
4 'I can never decide what to wear in the morning.'
5 'I like lots of clutter around me.'

You are going to read about five people who have chosen a particular lifestyle. Answer the questions by choosing from the people A–E. The people may be chosen more than once. When more than one answer is required, these may be given in any order. There is an example at the beginning (0).

Which person says that he/she

now has a home which is quite unlike a previous one?	0 A
has not been influenced by popular ideas?	1
tends to buy the work of only a very few designers?	2
spends a lot of time selecting which things to buy?	3
finds it easy to get rid of things which are no longer pleasing?	4
tends to buy things in similar colours?	5
aims to provide a relaxed atmosphere for guests?	6
tends to buy things at regular intervals?	7
aims to create a less stressful working environment?	8
no longer buys things which don't get used?	9
likes to buy things made from certain materials?	10
believes that keeping things in order can make you feel better?	11
has designed something to serve more than one purpose?	12
wants to keep work and home life very separate?	13
aims to get good value for money when buying things?	14 15

The simple life

Five people talk about how they have cleared the clutter from their lives and are now living in style with relatively few possessions.

A Toby Thomson

I'm a perfectionist and this is reflected in my apartment. I used to live in a small flat that was quite cluttered with lots of possessions scattered all over the place. By contrast, my present place is wonderfully empty and spacious. The rooms are all painted white and when you're inside them, you feel great because you get maximum use of the natural daylight. I have no pictures on the walls. As an architect, I work with drawings all day and I don't want to look at them in the evening. Everything in the apartment has to be just right. I take ages choosing each piece of furniture or lamp because I think it through carefully and know exactly what I'm after.

B Melanie Martin

Having a simple orderly wardrobe makes life less complicated. These days I am much more careful about clothes than I used to be. I buy one well-made piece of clothing that I'm going to love and cherish, rather than several inexpensive items which will soon wear out. I've refined my wardrobe down to a couple of well-known labels and I take a lot of care whenever I buy something to make sure it's right for me. A few years ago, I would just take clothes off the rails without really thinking about whether they'd suit me. Inevitably, some of them would get thrown away unworn. Having fewer clothes means you know exactly what goes with what. When I get dressed in the morning I don't spend half an hour rummaging through stuff trying to figure out what will look right.

C Annabella Bevan

My flat is uncluttered, I have wooden floors and only a few pieces of furniture, but I have chosen what I own with care. But if I go off something, I won't hesitate to throw it out because, for me, things have to be right. I work from home and I'm setting up my own company to sell things on the Internet, but I'd like to work in a soothing, relaxing environment. Having an orderly home and wardrobe helps me to cope with the frantic lifestyle people around me lead in London. It sounds strange, but when I switch on my computer here, I feel a lot calmer than I would in an office. Of course, the look of things does come into it too, but I think if you keep your clothes and possessions tidy, it can improve your mood.

D Graham Knight

The design of my flat is not a fashion statement. It's meant to be modern and contemporary, but I did it because I like it, not because it's the current trend. It's very much my space because I designed the interior myself. It's very sparse, but very homely. It's also very functional. I love cooking and the focal point of the flat is the steel worktop in the kitchen area. There's no dining table, so I both cook and eat on the worktop. I'm always having people round for dinner and they seem to like the informality of it. In the living room, there are two cream sofas and a black side table. I don't feel the need for anything else because I'm not a very materialistic person really.

E Barbara Clayton

I don't have a wardrobe. My clothes hang behind a see-through curtain so that I can take in everything at a glance. Above the rail is a transparent plastic shelf on which I put my scarves and jumpers. I buy a lot of cream-coloured and beige-coloured things and I'm prepared to spend quite a lot of money on one item. But it lasts so much longer than cheaper clothes that I think the expenditure evens itself out over time, because I end up buying fewer things overall. I usually have a shopping spree at the start of each season and resist the temptation to buy things on impulse in between. I will only buy things in one or two quality fabrics and, as I get older, I think I know what suits me, so I don't make many mistakes.

Vocabulary

1 Choosing the right word

Underline the correct word in each group. Then ask and answer the questions in pairs.

1 Do you *spend / pay / buy* much money on CDs?
2 How much do they *cost / charge / demand* for cassettes where you shop?
3 What *mark / class / make* of mobile phone do you think is the best?
4 What do you normally do if a store hasn't got the video you want in *store / stock / shop*?
5 Would you spend all night in a *rank / queue / file* if there were a chance you could buy a real sale bargain?
6 When you buy goods, do you usually pay by cheque, by credit card, or in *money / cash / coins*?
7 Do you always keep the *voucher / receipt / bill* when you buy something as proof of purchase in case you have to return it?
8 Have you made a purchase that you were not happy with recently? If so, did they give you a *rebate / refund / return* or were you able to *change / exchange / replace* it for a new one?

2 Countable or uncountable?

1 Underline the uncountable nouns in each set below. (Sometimes there is more than one word in the set.)

1 money   coin   change   cash
2 table   furniture   curtain   shelf   ornament
3 sweater   jewellery   suit   clothes
4 cotton   needle   silk   material
5 luggage   bag   equipment   shopping
6 staff   receipt   advice   information

2 Now underline the correct word in each pair.

1 I need *a/some* new curtains to brighten up my room.
2 The problem is, I've only got a *few/little* cash left.
3 I've already spent too *much/many* money on *a/some* new furniture.
4 I also bought *this/these* new stereo equipment last week, so I'm pretty broke.
5 Even if I could buy *the/a* curtain material now, I'm not sure which colour I'd choose. Can you give me *an/some* advice?
6 On the other hand, I hate buying sensible things. Why don't I forget about new curtains? I'd much rather have *a/some* piece of jewellery or *a/some* CDs.

3 Complete the rules.

With .... nouns we can use: *a/the, some/any, many/(a) few, those/these*.
With .... nouns we can use: *the, some/any, (a) little/much, this/that*.

3 Describing objects: order of adjectives

1 Read the following descriptions of objects and underline the adjectives (words and phrases).

1 My favourite possession is a present that my uncle brought me back from Tokyo. He had it made specially for me. It's a very beautiful, handmade Japanese kimono, and it's made of silk. It's full-length and very ornate – with huge purple dragons hand-painted onto a pale cream background. It's got wide sleeves and a thick belt made of very stiff fabric, which you have to pull very tight.

2 My favourite possession is an amazing old Indian drum. My brother bought it for me as a gift when he was on holiday over there. It's got a round clay base and a covering of different types of leather. At the top there's a small black circle made from iron dust, which helps to create the tune. It's painted in a dye made from plants and other natural ingredients. The sound it makes is great.

2 Copy and complete the table with appropriate adjectives from the descriptions.

Descriptions						
opinion	dimensions/size	age	shape	colour	origin	material

3 Now add more adjectives to the tables

Over to you

4 Describe your own favourite possession and say why it is special to you. Try to include words from the table in Exercise 3.2. Do not use more than three adjectives before a noun.

> **! *made* + preposition**
>
> Notice the prepositions.
> 1 It is **made from** natural ingredients.
> 2 It is **made of** leather.
> 3 It was **made by** craftsmen.
> 4 It was specially **made for** me.

Use of English 2: *lexical cloze*

▶▶ *exam strategy*
Paper 3, Part 1 ▶ p.13

1 **Discuss these questions.**

1 What are the advantages for the consumer of having a lot of products to choose from?
2 What are the disadvantages?
3 How can consumers deal with the problem of too much choice?

2 **Look at the exam task opposite. Read the text below all the way through, ignoring the gaps for the moment.**

1 Find the answers to the questions in Exercise 1.
2 Explain what the title of the text refers to.

▶▶ *exam tip!*

Read the **whole** sentence before deciding how to fill in the gap. The word you choose must fit the meaning and the grammar of the sentence as a whole. ◀◀

3 **Now complete the exam task. Use these clues to help you.**

Question:

1 Only one adjective collocates with *selection*.
3 This is a phrasal verb. Which verb fits with the particle *of*?
5 Which verb can be followed by a *to*-infinitive?
7 This is a fixed phrase.
12 Look at the form of the verb that follows.
14 This is a phrasal verb. Which verb goes with *up* and fits the context?
15 This is a collocation.

Read the text below and decide which answer A, B, C or D best fits each space. There is an example at the beginning (0).

0 A carried B held C done D worked

SPOILT FOR CHOICE

Some research which was recently (0) *A.* out in Britain has confirmed what many ordinary shoppers have suspected for quite a long time. Having a (1) ..... selection of goods to choose from is not necessarily a (2) ..... to consumers. The average supermarket in Britain has around 40,000 different products on sale at any one time and if you're (3) ..... of buying a car, then there are actually around 1,600 different (4) ..... on the market.

In one sense, choice is a good thing because it (5) ..... us to buy those products which best suit our needs. But choice can also (6) ..... something of a problem. With over 400 brands of shampoo on the market, how does the consumer (7) ..... hold of the information necessary to choose between them?

For some people the solution is to buy only well-known brands, whilst others are happy to be (8) ..... by advertising. There is evidence, (9) ....., that for some people the (10) ..... of choice available to them in Britain's consumer society is actually a (11) ..... of anxiety and stress. One man interviewed by the researchers admitted that he had (12) ..... to buy his girlfriend a mobile phone for her birthday, but was so (13) ..... by the number of different types on offer in the shop that he (14) ..... up and decided to buy her a (15) ..... of flowers instead!

1	A deep	B wide	C long	D tall
2	A profit	B favour	C benefit	D value
3	A considering	B thinking	C planning	D hoping
4	A styles	B patterns	C models	D labels
5	A allows	B lets	C makes	D leaves
6	A report	B respect	C review	D represent
7	A get	B come	C have	D take
8	A suggested	B persuaded	C proposed	D recommended
9	A therefore	B moreover	C however	D whether
10	A rank	B height	C total	D amount
11	A spring	B reason	C source	D motive
12	A set out	B looked for	C made up	D gone after
13	A confused	B complicated	C disorganised	D misunderstood
14	A hung	B gave	C held	D kept
15	A heap	B handful	C bundle	D bunch

Writing: *letter of complaint*

exam file

In **Paper 2**, **Part 1**, you may be asked to write a letter of complaint or a letter in which you correct inaccurate information. You will usually need to include a request for action or a suggestion.

▶▶ *exam strategy*

Make sure you:
- give your reason for writing in the first paragraph.
- avoid using a very aggressive tone or your letter will have a negative effect.
- write a topic sentence for each main paragraph.
- use linking words to connect sentences and paragraphs together.

1 **Read the writing task below.**

1 Underline the points you must include in your letter.

You bought a computer game from a mail–order catalogue but you were disappointed when it arrived. Read the advertisement carefully and the notes which you have made. Then write a letter to the manager of the company, complaining about the game and asking for your money back, or a better game.

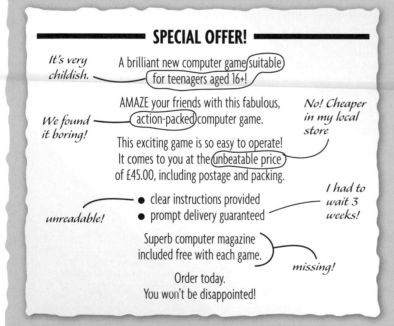

Write a letter of between 120 and 180 words in an appropriate style. Do not write any postal addresses.

2 Who are you going to write this letter to?
Should your style be formal, neutral or informal?

Focus on paragraphing

2 **1 Read the paragraphs of the sample letter below and put them in the correct order. Underline any words or phrases that help you.**

Dear Sir or Madam,

☐ The problems do not stop here. The instructions you claimed were 'clear' were actually unreadable. Furthermore, the free magazine was missing.

☐ I look forward to hearing from you.

☐ My second complaint is about the price quoted in your advertisement. In your advertisement, you said it was 'unbeatable' but I can buy the game cheaper in a local store. I could sue you!

☐ *1* I am writing to complain about the game which I ordered from your catalogue. I was very disappointed when it arrived.

☐ While we are on the subject of advertising, I discovered another problem when the game arrived. You said that it was for older teenagers but that was a lie – the game was very childish. You also said that the game was 'action-packed'. However, my friends agree it's really boring.

☐ To sum up, I would like a refund or another game, otherwise there'll be trouble.

☐ To begin with, you said the game would arrive promptly but I had to wait three weeks. When I rang and asked where it was, they suggested I should be more patient!

Yours faithfully

Kate Brown

Kate Brown

2 A paragraph should normally contain a topic sentence that tells you what it is about. Underline the topic sentence in five of the paragraphs.

3 **A letter of complaint must be polite. Find three phrases in the sample which are too rude or aggressive. How could you rephrase these sentences in a more appropriate way?**

Focus on grammar ▶ *pp.180–1*

4 **1 Underline all the examples of indirect speech in the sample letter in Exercise 3. What do you notice about the use of tenses and word order?**

2 Match the examples in the letter to the uses in the grammar file opposite.

3 Put this conversation into indirect speech.

1 'I'm really fed up!' Alex said.
  Alex *said that he was really fed up* .

2 'The new video recorder doesn't work properly,' he explained.
  He explained ....

3 'Where did you buy it, Alex?' asked Clare.
  Clare ....

4 'Why don't you take it back to the store tomorrow, Alex?' she suggested.
  She ....

5 'Can I have a refund on my video recorder?' Alex asked the assistant.
  Alex ....

6 'We've never had any complaints before,' claimed the assistant.
  The assistant ....

7 'I won't leave the shop until you give me a refund,' insisted Alex.
  Alex ....

8 'I will refund the money but my manager won't be very happy with me,' said the assistant.
  The assistant ....

4 Look at the exam task opposite. Read the advertisement and the handwritten notes. For which four points in the notes can you write sentences as in the example?

Example:
Your advertisement stated (said/claimed) that the jeans would be delivered promptly **but** in fact they were delivered late.

Over to you

5 **Write your answer to the exam task. Follow the advice in the exam strategy box. Remember to:**

• make a plan before you start to write.
• include all the points you are asked to write about.
• divide your letter into clear paragraphs.
• use an appropriate style for the target reader.
• check your writing for errors when you have finished.

---

grammar files 13, 14

A Indirect statements

When the reporting verb is in the past (e.g. *said*), we usually
● move verbs one step back into the past.
● change pronouns and words related to time and space.

Direct speech	Indirect speech
1 *'That new make of stereo only **arrived** in the store **this** morning.'* →	The salesman **said that** new make of stereo **had only arrived** in the store **that** morning.
2 *'**We haven't had** any dissatisfied customers until **now**.'* →	He stated/claimed **they hadn't had** any dissatisfied customers until **then**.

B Indirect questions

● have the same word order as statements.
● follow the same rules for tense changes as statements.

1 *'**Can you** give me a refund?'* →	I asked the assistant **if/whether he could** give me a refund.
2 *'Where **do I need** to go to make a complaint?'* →	I asked him **where I needed** to go to make a complaint.

C Suggestions

We use *suggest* + noun clause to report suggestions.

*'**Why don't you** write to **our** Head Office?'* →	The salesman **suggested (that) I (should) write** to **their** Head Office.

You recently bought a pair of jeans from a mail-order catalogue, but you are not happy with them. Read the advertisement carefully and the notes you have made. Then write a letter to the manager of the company, complaining about the jeans and asking for your money back.

Write a letter of between **120** and **180** words in an appropriate style. Do not write any postal addresses.

6 Family life

Lead-in

Look at the photo opposite and use words and expressions in the box to discuss these questions.

1 What is happening in the photo?
2 How do you think the people feel about each other?
3 What kind of things do you and your parents argue or disagree about? Make a list.

> to quarrel/fall out   to tell someone off for -ing
> to lay down the law   to nag   to go on at someone
> to interfere   messy   to be a tip   to tidy up
> to clean up after yourself   household chores
> to disapprove of   to feel resentful/annoyed
> to do the washing-up   to blame someone for -ing

Reading 1: *multiple-choice questions*

▶▶ *exam strategy*   Paper 1, Part 2 ▶ p.22

1 1 **Look at the exam task opposite and read the instructions. What strategy will you use to do this task? Put the following steps in the best order. Then compare your answers with a partner.**

☐ Read the questions but not the options, and underline key words.
☐ Read the text carefully.
☐ Read the options **A–D** and choose the one that best matches the ideas in the text.
☐ Find the parts of the text that you think answer the questions, and underline key words there.
1 Read the text quite quickly for general understanding.

2 **Check your answers by looking back at Unit 2, page 22.**

2 **Read the text once quite quickly and answer these questions to check your general understanding.**

1 What is the psychologist's view about teenagers' bedrooms?
2 Why did the teenager and his mother quarrel?
3 What is the teenager's point of view?
4 What is his mother's point of view?
5 How did they solve the problem?

3 **Use the exam strategy to answer the multiple-choice questions. Be prepared to justify your answers. Use these clues to help you identify the right option.**

Question:

1 Remember that the correct option will express the same ideas as the text but use different words.
2 Remember, the questions often test specific details in a paragraph. Look for a linking expression in the text which will help you eliminate one of the options.
4 Look carefully at the words which come before the pronoun to check what it refers to.
6 Is there a word in the previous sentence that has a similar meaning?

Over to you

4 1 **Look again at Tim's advice to parents in the text (lines 41–45). Do you agree with it?**

2 **Look at the list you made in Question 3 of the Lead-in. What advice would you give parents on how to solve these conflicts?**

Vocabulary: *collocations*

5 1 **Fill in the missing words in these tables. Most of the words can be found in the text or the questions.**

Verb	Noun	Adjective	Noun	Verb	Noun
decide	....	anxious	....	insist	....
agree	....	private	....	argue	....
solve	....				

2 **Complete these phrases with a word from the tables. Then add them to your vocabulary notebook. Write an example sentence for each one.**

1 to find a ....
2 to come to an ....
3 to have an ....
4 to respect someone's ....
5 to feel .... about something
6 to .... on doing something
7 to make a ....

Tidy your room *NOW!*

As a psychologist, my view on teenagers' bedrooms is quite straightforward. Personal space is very important in adolescence and privacy should be respected. If a teenager has his or her own room, then this space is for that teenager to arrange as he or she wishes. On no account should parents be tempted to tidy a teenager's room. If arguments arise, patience and understanding are required on both sides.

Unfortunately, this doesn't always happen. Let's take the example of a typical English teenager called Tim. He and his Mum fell out about the untidy state of his room because they were looking at the problem from two completely different points of view. This is what Tim had to say:

Bedrooms are incredibly important when you're a teenager. Everyone needs space, but at that time you need it most of all. I don't mind Mum coming into my room as long as she knocks. The problem is that she goes round looking for things to put away and saying things like 'Tidy room, tidy mind'. I tell her I don't want a tidy mind. She thinks it's strange that although I'm hoping to study Interior Design at college, I don't seem to bother about my own room at home. But what she fails to understand is that I like the mess. It's interesting watching it grow, because it's full of shapes and patterns. I like my Mum, but when she goes on at me about tidying my room, I just get more determined not to do anything about it. My advice to parents would be to leave their teenagers' rooms till they are so bad that it's impossible to walk in. Then the kids will have to tidy up.

And of course, Tim is right. In my experience, teenagers left to live in their own mess will eventually reach the stage where they clean it up. We have to remember that this is an important period of experimentation for them and they need to make their own decisions about things. Parents' anxiety never solves anything during this period and **it** can actually have the effect of making things worse. This is what Tim's Mum had to say:

*I encouraged Tim to clean up after himself when he was young and he was happy to do it then. But when he got older, he simply started to refuse. His room became a complete tip. He had lots of expensive designer clothes all thrown on the floor, along with waste paper, empty cans and leftovers of food he'd taken up there secretly. When I started being more insistent, I was very shocked by Tim's response. He isn't normally very rebellious but he just exploded, saying it was none of my business what he did in his room. When I tried to tidy it up myself, he just **hit the roof**, insisting that he wanted it like it was. After this, my husband, who is also horribly untidy, had a man-to-man chat with Tim about it. He didn't get very far but he got a better reaction than me, which was irritating.*

Things are better now for Tim and his Mum, although this is still not a subject which they can laugh about. Tim is just as messy, and still doesn't want his Mum cleaning his room. She, however, came to realise that it was better not to interfere and so she has ignored the problem for the last six months. Tim, meanwhile, has taken to cleaning his own room once a week. His Mum daren't ask him why or say how pleased she is in case he stops. Although it seemed like a big problem at the time, it looks like Tim and his Mum have found a solution.

1 What point does the psychologist make about teenagers in the first paragraph?

A They are often unreasonable.
B They should respect their parents.
C They need their own private space.
D They should keep their rooms tidy.

2 Why does Tim get annoyed when his mother comes into the room?

A She doesn't knock before entering.
B She makes comments about the state of the room.
C She expects him to know where things are.
D She takes away the things that he needs.

3 How does Tim feel about his bedroom?

A He's too lazy to tidy it up.
B He's guilty about not looking after it.
C He's pleased with how it looks.
D He doesn't see it as his responsibility.

4 What does 'it' in line 55 refer to?

A a period
B an experiment
C an effect
D a feeling

5 What aspect of Tim's behaviour surprised his mother most?

A the way he treated his clothes
B the fact that he used to be tidy
C the fact that he had secrets
D the way he reacted to her

6 'hit the roof' in line 72 means that Tim

A lost his temper.
B tried to explain.
C refused to speak.
D was very rude.

7 Why is Tim's bedroom tidier now?

A He has developed a new routine.
B His mother has changed her attitude.
C His mother is now allowed to clean it.
D He has reached an agreement with his parents.

Grammar: *structures after reporting verbs* ▶ *pp.181–2*

grammar file 15

A Verb + *that*-clause

- **verb + *that*:** admit, realise, remember, reply, think, etc.

1 *'I can't blame my Mum for getting upset.'*	➤ He **admitted** (that) he couldn't blame his mother for getting upset.
2 *'Oh, no! I forgot to leave a note for my parents!'*	➤ He **realised** (that) he had forgotten to leave a note for his parents.

- **verb + object + *that*:** remind, tell, etc.

3 *'Remember you must finish your homework.'*	➤ Her parents **reminded her** (that) she had to finish her homework.

- **verb + *that* + *should*:** advise, demand, recommend, suggest, etc.

4 *'Why don't you discuss your problems with me?'*	➤ My Dad **suggested** (that) I **should** discuss my problems with him.

B Verb + *-ing* or infinitive

- **verb + *to*-infinitive:** agree*, offer, promise*, refuse, threaten*, etc.

1 *'I'll stop your pocket money if you don't work harder!'*	➤ Mum **threatened to stop** my pocket money if I didn't work harder.

- **verb + object + *to*-infinitive:** advise, forbid, persuade*, remind*, tell*, warn*, etc.

2 *'I wouldn't disturb your Dad if I were you.'*	➤ Mum **advised me not to disturb** my Dad.

- **verb + *-ing*:** admit*, deny*, suggest*, etc.

3 *'I did not break my promise!'*	➤ My friend **denied breaking** her promise.

C *-ing*/infinitive or *that*-clause?

The verbs marked * above can also be followed by a *that*-clause. We have to use a *that*-clause with a change of subject.

1 *'You have to be back by 10 p.m.'*	➤ Dad told **me to be** back by 10 p.m.
2 *'Your sister has to be back by 10 p.m.'*	➤ Dad told **me** (that) **my sister** had to **be** back by 10 p.m.'

---

1 **Find and correct the mistakes in these sentences. There may be two ways to write the sentence correctly.**

1 The other day Mum and I had a row. She said me I had to work harder.
2 She suggested me spending more time studying and less time socialising.
3 She reminded that I had a lot of work to do if I wanted to pass my exams.
4 She made me promise that I not go out more than two nights per week.
5 She also warned me to not invite friends round to the house too often.
6 She advised me that I come in earlier at night.
7 I tried to persuade her that she let me go to a party the following Friday but she refused letting me go.
8 She forbade that I go out again this week.

2 **1** **Read the following extract from a reported conversation between Ginia and her father. Choose the appropriate verb from each pair and write it in the correct form in the text.**

1 tell/explain	3 persuade/threaten
2 promise/warn	4 demand/order

❝ I got home really late last night. My Dad was very angry and wanted to know why I was so late. I (1) .... him that I had forgotten the time and had missed the last bus. He (2) .... me not to let it happen again. He (3) .... that I wouldn't be allowed out for a month if it did. He (4) .... me to apologise to my mother for worrying her. ❞

2 **What were the original words that Ginia and her father used?**

3 **Match each of the sentences (1–8) with an appropriate reporting verb a)–h). Use each verb once only. Then rewrite the sentences in indirect speech, as in the example below.**

Example:
1h *I promised to tidy my room.*

1 'I'll tidy my room, honestly!'
2 'I don't think you should buy a motorbike.'
3 'Why don't you talk things over with your parents?'
4 'Do you think you could tell your friends not to phone so late?'
5 'Please, please, Mum, let me go out.'
6 'Don't come home late or there'll be trouble!'
7 'Go on! Come to the club with me.'
8 'Shall I pick you up after school?'

a) I begged ...
b) My friend tried to persuade me ...
c) My uncle offered ...
d) My father asked ...
e) My aunt advised ...
f) My parents warned ...
g) My best friend suggested
h) I promised ...

Over to you

4 **Work in pairs.**

Student A: Think of an area you and your parents often disagree about, e.g. late nights. Report a recent conversation on the subject to a partner. Use a range of reporting verbs.

Student B: Listen to your partner and encourage him/her by asking questions or making comments:
Did they tell you to ... ?
What did you say when they ... ? etc.

Use of English 1: *error correction*

1 **Look at the exam task below. Read the text to find out:**

1 What was the survey about?
2 What were the results of the survey?
3 Do you agree with what the survey found out or not?

2 **Now follow the rest of the exam strategy to do the task. What types of errors does the text contain? Look at this list as you go through the text, and note down the line numbers.**

Unnecessary:

pronoun (subject/object) ....   preposition ....
particle (part of a phrasal verb) ....   *to*-infinitive ....
adverb (e.g. *so, too, very*) ....   linking word ....
verb form ....

▶▶ **exam tip!**
An extra word only occurs once in the same line. If you see a word twice in one line, both will be correct.
◀◀

Read the text below and look carefully at each line. Some of the lines are correct, and some have a word which should not be there. If a line is correct, put a tick (✓) in the space by the number. If a line has a word which should not be there, write the word in the space. There are two examples at the beginning (0 and 00).

A SURVEY

0	*to*	A recent survey found that the majority of teenagers tell to their parents
00	✓	most things about their lives, but not everything. Parents are often heard
1	....	to say that as well their teenage children become more independent, so they
2	....	tend to become less communicative. If the survey is it to be believed, this
3	....	seems to be true. When asked about why they kept some things from
4	....	their parents, many teenagers explained us they were afraid their parents
5	....	would not understand. This is because adolescence is said a time when
6	....	young people are experimenting and searching for their individual identities.
7	....	As a result, they often turn to friends when they are in have need of advice
8	....	and support, but rather than to parents. Privacy is often a big issue with
9	....	teenagers, and some parents may ask too many questions, giving up the
10	....	impression that they want trying to control their child's life. In an attempt to
11	....	be helpful, some parents may suggest to doing things that would not
12	....	be acceptable in the teenage social group. Other parents not only avoid
13	....	asking questions, but may also keep off them certain embarrassing topics
14	....	of conversation altogether. In this way, they do not have got to accept the fact
15	....	that their child is fast turning into an adult, with all the problems that brings.

Speaking: *individual long turn*

▶▶ **exam strategy** Paper 5, Part 2 ▶ p.21/59

1 **You are going to practise Part 2 of the Speaking Test, in which you are given one minute to compare, contrast and comment on two photos. What must you do? What should you avoid doing? Think of three DOs and two DON'Ts.**

DO	DON'T
listen	*describe each* ....
....	....
....	

2 **Work in groups of three.**

Student 1: You are the examiner. Give the candidates the instructions on page 204. Time each candidate. If necessary, interrupt Candidate A after one minute. Don't give Candidate B more than about 20 seconds to comment.

Student 2: You are Candidate A. Compare and contrast the two photos on this page, according to the examiner's instructions. You have one minute.

> wedding reception   to get married (to)
> wedding dress   to celebrate   to kiss sb
> bride   bridegroom   bridesmaid   best man
> mother/father-in-law   grandchild
> nephew/niece
> birthday party   party hats
> to give/receive presents   to enjoy yourself
> to have fun/a great time   to play games

▶ **Functions files 1 and 3 p.200**

Student 3: You are Candidate B. The examiner will ask you to comment on the two photos briefly after Candidate A has finished. You should take about 20 seconds for this.

> **▶▶ exam tip!**
> Remember: if you don't know the English word for something in one of the pictures, describe it using different words.

◀◀

3 **Turn to the photos on page 204. Work in groups of three as in Exercise 2. The examiner should give the instructions on page 207.**

▶ **Functions files 1 and 3 p.200**

Listening: *multiple matching*

▶▶ **exam strategy**   Paper 4, Part 3

- Read the instructions carefully to find out what the speakers will be talking about.
- Before you listen, read the options **A–F** and think about what you might hear.
- During the first listening, listen for the main idea and mark the option that seems closest.
- Check your answers during the second listening.

1 **Read the instructions for the exam task opposite and the options.**

1 How do you celebrate the events listed A–F?
2 What words do you think you might hear? Make a list.

2 🔊 **Listen to the recording once. Try to get the gist of each speaker's words. Mark the options you think are closest to this.**

3 🔊 **Read the following questions and then listen again to check you haven't made an error. Sometimes a word in the options is mentioned by more than one speaker. Make sure this hasn't misled you.**

1 Three speakers mention the word *birthday*. But which speaker talks about *celebrating* a birthday (see the task instruction)?
2 Three speakers mention a *public holiday*. Are they talking about *celebrating* a public holiday as a *social event*?

▶▶ *exam tip!*

Make good use of the second listening even if you've answered every question the first time. If you discover an error, you may need to change more than one answer. One wrong answer can have a knock-on effect on the others.

◀◀

You will hear five different people talking about social events. For questions **1–5**, choose from the list A–F what is being celebrated at each of the events. Use the letters only once. There is one extra letter which you do not need to use.

A	The end of term	Speaker 1	1
B	Someone's birthday	Speaker 2	2
C	An engagement		
D	Somebody leaving	Speaker 3	3
E	A new flat	Speaker 4	4
F	A public holiday	Speaker 5	5

Over to you

4 **An English friend of yours wants some information about your country. Answer his/her questions.**

1 What social occasions do you celebrate every year?
2 Are long engagements common in your country?
3 What public holidays do you have? What is the most important one? How is it celebrated?
4 How popular are the celebrations with young people?

4th July, Independence Day in the USA

May Day in Britain

Lead-in

Look at the photos, which show famous parents and their children, and discuss these questions.

1 Can you name the celebrities and say what they are famous for?
2 What do you think are the advantages and disadvantages of having a famous parent?
3 Would you like to have famous parents?

Reading 2:
gapped text (sentences)

▶▶ *exam strategy*   Paper 1, Part 3 ▶ p.34

1 1 Look at the exam task opposite and read the instructions. What strategy will you use to do this task? Put the following steps in the best order. Then compare your answers with a partner.

☐ Read the extracted sentences and look for one that fits the meaning of each paragraph.
[1] Read the whole of the base text including the example answer.
☐ Check for language links and associated words before and after the sentence.
☐ Read the text around each gap carefully.
☐ Read the whole text again.

2 Check your answers by looking back at Unit 3, page 34.

2 Read the base text and the example answer. Then answer these questions to check your understanding.

1 What are the writer's earliest memories of the theatre?
2 Why did she have doubts at first about becoming an actress?
3 Why didn't her parents want her to take up an acting career?
4 What is the disadvantage of a famous parent according to the writer?

▶▶ **exam tip!**

Make sure you have a good understanding of the base text before looking at the extracts. If you don't fully understand the main message, you may get confused later.

◀◀

3 Use the exam strategy to complete the task. Remember, there is one extract that doesn't fit anywhere. Pay attention to:

• meaning.
• noun/pronoun sequences.
• the use of *this/that* to refer to a previous idea, not just a single word.
• linking expressions that show the connection between ideas.
• associated words and ideas in the extracted sentences.

Use these clues to help you.
Question:

1 Look for a sentence in the box that refers to the writer's age.
2 Look for a pronoun that can replace *father*.
4 Does the missing sentence refer to an alternative ambition? Does the word *That* in the sentence after the gap refer to a word or a whole idea?
5 What does *it* refer to in the first sentence? (Look at the previous paragraph.) Which sentence extract refers to a similar idea?

Vocabulary: *synonyms*

4 1 Which words in the text mean the same as:
1 very (= intensifier) (paras. 1, 3 and extracts)
2 idea (extracts)
3 to cry (para. 3)
4 at first (para. 5)
5 ambition (extracts)
6 to persuade someone not to (para. 8)

2 Why do you think the writer chose the words used in the text?

Over to you

5 Discuss these questions.

1 Have you ever done any acting? Would you like to? Why/Why not?
2 Do you enjoy going to the theatre? How popular is theatre-going in your country?
3 What is the most popular TV series on at the moment? Why is it so popular?

I'M FOLLOWING IN FATHER'S FOOTSTEPS

What is it really like to live up to a famous parent? Lucy Briers, the daughter of actor Richard Briers and actress Ann Davies, reveals the benefits and pitfalls.

The strangest thing about having a famous actor as a father was that, when I was about seven, my friends at school got confused about it. When they saw my Dad acting on the television, they assumed that the actress who played his wife in the series was my mother. They used to ask me really daft questions. **0** **I**

> ❛ **The minute I walked onto the stage, I knew that I loved it and began to consider acting as a career.** ❜

I have always understood about my parents' work because they used to take me to see plays with them from a very young age. When I was a child, I would go to the theatre every six months or so. **1**

In one scene that I saw my father in, he ran on stage wearing a bright red curly wig, pushing a table on wheels. I thought this was hysterically funny, and so did the audience. **2** I also loved going backstage and, at the end of the night, I would weep because I didn't want to go home.

There is something compelling yet homely about the backstage of a theatre. **3** It is a protected environment which I have known all my life and find comforting.

Nonetheless, initially I did not want to follow in my parents' footsteps. **4** That passed and, by the time I was ten, I knew I wanted to be an actress. I'm convinced that I was born with the need to act.

At first I tried to ignore it because my parents were both actors and I thought it would be too boring if I became one too. **5** My first role was in Shakespeare's *A Midsummer Night's Dream* when I was sixteen at school. The minute I walked onto the stage, I knew that I loved it and began to consider acting as a career.

My parents tried to dissuade me, endlessly telling me what a hard life it can be. **6** While my Dad had enjoyed a consistent and successful career, my mother had had a very hard time.

Being the daughter of a famous actor is a double-edged sword. You are brought up with a certain amount of success around you and so you have high expectations. **7** I have worked through those feelings now though, and decided that it is all right. I am very proud of the work I do, as are my parents, and that is what counts.

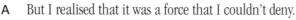

A   But I realised that it was a force that I couldn't deny.

B   As a child, I found it thrilling to see him at the centre of so much attention.

C   A theatre company is like a family.

D   But I already knew that and was under no illusions.

E   My first real aspiration was to be an underwater sea explorer.

F   I remember first seeing my Dad on stage when I was about four.

G   Since then, I have had only one other period of unemployment.

H   If you don't live up to those, there are moments when you think, 'I am not as good as my father.'

I   I just thought they were all incredibly silly not to understand the concept of television.

Vocabulary

1 Adjectives describing personality

Look at the adjectives in the box. Put a cross (X) next to the ones that usually have a negative meaning.

argumentative X	honest*	polite*
arrogant	intelligent*	rude
bad-tempered	jealous	sensitive*
~~confident~~*	loyal*	sincere*
easy-going	mean	sociable*
~~funny~~*	original*	stubborn
~~generous~~*	patient*	

2 Nouns for personal qualities

1 Make nouns from the adjectives in Exercise 1 that are marked * and add them to the qualities in the box. Three adjectives have been done for you.

-ence	-ity	others
confidence	*generosity*	*sense of humour*
....	....	....
....	....	....
	....	....
	....	

2 Which qualities in the box:

a) do you prize most in your parents?
b) do parents prize most in their children?

3 Your ideal partner

1 Fill in the extract from a computer dating form below.

2 Is anyone in the class your ideal partner? Interview other members of the class to find out what their best qualities are. Compare them with your wish list.

MY IDEAL PARTNER

My best qualities are:

1 *a sense of humour*
2 ....
3 ....
4 ....
5 ....

The qualities I would like my ideal partner to possess are:

1 *originality*
2 ....
3 ....
4 ....
5 ....

4 Choosing the right word

Underline the correct word in each group.

1 My father was a foreign diplomat so, although I am English, I was born and *developed / brought up / educated* in a big house in Buenos Aires.
2 I always thought I'd *become / grow / grow up* to be a diplomat, just like my father.
3 The problem is I'm really shy with strangers, although I'm fine with people once I *know / get to know / meet* them.
4 If I had to write myself a *character / personality / temper* reference, I'd describe myself as quiet rather than outgoing.
5 Actually, I have a lot *similar to / alike with / in common with* my mother.
6 She has *made / done / managed* a great success of her role as a diplomat's wife, so perhaps I have the right personality after all!

5 Linking words

Read the following story. Then fill the gaps with one of the linking expressions in brackets.

1 The party was a great success. ...., David walked Sonya home as they lived in the same street. (*After / Afterwards / After that*)
2 .... it was a warm night, Sonya started to shiver and David lent her his jacket. (*Although / However / In spite of*)
3 They didn't speak much ...., but, as their shyness wore off, they started to chat. (*firstly / at first / first of all*)
4 .... their walk, they discussed music and fashion, and found they had a lot in common. (*While / Meanwhile / During*)
5 Sonya confessed that she had wanted to speak to David .... of the evening but had not had the courage. (*at the beginning / in the beginning / for a start*)
6 When they .... reached Sonya's house they exchanged phone numbers. (*at the end / after all / eventually*)
7 They stood outside the house for a while but .... Sonya's Mum called her indoors. (*at the end / in the end / lastly*)
8 .... of the evening, David knew that he was falling in love with Sonya. (*In the end / At the end / At last*)

Over to you

6 Work in pairs or groups.

How did you meet your first girl/boyfriend? Tell the group what happened.

7 Make up a story using the phrasal verbs in the box.

ask someone out
to approve of someone
to go out with someone
to split up   to make up
to fall for/fall in love with
  someone

Use of English 2: *lexical cloze*

▶▶ *exam strategy* Paper 3, Part 1 ▶p.13

1 **How would you answer this question?**

'What do most teenagers want from a high school romance?'

2 **Look at the exam task opposite. Read the text all the way through, ignoring the gaps for the moment. What is the answer to the question in Exercise 1, according to the text?**

3 **Now complete the exam task. Remember, to help you choose the right word, you should:**

• pay careful attention to the meaning of the whole sentence.
• look for common collocations (words that go together).
• make sure that linking words fit the meaning of the text.

Use these clues to help you.

Question:

1–3 These are collocations. Which verb + noun combinations go together?
  4 Do you need a conjunction that expresses contrast or result?
  7 Look at the preposition after the gap. Which verb fits?
 10 The verb that fits here is a phrasal verb with *by* meaning to *remain loyal to someone*.

4 **Look for all the expressions in the text made with the verbs *come, get, make, play* and *put*. Add them to your vocabulary notebook. Write an example sentence to help you remember the meaning.**

Example: to **get** ready for something
I have to get ready for a tennis competition.

▶▶ *study tip!*

The verbs *do, come, get, make* and *put* collocate with many other words to form fixed phrases and phrasal verbs. It's a good idea to allocate a page in your vocabulary notebook to each verb, and add phrases as you come across them.

Read the text below and decide which answer A, B, C or D best fits each space. There is an example at the beginning (0).

0   A regarded   B reviewed   C respected   D recorded

IT MUST BE LOVE

The final years of secondary school are generally (0) ..*A*. as a fairly stressful period for students. There are exams to (1) ..... ready for, decisions about the future to be (2) ..... and many other aspects of growing up to come to (3) ..... with. It may seem surprising, (4) ....., that students of this age have enough time and energy left for (5) ..... relationships. For many, however, such relationships (6) ..... an important part of both their social life and their personal development. But what are most teenagers (7) ..... for in a high school romance?

For some, it's the chance to (8) ..... this wonderful period of discovery and adventure with somebody else. They (9) ..... having a loyal friend who will be there to (10) ..... by them in times of need or difficulty. It's also someone they can (11) ..... their trust in, someone to whom their deepest secrets can be (12) ....

For others, it's an opportunity to experiment with emotions and ideas. (13) ..... of being in a relationship, they learn what it is like to feel committed to one other person. (14) ..... a feeling of security, such relationships can also give a (15) ..... of what marriage must be like.

1	A come	B set	C learn	D get
2	A made	B done	C had	D brought
3	A face	B terms	C rights	D agree
4	A given	B although	C whether	D therefore
5	A forming	B raising	C growing	D shaping
6	A play	B result	C remind	D recommend
7	A wanting	B looking	C liking	D seeking
8	A give	B join	C share	D know
9	A approve	B relate	C identify	D appreciate
10	A stand	B remain	C support	D return
11	A mind	B put	C lay	D let
12	A said	B told	C kept	D placed
13	A As a result	B Despite	C Instead	D In case
14	A As far as	B As long as	C As well as	D As soon as
15	A slice	B thought	C sense	D touch

Writing: *story (first line)*

exam file

In **Paper 2**, **Part 2**, you may be asked to write a short story for a student magazine or for a competition. You will be given one sentence from the story. You may be instructed to use this as the first line or last line, or you may be asked to include it anywhere in the story.

▶▶ *exam strategy*

Make sure you:

- use the sentence you are given in the task in the correct position. DON'T change it in **any** way.
- use your imagination. Your story should be intriguing/original so your reader will want to finish the story to find out what happens.
- work out the plot carefully before you start to write. DON'T make the plot too complicated or far-fetched.
- begin the story in an interesting way.
- recount events in chronological order where possible and use a good range of narrative tenses.
- use linking words to sequence events and to signal time changes.
- use vocabulary imaginatively. Try to use words that paint a picture for your reader.

1 Read the writing task below.

1 Who is the main character? How many people are involved? Underline the names or pronouns you must use in your story.

You have been invited to write a short story for a students' magazine. The story must begin with the words:

As soon as they met, John knew that they would become good friends.

Write your story in 120–180 words in an appropriate style.

2 Answer these questions.

1 Who is going to read your story? Where is it going to appear?
2 What kind of story will your reader expect – a love story, a mystery story, another type of story?

Focus on working out a plot

2 Work in groups. The questions below are useful to ask when planning any story. Use them to help you work out a plot for this story and note it down. Use your imagination!

Background	Who was John? What sort of person was he? How old? Who was the other main character in the story? What was he/she like?
Events	How did the characters meet? Where did the story happen? When? Why? What happened exactly?
The ending	How did the story end? How did the main characters feel/react?

▶▶ *exam tip!*

Keep referring back to the first sentence of the story while you are planning and writing. Make sure that your plot fits in with that sentence all the way through.

◀◀

3 Read the story one student wrote, ignoring any verb form errors for now. Compare the plot you worked out in Exercise 2 with the one in the sample. Which do you think is better? Why?

As soon as they met, John knew that they would become good friends. Of course, he's seen Maria before. They lived in the same village so he would occasionally <u>seeing</u> her at the bus stop. But they had never spoken. *wrong form*

The truth was that John never thought <u>he needed</u> friends. He <u>was use to being alone</u> – he thought he preferred it. He <u>used to sitting</u> by himself in school and would never join in with the other kids. They <u>wondered</u> about him at first but soon ignored him. *wrong form*

One evening, John walked home when he saw a circle of girls. They were shouting and laughing but the girl in the centre was crying. The others were picking on her. John felt sorry for her so he warned the girls to stop. They were furious but eventually they ran off.

When Maria realised that the girls went, she smiled. She asked John to walk home with her. He agreed and, as they walked, he discovered that they had a lot in common. They were both shy, and had similar hobbies. By the time they reached her house, he knew this girl was different. This was a friendship he couldn't turn away from.

Focus on grammar ▶ *p.179*

4 **1 Read the information in the grammar file. Then correct the underlined errors in the story in Exercise 3.**

grammar file 7

A Past habits and actions

● *used to*
1 *My brother **used to hate** girls when he was young.* (= but not any longer)
2 *My friend **didn't use** to go to the same school as me.* (= but she does now)
3 ***Did** you **use to play** football in your last school?* (= was it your habit?)

● *would*
*My best friend and I went to the same school. We **would** always **walk** to school together. We**'d sit** next to each other all day and we**'d play** together at break times.* (= past habits/actions)

B Past states: *used to* (NOT *would*)
*I **used to be** shy when I was little.* (= past state)
NOT *I ~~would be~~ shy when I was little.*

C *Used to do* or *be/get used to*?
Compare:
1 *I **used to live** in the city but I don't now.* (= past habit)
2 *I**'m used to living**/I've **got used to living** in the country now. It's not strange anymore.* (= I'm accustomed to it now.)

2 Describe some of the routines or habits that you had as a child that you don't have now.

Example:
I used to tell my parents everything but I don't now.

3 Think back to the day you started coming to this class. Tell a partner about the things that seemed strange to you then that you are accustomed to now.

Example:
I've got used to working in pairs.

4 Imagine you are getting married soon. What things will you have to get used to?

Example:
I'll have to get used to sharing everything.

5 **There are three other tense errors in the story in Exercise 3. Find and correct them.**

❗ *tense sequences*

Remember, in clauses introduced by *I thought / realised / knew that* … the verb must move one step back in the past. Which tense is correct?

*I knew that I **made/had made** a terrible mistake.*

Over to you

6 **1 Read the exam task in Exercise 6.2. Then work with a partner to make notes for the task. Use the questions below to help you develop ideas.**

Introduction
Who was your friend? What was his/her name? What sort of person was he/she? How old?

Main events
Why were you planning a surprise? For a birthday? For some other occasion? What sort of surprise were you planning? Where did you plan to hold it? When? What happened exactly? How did your friend react to the surprise? How did you feel? If your plans failed, say why. What happened? How did other people react?

Ending
How did the story end? How did you all feel? Is there a lesson to be learned from what happened?

2 Write your answer to the following task in 120–180 words in an appropriate style. Follow the advice in the exam strategy box.

You have been asked to write a short story for an international young people's magazine. The story must begin with the words:

I was planning to give my friend a surprise.

Write your story.

Remember to:
● make a plan before you start to write.
● divide your story into clear paragraphs.
● check your writing for errors when you have finished.

7 Fitness

Lead-in

1 **Read the title and sub-heading of the article opposite. How far do you agree with the statement in the sub-heading?**

2 **What factors stress teenagers out?**

1 Look at the table TOP CAUSES OF STRESS opposite. Number the causes of stress 1–5 in order of importance for you (number 1 = most important). Then compare your answers with the survey results on page 199.
2 What other stress factors would you add to the list?

Reading 1:
gapped text (sentences)

> **exam file**
>
> In **Paper 1**, **Part 3**, the gapped text may be discursive. Discursive texts are organised according to the development of ideas, so it's especially important to understand the meaning of the text as a whole and to notice how the writer moves from point to point.

1 **Read the base text once including the example sentence. (Leave the missing sentences until later.) Find the answer to these questions.**

1 What causes of stress are mentioned in the article?
2 What positive aspects of stress are mentioned?
3 What ways of coping with stress are described?

2 **Read paragraph 1 again without looking at the example extract.**

1 What must *It* in the first sentence refer to?
2 Now look at the example answer (I) and underline the words that refer back to *It* in the first sentence.
3 Why do you think the writer has begun in this way?

3 **1 Use these clues to help you find the missing sentence for gaps 1–3.**
Question:

1 *Think about meaning.* If something is *blown out of all proportion*, we think it is more important or serious than it really is. Look at the sentences after the gap. Does the writer think stress should be taken seriously or not? *Check your answer.* Underline the pronouns in your answer. What does each pronoun refer to? (Remember, *this* and *that* can refer to a whole idea.)
2 *Think about meaning.* Look at the sentence after the gap. What <u>kind</u> of pressure is suggested by the references to *the right mobile phone* and *trainers*? *Check your answer.* Underline any linking words and associated words.
3 *Think about meaning.* Causes of stress at <u>school</u> and <u>home</u> have been mentioned. What other causes could the writer mention? *Check your answer.* Look for a linking word that introduces another example or relates to the previous idea.

2 Now continue with the rest of the gaps. Use the underlined words in the text and extracts to help you. Pay attention to topic links:
- ideas which are expressed over several sentences.
- examples that illustrate or support ideas in the paragraph.

Vocabulary: *phrasal verbs*

4 **1 Find these phrasal verbs in the text and fill in the missing particle. What do the verbs mean in the text?**

1 face .... to
2 give ....
3 live .... to
4 end ....
5 come ....
6 put .... with

2 Add the verbs to your vocabulary notebook. Write an example sentence for each, preferably one that is true for you.

Over to you

5 **Work with a partner. Find out what stresses your partner out and suggest some solutions.**
- *Have you tried … ?*
- *Have you thought of … ?*
- *I'd really recommend … -ing.*
- *What works best for me is …*

relaxation therapy	meditation	yoga	to go on a diet
to take up (pottery)	to enrol in an evening class		
to keep a diary	to share your worries with friends		

You are going to read an article about stress and how to cope with it. Eight sentences have been removed from the article. Choose from the sentences A–I the one which fits each gap (1–7). There is one extra sentence which you do not need to use. There is an example at the beginning (0).

Coping with stress

Teenage stress is a real problem but it can be beaten. Just don't suffer in silence.

It affects us all sometimes. **0** **I** It can make the most minor problem (what am I going to wear for that party?) feel like a matter of life or death and the prospect of a big event such as an exam seem like the end of the world.

OK, so stress blows problems out of all proportion. **1** When it's dismissed with comments like 'she's going through a phase' or 'he's being moody', this doesn't help either. Not recognising the fact that young people are under more pressure – and stress – than ever before isn't facing up to what teenagers today have to deal with.

'The world has changed a lot over the last thirty years,' says Gavin Ward of the Health Education Authority. 'There are more pressures on young people to succeed. **2** It's not even about having the right jeans any more but the right mobile phone or expensive pair of trainers.'

For many teenagers, daily stress starts at school. 'I only have to hear the word "exam" and I begin to panic,' says 16-year-old Joanne. 'I feel sick and I just want to give up. And there is always a new story in the newspapers about someone with a string of A grades to torment me.' There's also the pressure of large workloads and long days, and just wanting to be liked. At home there might be family problems such as arguing with parents or siblings. **3**

'I'm a typical teenager – bored unless I'm doing something out of the ordinary,' says Joanne. 'I get stressed by being stuck in a routine. Sometimes I don't know if I'm coming or going. I also feel that there are so many expectations to live up to and if you're not rich, famous or successful, then you don't stand a chance.' **4** If you've ever had one too many late nights and ended up in tears over 'nothing', you'll know what she means.

Just as there are many causes for stress, the way it shows itself also changes. Stress can make you feel as if you don't want to be around other people. It can put you off your food or lead to eating disorders like bingeing, stop you sleeping properly and even be the reason for stomach pains, backache or a stiff neck. **5** That's when getting one bad mark makes you think you're a total failure.

But for all the negative effects, stress can actually be good for you. A small amount can give you the feeling of excitement and the adrenaline rush you need to perform. **6** The key is achieving the right balance between not enough and too much, and learning how to beat off unhelpful levels of anxiety.

It's also good to know that many of us use stress-busters. 'We do things to beat stress every day without knowing it,' Gavin Ward explains. 'Going to your room and putting the music on really loud, going out to kick a ball around or just chatting to a friend on the phone can all do the trick.' **7** Whatever you do, recognising and dealing with stress is vital. As Joanne knows: 'Problems will come up all through life and I think you have to experience the downs to appreciate the good bits.'

TOP CAUSES OF STRESS
Boys and girls in two UK schools were asked to list their top five stress factors.

Boys	Girls
☐ **girls:** looking good and acting cool in front of girls	☐ **parents:** imposing restrictions
☐ **competition:** exams, sport	☐ **being organised**
☐ **image:** pressure to look good/wear the right clothes	☐ **peer pressure:** what to wear/look like
☐ **toughness:** trying to be tough and mature	☐ **exams:** coursework and homework
☐ **classmates:** peer pressure	☐ **friendships:** arguments and problems

---

A In particular, there is a lot of commercial pressure on young people to live up to expectations and conform.

B Then on top of all that, there's the 'bigger picture', with young people more likely to worry about the environment, crime and unemployment problems.

C Irrational fears are <u>also</u> common.

D If you feel awful, remember you won't feel this way forever.

E <u>Too little</u> stress can result in boredom and feeling frustrated with life.

F <u>Regular exercise, a good diet and activities like dancing</u> can even stop you getting stressed in the first place.

G But <u>despite</u> the big pressures Joanne feels, she also admits stress can come down to something as simple as <u>being tired</u>.

H But that doesn't mean it isn't real and it definitely doesn't mean you have to put up with it.

I That anxious, gloomy feeling called stress is something everyone has experienced.

Grammar: *the passive* ▶ *p.184*

A Form

We can only form the passive with transitive verbs (verbs followed by an object).

1 They **teach** teenagers how to cope with stress nowadays.
   → Teenagers **are taught** how to ...
2 They **are helping** young people to recognise the symptoms.
   → Young people **are being helped** to recognise ...
3 Doctors **didn't recognise** the dangers of stress in the past.
   → The dangers of stress **weren't recognised by doctors** ...
4 People **have written** a lot about stress recently.
   → A lot **has been written** about stress recently.

● **verbs with two objects:** give, lend, send, etc.
5 They have given **us tips** on how to relax.
   → **We** have been given **tips** on how to ...
      NOT Tips have been given to us ...

● **verb + preposition/particle**
6 Exams **put** my friend **off** school.
   → My friend was **put off** school by exams.

● **passive infinitives**
7 Exam pressure **will / can / may cause** stress.
   → Stress **will / can / may be caused** by exam pressure.
8 They **need to help** teenagers to relax.
   → Teenagers **need to be helped** to relax.
9 'Please **don't disturb** me,' he said.
   → He asked **not to be disturbed**.

B Use

We use the passive:

● when we are more interested in the action than who did it (the agent).
● when the agent is obvious, not important or unknown.
● to avoid vague subjects like *they, someone,* etc.

We use *by* + agent when it is important to know who or what did the action.

---

1 Read these sentences and underline the correct form of the verb, active or passive.

1 A lot of students *suffer/are suffered* from stress.
2 Social pressures on teenagers *have not always recognised/have not always been recognised*.
3 The causes of teenage stress *examined/were examined* at a conference last week.
4 The experts *will publish/will be published* a report of their findings soon.
5 Ways of dealing with stress *are researching/are being researched* by another group of experts.

2 Rewrite these sentences in the passive, using the words underlined as the subject of the sentence. Omit the agent if it is not necessary.

Example:
Exams cause <u>a huge amount of stress</u>.
A huge amount of stress is caused by exams.

1 Arguments with friends frequently worry <u>teenagers</u>.
2 Pressure from parents has stressed out <u>many teenagers</u>.
3 Advertisers are always pressurising <u>young people</u> to spend money.
4 They have recently issued <u>new guidelines</u> on coping with stress.
5 They should advise <u>students</u> to do regular exercise.
6 You can reduce <u>stress</u> by chatting to a friend.
7 Positive stress will improve <u>your performance</u>.
8 They showed <u>us</u> a video on yoga and head massage.

3 Complete the second sentence so that it has a similar meaning to the first sentence, using the word given. Do not change the word given. You must use between two and five words including the word given.

1 Ana's parents don't let her study on Saturdays. **is**
   Ana .... study on Saturdays.
2 'Don't give up your yoga class, Sarah,' they advised her. **not**
   Sarah .... give up her yoga class.
3 They have made Paul do sport more regularly. **has**
   Paul .... sport more regularly.
4 Many people have taken yoga up in recent years. **by**
   Yoga .... many people in recent years.
5 My friend was upset when they accused her of cheating. **was**
   My friend was upset when .... cheating.
6 It was unfair that Ana was dropped from the swimming team. **deserve**
   Ana didn't .... from the swimming team.

┌ ! *make / let / allow* ──────

What happens to *make* and *let* in the passive?

Active	Passive
1 They **made** me study every night. →	I **was made to** study every night.
2 They **didn't let** me go to the disco. →	I **wasn't allowed to** go to the disco.

Over to you

4 A new sports centre is to be built in your school/college.

You are members of the students' committee. You have been asked to meet the architect, then report on what stage has been reached. Write sentences for your report under the following headings, using the cues given.

What is being done at the moment?

Example:
students / still / ask for / their ideas
Students are still being asked for their ideas.

1 old building / pull down
2 plans for the sports hall / draw up

What has/hasn't been done?

3 the running track / not finish / yet
4 swimming pool / just / dig out

What will/is going to be done soon?

5 the tennis courts / finish / in one month
6 the changing rooms / open / soon after that

Use of English 1: *structural cloze*

▶▶ *exam strategy*　　　　　　Paper 3, Part 2 ▶ p.57

1 You are going to do a cloze task like the one in Paper 3, Part 2 of the exam. What is the best way to do the task? Put these steps in the right order. Then compare your answers with a partner.

☐ Fill in the gaps.
☐ Read each sentence carefully.
1 Read the whole text for general understanding.
☐ Try to decide what type of word is missing: noun, verb, adjective, etc.
☐ Read the whole text again.

2 Read the text below and answer these questions.

1 What methods of dealing with stress are described?
2 Why are these methods effective?

3 Now read the text again and fill in the gaps. Which of the following types of word are missing? Tick (✓) them. Which word types occurred most often?

- prepositions
- auxiliary verbs
- verbs

- pronouns
- phrasal verbs
- question words

- linking words
- quantifiers
- adjectives

Read the text below and think of the word which best fits each space. Use only **one** word in each space. There is an example at the beginning **(0)**.

BEATING STRESS

How can we combat the stresses of everyday life **(0)** *while* still maintaining an optimistic attitude and good physical health? It could be as simple as laughing **(1)** .... a joke, wearing the right colours **(2)** .... eating a chocolate bar.

It's well known that having a positive attitude is good **(3)** .... your state of mind, but **(4)** .... would have believed **(5)** .... could affect your health as well? It's true! According **(6)** .... recent research, laughter strengthens your immune system and improves your intellectual performance.

How much thought do you **(7)** .... to the colours that surround you in your daily life? It seems that each colour affects us **(8)** .... a different way. For example, yellow **(9)** .... thought to stimulate the mind and may help you to think on your feet. Blue, on the **(10)** .... hand, may help you to think more clearly, while green is good **(11)** .... your nerves need to be calmed. One colour that might best **(12)** .... avoided, however, is red, because this can make you feel impatient and aggressive.

And next time your mother **(13)** .... you off for eating your favourite snack, inform her that chocolate can help protect you **(14)** .... heart disease. Rather than avoiding it at **(15)** .... costs, it seems you should eat it more often!

Speaking: *collaborative task and discussion*

1 **Look at the photographs opposite.**

1 Where do the activities take place? Match a word in Box A with a word in Box B to form compound nouns.

A		B	
football	basketball	track	centre
running	sports	hall	court
swimming	fitness	pitch	pool

2 Put the names of the sports or activities in the correct column. Can you add any more examples?

do	play	go
athletics	*football*	*jogging*

▶▶ *exam strategy* Paper 5, Part 3
- DO make full use of the visual prompts.
- DON'T make a decision too soon, or you will run out of things to say.

2 **Part 3 task**
Work in groups of three.

Student 1: You are the examiner. Give Students 2 and 3 the instructions on page 207. Time them and interrupt if necessary after three minutes.

Students 2 and 3: Listen to the examiner carefully and do the task.

> (running) is good exercise   to lose weight
> to tone your muscles   to calm you down
> to make you feel good/better
> to help you relax   to get fit
> to improve general fitness
> to increase your sense of well-being

▶ **Functions files 8, 9,12 and 13 p.200–201**

▶▶ *exam strategy* Paper 5, Part 4
- DO initiate discussion as well as answering the examiner's questions.
- DO make use of strategies to ensure you and your partner share equally in the discussion.

3 **Part 4 discussion**
The examiner should now join in the discussion.

Student 3: You are the examiner. Ask Students 1 and 2 the questions below to develop the topic further. Stop the discussion after four minutes. (Don't worry if you don't manage to ask all the questions.)

Students 1 and 2: Discuss the examiner's questions.
1 What other things can you do to stay fit and healthy?
2 What things should you avoid doing?
3 What facilities are available where you live for exercise and relaxation?
4 How often do you make use of these facilities? What improvements would you suggest?

Listening: *multiple-choice questions*

1   Look at the words and expressions in the box and explain how they relate to the topic of football.

a man's game   club   to toss a coin   sponsor(ship)   coach   fans
transfer deal   to score   referee   a back-up career   the press

Example:
Football is often considered to be a man's game.

2   **1**   Read the instructions for the exam task. Discuss:

What do you think a football agent does? Why does a football player need an agent?

2 Read through the questions and underline key words.

What do the questions tell you about the work of a football agent?

3   **1**      Listen to the first part of the recording and decide what you think is the best answer to Question 1.

2 If you chose C, read the question again carefully.

What information does it ask for? Why is **C** the wrong answer?

4      Now listen to the rest of the recording and complete the exam task. Check your answers during the second listening. Then compare with other students.

You will hear an interview with Rachel Anderson, who talks about being a football agent. For each of the questions, choose the best answer, A, B or C.

1   For Rachel, what was the first step on the road to her present career?
   A   She met a relative of a footballer.
   B   She read an article in a newspaper.   ☐ 1
   C   A footballer offered her a job.

2   Which of these is part of Rachel's job?
   A   She represents fifteen clubs.
   B   She writes articles for newspapers.   ☐ 2
   C   She gives advice about money.

3   In her job, Rachel
   A   always knows how much she will earn.
   B   is not always paid immediately by her clients.   ☐ 3
   C   works as part of a large team.

4   Rachel's first contact with football came through
   A   her family.
   B   her friends.   ☐ 4
   C   her first job.

5   Rachel complains about a social event because
   A   she was prevented from attending.
   B   she was not invited to attend.   ☐ 5
   C   she was not a member of the club.

6   Rachel says that a woman working in football must
   A   act like a man.
   B   be good at football.   ☐ 6
   C   work harder than men.

7   Rachel says her family benefits from her
   A   professional contacts.
   B   international experience.   ☐ 7
   C   knowledge of football.

Over to you

5   **Discuss in pairs or groups.**

1 What sports are most popular in your country?
2 What sports do you like
   a) to play? b) to watch as a spectator?
3 How has professional sport changed in recent years? Talk about:
  • women in sport   • sponsorship
  • money earned by sportspeople
  • sports personalities as role models

7 Olympic sports

Lead-in

You are going to read an article in which five Olympic athletes describe how they train. Look at the photos and discuss these questions, using words and expressions from the box.

1 What special equipment and facilities do you need for each sport?
2 What physical and mental skills do you need for each sport?
3 How do you think each athlete trains for competitive events?

> goggles   net   whistle   trainers   flippers
> rowing machine   running machine   helmet
> weight-lifting equipment   cycling machine
> racquet   gloves   stick   punchbag   speed
> fast reflexes   stamina   a good sense of balance
> hand–eye coordination   determination
> motivation   dedication   courage

Reading 2: *multiple matching*

▶▶ *exam strategy*   Paper 1, Part 4 ▶ p.46

1 Do the multiple-matching task. If you can't remember how to tackle this task, look back at the strategy recommended in Unit 4, page 46.

2 Compare your answers with other students.

> ▶▶ *exam tip!*
>
> Remember, there may be similarities between sections of the text. As well as similarities in the topic, there may be similarities in the words and expressions used. When you choose your answer, make sure it matches the question. ◀◀

Vocabulary: *using context*

3 Work out the meaning of the words in bold in the text (1–8). Use context clues to help you. Then explain the meaning to other students using a definition or examples.

Over to you

4 Discuss.

1 Look at the text again. Which athlete seems to have the hardest routine?
2 Which sport do you find most exciting?

You are going to read an article about the diet and training programme of five athletes. Answer the questions by choosing from the athletes A–E. The athletes may be chosen more than once. When more than one answer is required, these may be given in any order. There is an example at the beginning (0).

Fitness of purpose

Different Olympic events require specific training and diets.

A The Swimmer

The strength I need is mainly upper-body, because 90% of a swimmer's **momentum**[1] comes from there. You'll notice that most swimmers have very big
5 shoulders. Chest muscles are less important. My arm muscles are not **bulky**[2] either, they're **lean**[3].

My diet is pretty much what I like, within reason. For breakfast I have scrambled eggs on toast, or porridge. I have a
10 mid-morning snack and sandwiches or pasta for lunch. I normally eat a cooked meal after I've finished training in the evenings.

For fitness, I do weight-lifting so as to strengthen certain muscles. I can't run to save my life and I'm not keen on it anyway; it puts too much stress on the joints. I play basketball for general fitness. I swim
15 five or six miles a day five days a week. Once you're fit, you should really be doing the distance you're swimming in competition.

B The Boxer

I need all-body strength. I build myself up with a lot of running, eight kilometres every morning. Then I go and train at a local
20 sports centre – weight machines, plus running, rowing and cycling machines. I box from six to eight in the evenings, either a punchbag or training with another boxer, whatever my coach says. It's difficult to find a good way to make
25 my footwork faster except to keep working on it. I've never done ballet, though many boxers are keen on ballet as a way to improve their **agility**[4].

I have some cereal and a glass of orange juice for breakfast. At lunchtime, I have fruit. When I've finished training, I have rice
30 or pasta, with white meat. It may not sound much, but as a feather-weight I've got to keep my weight below 57 kilograms.

Which athlete

tries to eat a varied diet?	**0**	**C**
dislikes a certain activity?	**1**	
doesn't pay special attention to what he/she eats?	**2**	**3**
mentions the time it takes to build the right muscles?	**4**	
has to be careful how much he/she eats?	**5**	
carefully measures his/her improvement?	**6**	

mentions taking advice about his/her training?	**7**	**8**
does some training at home?	**9**	
mentions an activity practised by others in his/her field?	**10**	
avoids certain types of food?	**11**	**12**
is careful not to spend too much time training?	**13**	
compares training and competing?	**14**	
doesn't like to eat at regular times?	**15**	

C The Runner

For marathon running, I mainly need lower-body muscles, chiefly the legs. They're developed over very long periods, I mean years. The upper body doesn't need so much development. I run 200 kilometres a week, so the most important thing for me is to **replenish**[5] my energy source because I'm burning up a lot of calories. I need a large amount of carbohydrates and plenty of fluids. I make an effort to eat a really good variety of foods, but not too much high-protein food, so that I'm taking in all the necessary vitamins and minerals. And that makes my diet interesting as well. 35 ... 40

On long training runs I think about a variety of things, just like someone out for a walk. But in a race, it's very different. The focus is on what's happening, your plans and responding to what people are doing around you.

D The Cyclist

It might sound strange, but when pedalling a bike you don't use that much actual strength. Cycling is about energy output, so you need stamina, not strength. 45

As for diet, I need the highest amount of carbohydrates I can get. I steer clear of fatty food as much as I can. For breakfast I have cereal and a glass of orange juice. I eat again when I feel hungry. I don't stick to traditional mealtimes because I don't think the human body is designed to have three big meals a day. 50 Mid-afternoon I might eat some fish and then a couple of hours later I might have another bowl of cereal. So the whole thing can vary.

My training is very **methodical**[6] and it hurts a lot! I've got a **static**[7] bicycle in my garage, and I try and do a **fraction**[8] more each time. When you look back at the record over a long period of time, the difference is quite appreciable. 55

E The Hockey Player

For hockey, you need to be really fit. It's speed that counts as well as skills on the field. I always do about thirty minutes running or cycling first thing in the morning. That's followed by a session in the gym, but I never do more than two hours a day. My coach warned me against overtraining. I once became ill through training too much and missed out on an important 60 competition. As well as general fitness training, I practise hockey skills with the rest of the team about three times a week.

I'm still at university, and living on campus, so I don't get much choice about my diet. I eat more or less whatever they put in front of me. There tends to be a lot of high-carbohydrate food like pasta, bread or mashed potatoes. I burn off the calories during training! 65

Vocabulary

1 Healthy eating

1 Find all the examples of foods in the text on pages 84 and 85. Put them into the correct group in the table below, according to the nutrients they are richest in. Some items may go in more than one group.

Carbohydrates	Proteins	Vitamins
pasta	*eggs*	

Fat	Fibre	Salt

2 Now add more items to the table from the box below.

> cream   salad vegetables   crisps   nuts
> green vegetables   French fries   butter
> lentils   chocolate   cheese   milk
> shellfish   root vegetables

3 The words in Box A describe how we can cook things. Match them to as many types of food as possible in Box B. Then say which way of cooking you think is the healthiest and why.

> **A**
> baked   roast   barbecued   boiled
> grilled   stewed   microwaved   steamed

> **B**
> fish   meat   sausages   vegetables
> snacks   steak   beef   potatoes

4 A balanced diet is important for health and fitness. Make a list of the foods you eat regularly. Compare your list with other students.

1 Who has the healthiest diet?
2 What advice would you give to the others?

Examples:
If I were you, I would cut out … They're very high in salt, and too much salt is bad for you. You should really eat more green vegetables. You're not getting enough vitamins.

forehead — (1)
(13)
(12)
(11)
(10)
(9)
(8)
(2)
(3)
(4)
(5)
(6)
(7)

2 Parts of the body

1 Look at the words in the box, which describe the parts of the body.

1 Which are:
   a) inside the body?   b) limbs?   c) joints?   d) other?
2 Which could you break? Which could you sprain?

> wrist   thumb   toe   heart   leg   muscle   ankle   elbow
> knee   arm   vein   forehead   lung   thigh   calf   shoulder
> finger   hip   chest   tongue   stomach

2 Label the man in the photo above choosing words from the box in Exercise 2.1, as in the example.

3 Read these sentences. What other parts of your body can *ache*? Which can *hurt* or be *sore*?

1 I went to aerobics last Thursday and my legs are still aching.
2 My feet are hurting. Can we stop for a rest?
3 My eyes are sore from sitting at the computer too long.

**4 Talk to a partner.
Find out:**

Have you ever broken, sprained, bruised or cut any part of your body? How was it treated?

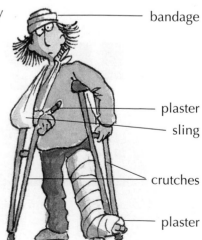

bandage
plaster
sling
crutches
plaster

Use of English 2: *word formation*

3 Choosing the right word

1 Underline the correct word in each pair.

1 A sore throat and a headache are *signs/symptoms* of flu.
2 You'd better go to bed. You've got a *temperature/fever* of 103!
3 My friend *injured/wounded* his shoulder when he was playing football.
4 He's been complaining of a sharp *ache/pain* in his back.
5 The best way to treat a sprained ankle is to put a tight bandage round the *wound/injury*.
6 My sister is in bed with a chest *disease/ infection*.
7 Did you know that herbal therapists use poisonous plants to *cure/heal* headaches?
8 It takes time to *cure/recover* from an operation.
9 Flu cannot be *treated/operated* with antibiotics.
10 Quick! Stop the car! I'm going to be *ill/sick*!

2 What treatment would you recommend for:

1 a bad cough?	3 a headache?
2 a sore throat?	4 a temperature?

Example:
You should take an aspirin if you have a headache.

▶▶ *exam strategy*   Paper 3, Part 5 ▶ p.49

1 Read the text once. Don't try to fill in the gaps yet. Answer these questions.

1 What are 'functional foods'?
2 Why are they becoming more popular?

2 Do the exam task. Remember to read the whole sentence, not just the line with the gap.

3 Compare your answers with other students. Which answers required:

a) a suffix?   b) a negative prefix?   c) a plural form?

Read the text below. Use the word given in capitals underneath to form a word that fits in the space in the text. There is an example at the beginning (0).

FUNCTIONAL FOODS

Good and plentiful food is one of the keys to human (0) *survival* , but for many people eating is no longer (1) ..... a way of satisfying their (2) ..... . In modern society, food is often viewed as something to look forward to, as a (3) ..... to be enjoyed in moments of relaxation or as a form of reward for some of life's (4) ..... . What's more, people are now choosing foods that are (5) ..... of both improving their mood and making them feel (6) ..... . And the (7) ..... of these so-called 'functional foods' is booming, particularly in the USA, where people are very interested in (8) ..... remedies of various kinds. If you can prevent (9) ..... by eating the right kind of food, they argue, then all the pills and medicines become (10) ..... .

(0) SURVIVE	(4) ACHIEVE	(8) NATURE
(1) SIMPLE	(5) ABLE	(9) ILL
(2) HUNGRY	(6) HEALTH	(10) NECESSARY
(3) PLEASE	(7) POPULAR	

Writing: *report (evaluating)*

exam file

In **Paper 2**, **Part 2**, you may be asked to write a report for a superior or for colleagues or other members of a club. You will have to supply information, for example about a place or a facility, and you may need to add recommendations or suggestions.

▶▶ *exam strategy*

Make sure you:
- use a neutral or formal style depending on your reader. DON'T use informal style.
- use the correct format for a report.
- divide information into separate sections. Use an appropriate heading for each section. The reader can then quickly and easily identify the information he/she needs.
- number points in a section if this helps to make things clearer.
- write a clear introduction and conclusion.
- use short sentences to make the information easier to understand.

1 **Read the writing task below.**

1 **Underline the points you need to keep in mind when you write your report. One important point has been underlined for you.**

> You are a member of a student club. The club secretary wishes to find out more about <u>a new sports centre</u> in your area so that he can inform club members about it. Write a report for the club secretary describing the sports centre and outlining some of its good and bad points.
>
> Write your report in **120–180 words** in an appropriate style.

2 **Answer these questions.**

1 Who are you writing your report for? What style will be appropriate?
2 Why are you writing the report?
   a) to compare different sports centres
   b) to give information about one sports centre

2 **Read the report one student wrote and answer these questions.**

Content

1 Has the writer included all the necessary information? Would the reader be fully informed about the subject?

Style/register

2 Is the report written in an appropriate style for the target reader?

Format

3 How could the writer make the topic of each section stand out more clearly?

To: The club secretary
From: Peter Kay
Date: 12 May 20—
Subject: Description of Kings Sports Centre

Introduction
Here is my report.

....
This centre is located in the city centre, so it is easy to reach. It opens every day from 6 a.m.–10 p.m.

....
There is a well-equipped gymnasium, indoor and outdoor football pitches and several tennis courts. There is also a large pool. (It was closed last week due to technical problems but reopens next week.)

....
Admission prices are reasonable, so all our members can afford them. A booking scheme is being introduced in order to limit numbers at peak times.

....
1 The centre is bright and well-equipped.
2 The instructors are well-qualified.
3 The changing rooms are excellent and there are secure lockers for belongings. A member of staff patrols the rooms regularly so as to discourage thieves.

....
The car park is tiny, so a lot of time could be wasted looking for a parking space.

....
In spite of minor drawbacks, I think all our members would enjoy using this excellent centre.

Focus on format

3 **1 Which of these two formats is more appropriate for a report? Tick (✓) it.**

1: memo   **2:** letter

To: **From:** **Date:** **Subject:**

Dear club members, Here is my report on the sports centre.

2 The writer of the report in Exercise 2 divided the information into sections, but didn't use headings. Read the suggested headings below and add them to the report in the correct position. The first item has been done for you.

General Information   Prices   ~~Introduction~~
Conclusion   Bad Points   Facilities   Good Points

3 The introduction to a report should tell the reader clearly what the report is about.

1 What is wrong with the introduction in the sample answer in Exercise 2?
2 Decide which of the following would make a more appropriate introduction and say why.

a)   This is my report on the Kings Centre.

b)   The purpose of this report is to describe the Kings Sports Centre and to outline any good or bad points.

c)   I popped into the Kings Centre last night and here is some information about it.

4 Depending on the exam task, your conclusion should round off the report with a) a general comment or b) recommendations or suggestions.

1 Which does the writer of the report in Exercise 2 do in the conclusion?
2 Look at the exam task again. Is the conclusion appropriate for this task?

Focus on grammar ▶ *p.185*

4 **1 Read the information in the grammar file. Then underline examples which describe purpose in the sample report in Exercise 2.**

grammar file 24

To express purpose, we use:

● *for* + noun.
1 *I went to the centre **for a game of tennis**.*

● the *to*-infinitive when the subject is the same in both parts of the sentence.
2 *I left early **to miss** the traffic.* (= because I wanted to miss the traffic)
3 *I went on a weekday morning **in order to/so as to avoid** the crowds.* (= formal)
4 *I took a taxi **in order not to/so as not to be** late.* (Be careful of word order!)

● *so that* when the subject of each verb is different.
5 *The centre is open to different groups on different days **so that** numbers don't get too big.*
6 *The taxi dropped me near the centre **so that/in order that** (= formal) I wouldn't have far to walk.*

2 Underline the correct expression in each pair.

1 I went to the centre *for to see/to see* the facilities.
2 I arranged to meet the manager first *in order to/so that he could* show me round the centre.
3 I interviewed a number of people *in order that/in order to* write this report.
4 You need to book in advance *so as not to/so that not to* be disappointed.
5 The instructors in the gym gave me gentle exercises *so that I wouldn't/for not to* overdo things.
6 They are going to close the centre for a month *so as to/so that* sort out the technical problems.

Over to you

5 **Write your answer to the following task in 120–180 words in an appropriate style.**

A group of students is going to study at your college for three months. You have been asked to write a report for their leader on a new leisure centre that has just opened in your area. You should describe the types of facilities available, mention some of the good and bad points about each, and include details on such things as opening times and prices.

Write your report.

Follow the advice in the exam strategy box. Remember to:

● read the question carefully and include all the relevant points.
● make a plan before you start to write.
● check your writing for errors when you have finished.

8 Travel

Lead-in

1 A well-known British tour operator decided to find out what teenagers really want on holiday. Six teenagers were invited to make their recommendations in exchange for a free family holiday. Read the 'wish list' they produced. Do you agree/disagree? What would you change?

2 Read this comment from one of the teenagers:

'If I hadn't won a free holiday, I would be going away with 12 mates to a villa.'

What about you? How do you prefer to spend your holidays?

The wish list

- freedom to choose whether or not to participate in activities
- shopping trips, non-alcoholic discos in real nightclubs
- discounts to bring friends
- water skiing, bungee jumping
- Blind Date and Karaoke competitions

Reading 1: *multiple matching*

▶▶ *exam strategy*   Paper 1, Part 4 ▶ p.46

1 **1** Look at the text opposite and read the instructions for the exam task to find out what it's about.

2 What type of holiday do you think each text describes? Choose from this list.

- beach holiday
- cultural holiday
- educational holiday
- walking and trekking holiday
- activity holiday
- sightseeing holiday

2 Now do the multiple-matching task opposite.

3 Compare your answers with a partner.

Vocabulary: *adjectives*

4 **1** Find these adjectives in the text. What nouns do they describe? Write them on the line.

1 undemanding ....
2 relaxing ....
3 family-run ....
4 taxing ....
5 tranquil ....
6 sensational ....
7 mouth-watering ....
8 fantastic ....

2 Can you think of more nouns that can be described by these adjectives?

Over to you

5 Tell a partner about the best holiday you have ever had. Use some of the adjectives in Exercise 4.1 to describe it.

You are going to read a magazine article about six different holidays. Answer the questions by choosing from the holidays **A–F**. The sections may be chosen more than once. When more than one answer is required, these may be given in any order. There is an example at the beginning (0).

On which of the holidays will you

have to get up early in the morning?	**0 B**
be able to choose how much to spend on meals?	**1**
find a fairly constant climate?	**2**
find a good environment for creative work?	**3**
get the chance to understand another culture better?	**4** **5**
have contact with wildlife?	**6** **7**
have a chance to take part in scientific research?	**8**
have a number of planned activities to choose from?	**9** **10**
be offered rapid training in an activity?	**11**
find it easy to get to know other holidaymakers?	**12** **13**
learn a skill that will be useful back home?	**14**

SIX of the BEST

Regina Newbold investigates six very different holiday options

A: DIVE INTO THE RED SEA

This holiday is perfect if you and your friends are after a seriously undemanding break with sun, pools and the option of a little sporty diversion if you want it. This is a relaxing beach resort which enjoys year-round good weather, some of the best diving in the world and just enough nightlife to keep you amused. If you take the optional course, it only takes four days to pick up the basics of scuba diving. It's not for everybody though, so try it out in your local pool back home before you commit yourself. Even if you hate the scuba diving, you can always take yourself off for a swim with the local dolphin population, or go sunbathing on the beach.

B: BE AN ECOTOURIST

If you have guilty feelings about what we're doing to the environment, you can lose them on this holiday. The work you do is as good for the world as it is for you. You can do your bit for the planet whilst enjoying some of the most beautiful sights of the natural world. Starting at daybreak, you'll be working from boats, albeit in the sunshine, as you study the behaviour of some amazing sea mammals. You'll be taking photos to identify individual animals, collecting skin samples for analysis and monitoring the animals' movements. You don't have to be too serious to enjoy this sort of working holiday, but you do have to be fairly fit!

C: WALKING OFF THE CALORIES

This is an ideal compromise for the food lover with a guilt complex. You can enjoy some of the best of French cuisine in a series of small family-run hotels, the ten-mile walk from one to another cancelling out the calories. At least that's the theory! The walks are divided into easy, average and difficult and as long as you select wisely, it shouldn't be too taxing. What's more, there's plenty of time to gossip non-stop with your companions both along the way and over dinner. Could there be a better way to make new friends?

D: AN INSPIRED CHOICE

If you feel there's a novel in you somewhere, try a fiction writing course at the Skyros Centre. If you're ever going to write, it will happen here. Skyros is a beautiful, tranquil setting in which to have a go at improving yourself and the courses are not confined to writing. The centre offers dozens of other self-improvement courses, including dance, music and theatre. If it all sounds a bit too arty, then you should leave your preconceptions behind you because these breaks are really what you make of them.

E: RECIPE FOR SUCCESS

'This holiday was sensational,' reported one person who'd signed up for two weeks in the ancient farmhouse in Italy. 'You meet people who all have something in common.' And that something is a love of good food and drink. Although there are opportunities to be on your own if you prefer, the long cooking sessions provide an ideal environment for getting to know your fellow guests whilst you gain an insight into the local way of life. The highlight of the course, naturally, is being able to eat the mouth-watering food you've prepared, and the knowledge that you'll be able to try your new-found expertise out on all your friends on your return.

F: CITY BREAK

People go to Bilbao mostly for the city's artistic highlights and you can manage to pack quite a lot in to even a short stay. There are, of course, fantastic shops and restaurants in the centre, but if you're prepared to stray just a short way off the beaten track, you'll find places that are much cheaper where the local people go to shop and eat. And those local people are exceptionally friendly, especially the café owners who are keen to tell you all the background to the sights and the local customs. Everyone who goes promises themselves that they'll soon be going back, and taking their friends along too.

Grammar: *determiners and quantifiers* ▶ *p.176*

grammar file 2

A some/any (of)

1 **Some** *holiday resorts are busy.* **Some (of them)** *are quieter.*
2 *It often takes* **some** *time to acclimatise.* (= a considerable time)
3 *There are* **hardly any** *big hotels in that area.* (= negative)

B all/none (of)

1 **All** *Greek islands are beautiful.* **All of** *the Greek islands I know are stunning.*
2 **None (of them)** *is/are disappointing.* (+ affirmative verb. Singular *is* = formal)

C several (of) / plenty of / a lot of / a great deal of

1 *It took* **several** *hours to reach our resort.* (= quite a few)
2 *There are* **plenty of/a lot of** *things to do.* (+ countable or uncountable nouns)
3 *Take* **a great deal of** *care when driving.* (+ uncountable noun)

D many, a few/few; much, little/a little; more/most (of)

1 *There aren't* **many** *signs of pollution.*
2 *There isn't* **much** *pollution.* (usually + negative verb)
3 **A few** *villages sell souvenirs.* (= a small number)
4 **Few** *inhabitants speak Spanish.* (= not many)
5 *Take* **a little** *water with you.* (= take some)
6 *There is* **little** *natural water to drink.* (= not much)
7 **Many villagers** *have never left the island.* (= more formal than *a lot of*)
8 *There is* **more nightlife** *in this resort.* (= an implied comparison)
9 **Most (of the)** *inhabitants are friendly.*

E each (of)/every

1 *There are many villages.* **Each (of them)** *has a market.* (= considered separately)
2 **Every** *house in the town is different.* (= each one of a group)

F both / either / neither (of)

1 *There are two hotels.* **Both (of them)** *are excellent.*
2 **Neither** *the locals* **nor** *the tourists want new development.* (+ affirmative verb)
3 *I want to visit* **either** *Crete or Corfu.*
4 *I haven't seen* **either of** *the two main towns.*

1 **Underline the correct word or words in each pair.**

Tourism can bring (1) *a lot of/much* wealth to a country. Unfortunately, it also causes (2) *many/much* problems. (3) None of us *don't want/want* to see beautiful places overdeveloped. But sometimes there seems (4) *little/a little* we can do about it. I go to Greece (5) *all/every* year for my favourite type of holiday. Relaxing! Like (6) *the most/most* of the Greek Islands, Cephalonia has become very popular. In the past, it attracted only (7) *a little/a few* foreign tourism. But recently there have been (8) *a great deal of/a lot of* changes. There were hardly (9) *any/some* hotels in my favourite resort ten years ago. Now there are (10) *so many/so much* I can't count them. Fortunately, however, (11) *much of/many of* the countryside remains undeveloped, so people can choose (12) *neither/either* a busy resort or peace and quiet.

2 **Look at the results of a holiday survey in the table below. Then complete the text on page 93 with words or phrases from the grammar file.**

HOLIDAY SURVEY
What type of holiday do you prefer?
Number of people interviewed: 300+ Age range: 15–20

		YES	NO
1	Do you like going abroad for your holidays?	280	26
2	Do you choose lively holiday resorts?	290	16
3	Do you prefer to spend all your holiday just relaxing?	180	126
4	Do you like your holidays to be action-packed?	200	106
5	Would you be interested in a wildlife holiday?	240	66
6	Is food an important consideration in your choice of holiday?	298	8
7	Is the weather an important factor?	297	9
8	Do you like to do a lot of sightseeing?	65	241
9	Do you want to meet new people on your holiday?	273	33
10	Is cost the most important factor?	302	4

In our survey, we asked over (1) .... hundred people about their holiday preferences. Nearly (2) .... those we questioned said that they liked going abroad. Only (3) .... people said they preferred to stay at home. (4) .... of the people that we questioned (90 per cent) said they liked lively resorts. Hardly (5) .... of them would choose a quiet area. People seem keen to spend (6) ...., but not all of their time, relaxing. Action holidays are popular, but not with as (7) .... people as we had expected. Only a small percentage of the people questioned had been on a wildlife holiday, but there was (8) .... interest in this area, which was nice to know. Not surprisingly, (9) .... food and the weather were seen as very important. In fact the vast majority, if not (10) .... the people we interviewed commented that if (11) .... of these two areas were not up to standard, their holiday would be ruined. Sightseeing is not a popular activity, it seems, and there was very (12) .... enthusiasm shown for this pursuit. However, it was pointed out that (13) .... resort has something different to offer, and that (14) .... are more interesting than others, so there was no easy way to answer the question. When it comes to meeting new people on holiday, there isn't (15) .... doubt that it is a major requirement. But the key factor, which is more important than (16) .... other, is the cost of the holiday.

Over to you

3 Interview your family and friends using the survey questionnaire in Exercise 2 and write about the results as in the text above.

Use of English 1:
error correction

▶▶ *exam strategy*

Paper 3, Part 4 ▶ p.69

1 Put the following steps in the right order for this task. Then compare your answers with a partner.

☐ Read each whole sentence, not just the numbered line.

☐ Underline words you think should not be there.

☐ Read the whole text again to check your answers.

☐ 1 Read the whole text to find out what it's about.

☐ Read the sentence again without the word.

2 Read the text once and answer these questions.

1 Who is the writer? Who is he/she writing to?

2 Would you accept his/her invitation? Why/Why not?

3 Now do the exam task. What types of errors does the text contain? Make a list.

Read the text below and look carefully at each line. Some of the lines are correct, and some have a word which should not be there. If a line is correct, put a tick (✓) in the space by the number. If a line has a word which should not be there, write the word in the space. There are two examples at the beginning (**0** and **00**).

WISH YOU WERE HERE

0	*it*	I am writing it this letter to you on the balcony of my family's new
00	✓	summer house. You would love it here. As I look out over the deep
1	....	green valley below, I can see lots farmers working on the small
2	....	fields that have been cut out of the hillside. It looks like a very
3	....	hard work. They grow up a lot of potatoes here as well as a great
4	....	many of different vegetables and fruit trees. Looking up the valley, I
5	....	can too see quite a few sheep on the rocky mountainside. We went
6	....	for a walk up there yesterday. The views are lovely and there are
7	....	lots of marked paths so you can't get lost! In case that you are thinking
8	....	that it all sounds a bit rural and boring here, let me remind you that as
9	....	we have a beautiful heated swimming pool. It's so warm here that we
10	....	have even gone swimming after the dark because there are lights under
11	....	the water. Also, we are only two kilometres from the beach which
12	....	it has got a fantastic open-air disco where you can dance all night. We
13	....	love of this place so much that we're planning to stay here the whole
14	....	through summer. Wouldn't you like to join us? There is plenty of room
15	....	and my parents say so you would be welcome to stay as long as you like.

Listening: *note-taking*

Another task in **Paper 4**, **Part 2** asks you to complete notes. Like the sentence completion task you did in Unit 2, this task tests your understanding of the main points and specific details.

▶▶ **exam strategy**

- Read the instructions and the questions before you listen.
- Try to predict what kind of information is missing.
- Write one to three words only in each space.
- Check your answers during the second listening.
- Check your spelling.

1 Read the instructions for the exam task and the notes below. What can you predict about 21st-century holidays?

You will hear a talk on the subject of travel in the 21st century. For questions 1–10, complete the notes.

World Tourism Organisation predicts:

- number of holiday trips will rise by [____1____] per year.

- tourism will become a bigger industry than [____2____]

How tourism will change:

- most 20th-century tourists chose [____3____] holidays.

- what 21st-century tourists will want:
  - type of accommodation: [____4____]
  - chance to try: local [____*and*____5____]
  - travel around by: [____6____]

Type of holiday that will become more popular:

- visiting more than one [____7____]

- activity included, e.g. [____8____]

Reasons for changing holiday habits:

- changes in people's [____9____] lives.

- information available from [____10____]

2 ▭ Do the exam task. Listen twice, and check your answers on the second listening. Don't forget to check your spelling.

▶ **exam tip!**

DO expect to write a word or words that you hear on the recording. You are not usually expected to rephrase what is heard and doing so can cause you to give a wrong answer even if you have understood the content.

Speaking:
collaborative task and discussion

▶▶ **exam strategy**

Paper 5, Part 3 ▶ p.33/82

- DO invite your partner's opinions.
- DO listen to your partner and try to develop his/her ideas.

1 Part 3 task

Work in groups of three.

Student 1: You are the examiner. Give Students 2 and 3 the instructions on page 207. Time them and interrupt if necessary after three minutes.

Students 2 and 3: Listen to the examiner carefully and do the task.

to go sightseeing / hiking / walking / skiing / horse-riding / scuba diving
to sunbathe
to go on a cruise
to go on safari
to visit a historic site

▶ **Functions files 5, 6, 12 and 13 p.200–201**

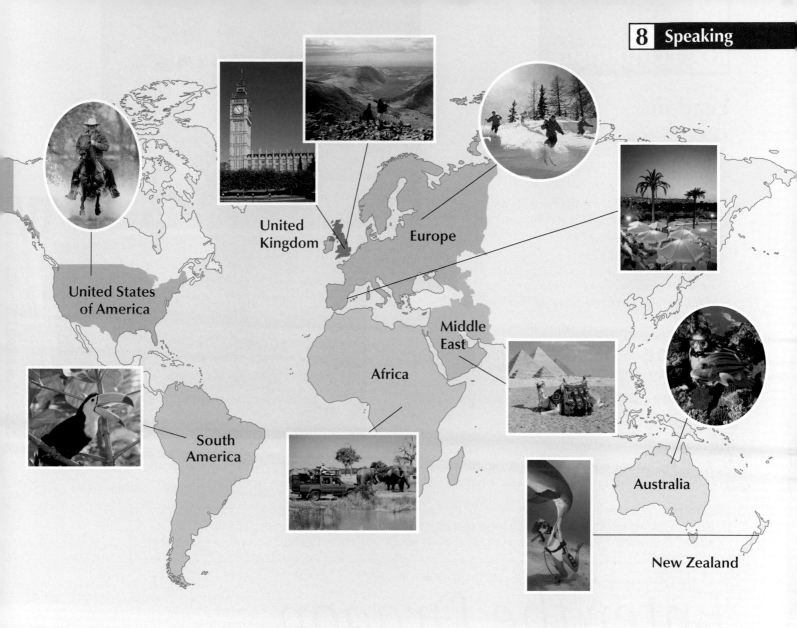

United Kingdom

Europe

United States of America

Middle East

Africa

South America

Australia

New Zealand

▶▶ *exam strategy* Paper 5, Part 4 ▶ p.45/82

2 **Part 4 discussion**

The examiner should now join in the discussion.

Student 3: You are the examiner. Ask Students 1 and 2 the questions below to develop the topic further. Stop the discussion after four minutes. (Don't worry if you don't manage to ask all the questions.)

Students 1 and 2: Discuss the examiner's questions.

1 What preparations would you need to make before going on a holiday like this?
2 What things would you need to take with you?
3 What kind of problems might you encounter on a holiday of this type?
4 What's the most interesting and enjoyable holiday you have ever had?
5 What places would you recommend a visitor to see in your country?

preparations:
to choose a good tour operator
to book well in advance
to get vaccinations
to confirm a booking/flight
to apply for a passport/visa
to make a hotel reservation
to arrange travel insurance

clothing:
wrinkle-free/easy-to-pack clothing
sunglasses   sun hat   walking shoes
to travel light

medical:
first aid kit   travel sickness tablets
insect repellent   suntan lotion
to get an upset stomach
to get sunburnt/sunstroke

equipment:
hand luggage   rucksack
binoculars   (video) camera   film

Lead-in

Look at the photos and discuss the questions, using the words and expressions in the box.

1 'Ecotourism' is a fast growing area. What is meant by 'ecotourism'?
2 What do you think are the benefits and drawbacks of tourism for wildlife and the local people? Make a list.

to bring in revenue / create jobs / improve facilities / protect species
to cause pollution / disturb wildlife / destroy habitats

Reading 2: *multiple-choice questions*

▶▶ *exam strategy*   Paper 1, Part 2 ▶ p.22

1 Look at the exam task.

1 Read the instructions and look at the title and sub-heading of the article to find out what it's about.

2 What strategy will you use to answer the multiple-choice questions?

You are going to read an article about a species of lizard that lives on a remote island. For each of the questions, choose the answer (A, B, C or D) which you think fits best according to the text.

Enter the Dragon

Visitors travel to a remote Indonesian island especially to see the world's largest lizard: the fearsome and unique Komodo dragon. Our reporter decided to investigate.

AT THE SMALL HOTEL 'Bajo Beach' on the Indonesian island of Flores, the talk was about goats and boats. 'How much did your boat cost?'

5 'Some Australians chartered theirs for just a few thousand rupiah.'

'Yeah, but it took five hours to get there and he left them stranded.'

'Is it really necessary to take a goat
10 with you?'

'Does the ranger kill the goat for you?'

These important questions are explained by the fact that the village of Labuan Bajo, of which the beach is a part, is the jumping-
15 off point for the island of Komodo, home to the Komodo dragon, the world's largest lizard. And these giants aren't satisfied with the normal lizard diet of insects, reptiles and small mammals. They eat goats,
20 horses, pigs and, given half a chance, you and me. After watching documentaries about this fearsome creature from the comfort of my own armchair, I had decided to see them for myself.

25 Having spent the previous night in luxury at a top-class hotel in Bali, the hotel on Bajo Beach was a shock to my system. My room was bare but spotless. It had an attached shower room with
30 cold water only and was the most expensive room in the hotel (less than £10 a night). Meals consisted of rice, fish, chicken and goatmeat.

The hotel was run by Mr Chandra. It was
35 home to an interesting bunch of travellers, including a team from the BBC, which comprised a zoologist, a producer and a writer. They were making a series on rare animal species. The zoologist filled me
40 in on dragons: 'They inhabit the islands of Komodo, Rinca and Flores. There are about 5,000 in all, and about 1,500 on Komodo.'

Komodo is a spectacular and beautiful
45 island, surrounded by coral and sandy beaches, and with a forbidding interior of deep valleys dotted with palms and jagged volcanoes. The villagers seem to respect rather than fear the dragons. The island is
50 a national park which has been open to regular tourists since 1970. The number of visitors has been small, but enough to disrupt the lives of an estimated 15 of the island's community of dragons. **The rest**
55 **remain in blissful ignorance of tourism.**

All the guidebooks I read were vague about what happens on Komodo – to you, the dragons and the goat. I soon found out for myself. You need a goat for bait. From
60 the jetty you walk about three kilometres in suffocating heat to the feeding area, dragging the goat. You are accompanied by a Komodo ranger, a teenager armed with nothing but a stick for protection.

2 **Read the text once quite quickly. Then answer these questions to check your general understanding.**

1 What is unusual about the Komodo dragon compared with other lizards?
2 How are visitors able to see the dragons close up?
3 What point is the writer making about tourism and wildlife in this article?

3 **Complete the reading using the exam strategy. Be prepared to justify your answers to the class.**

Vocabulary: -ing *adjectives and nouns*

4 **Find and underline the words 1–10 in the text.**

1 Are they used as **a)** adjectives **b)** nouns **c)** part of a compound noun?
2 Which of the nouns are countable?

  1 forbidding   3 viewing   5 thrilling   7 sighting   9 killing
  2 suffocating   4 bulging   6 disturbing   8 feeding   10 challenging

▶ **Grammar file 10, p.179–180**

Over to you

5 **What's your opinion? What is the best way to help endangered species?**

● encourage ecotourism   ● build more zoos

Make a list of pros and cons.

One of Komodo Island's dragons

65 We arrived at last at a natural amphitheatre, where a viewing platform overhangs a dried-up river bed three
70 metres below. There were two dragons in view. One was well over four metres long, with a bulging stomach. Our
75 goat was their second meal of the day. Although the Komodo dragon can live quite happily on a single pig or deer a week, this **elite** group was getting perhaps three goats a day in the high season between
80 May and September.

Sacrificing the goat allowed us to see a dragon close up. We were able to reach out and touch its scaly skin, admire its subtle markings, hear its wheeze and smell its
85 breath. It was a thrilling yet disturbing experience to see nature in the wild turned into a zoo, and to realise that I was now part of the process. The Komodo dragon is a protected species but the poor goat isn't. Is
90 the goat necessary? The revenue from the goats assists the inhabitants of Komodo, and were it not for the goats, visitors might never see a dragon. Komodo is a large and impenetrable island and sightings of dragons
95 are very rare; no one I met had ever seen one on Flores. If the supply of goats dried up, the dragons would abandon the feeding area and no sane person would hike, casually, into the interior.
100 Is the goat's death worth an hour's entertainment? For the islanders, who slaughter the animals they eat themselves, the killing of a few goats hardly matters. For us, who hunt in supermarkets and
105 find our prey in neatly cut joints or slices, it is a challenging question.

---

1 Where did the writer first hear about the dragons?
  A from some Australians
  B from the inhabitants of Flores
  C at home watching TV
  D in his hotel

2 Why did the writer get a shock at Bajo Beach?
  A He didn't like the menu.
  B His hotel cost more than he expected.
  C He was frightened by the animals.
  D He felt less comfortable than before.

3 How did the writer get more information on the dragons?
  A from a guidebook
  B from Mr Chandra
  C from a scientist
  D from a group of travellers

4 What does 'The rest' in line 54 refer to?
  A the dragons
  B the visitors
  C the villagers
  D the tourists

5 What does 'elite' in line 78 mean?
  A small
  B fat
  C contented
  D special

6 What does the writer suggest about the diet of the dragons he saw?
  A They eat only goats.
  B They eat too much.
  C They hunt human prey.
  D They prefer to hunt their own food.

7 On the island of Flores dragons are
  A not protected.
  B a serious danger.
  C not often seen.
  D smaller than on Komodo.

8 The writer is most worried because
  A what he saw was not realistic.
  B goats are treated cruelly for the benefit of tourists.
  C dragons deserve more protection.
  D tourism is bad for the islanders' way of life.

Vocabulary

1 Past participles + prepositions

1 Complete the text below using phrases from the box. Use each phrase only once. There are two phrases that you won't need.

> situated in   blessed with   linked to   built for   set on
> included in   designed by   surrounded by   lined with
> visited by   located off   twinned with   crowded with

ENJOY ... a weekend break in Scotland

Although Scotland borders England, and its capital, Edinburgh, is (1) .... London by a fast train service, it is very different from its neighbour. It has its own Assembly, its own flag, and makes many of its own laws. Scotland is also (2) .... truly breathtaking mountain and coastal scenery. It is (3) .... sea on three sides.

(4) .... cities in no fewer than eight other countries, Edinburgh is an international city with excellent cultural and shopping facilities. It is (5) .... millions of tourists every year who come to see the delights of the city – not least, Edinburgh Castle. (6) .... a hill high above the city centre, the castle is well worth a visit for its dramatic views. The cobbled streets around the castle, (7) .... tourists in summer, echo with the history of this great city.

You can also shop on wide streets (8) .... elegant buildings or in the bustling covered market at stalls selling everything from woollen sweaters to the Scottish delicacy, haggis.

For wildlife enthusiasts, a trip to the island of Skye is a 'must' and the distance from Edinburgh is surprisingly short. On this little island, (9) .... the west coast of Scotland, wildlife watchers can observe a range of animals in their natural habitat, including otters, eagles, dolphins and seals.

Why not book your weekend break now? Return air fare, bed and breakfast at a hotel (10) .... the city centre, and a guided tour of Edinburgh Castle are all (11) .... the price. Trips to Skye can be arranged as extra. Call us or visit our website at

2 Answer these questions from a tourist.

'What is your town/country especially famous for?'
'What places would you recommend I should see?'
'What local delicacies should I try?'

2 Choosing the right word

Underline the correct word in each pair.

1 We spent our last holiday on an island off the *coast/shore* of Scotland.
2 There were no *spaces/vacancies* in the local hotel so we stayed in a youth hostel instead.
3 The youth hostel advertised a number of sightseeing *excursions/journeys*.
4 We also took a short coach *voyage/trip* to a deserted beach to observe sea otters.
5 The sea otter is very nervous of humans, so sightings are quite *rare/odd*.
6 When we reached the beach, we all sat quietly and *waited/attended* impatiently.
7 We had almost given up, when suddenly the otters appeared and we were able to *make/take* some fabulous photos.

3 Phrasal verbs

Complete the dialogues using the phrasal verbs in the box in the correct form. Add a pronoun if necessary.

> check in   drop off   get to   set out
> hold up   get off   make for
> pick up   slow down   break down
> speed up   take off   turn back

1 A: You're driving very fast, Dan. There's a 70-mile-an-hour speed limit. Please .... !
   B: We need to .... the airport quickly. Our plane is due to .... at 11 a.m. We should have .... earlier.
2 A: Which terminal do we have to .... at?
   B: I don't know. Let's .... Terminal One.
3 A: Oh no! I've forgotten to bring my camera!
   B: Well, we can't .... now. We can buy one at the airport provided this traffic doesn't .... for too long.
4 B: Look! That car .... Can we offer the driver a lift? We could .... at the nearest garage.
5 A: Now we're really late.
   B: OK, I'll .... a bit.
6 B: Thank goodness there'll be no more driving once we .... the plane in Chicago. The taxi will .... at the airport and take us straight to the hotel.

Over to you

4 Ask and answer in pairs.

Have you ever …

1 … missed a plane or train? Why? (*oversleep / car/taxi break down / be held up in a traffic jam*, etc.)
2 … forgotten your passport? What did you do?

Has …

3 … your flight ever been delayed or cancelled? Why? What did you do? Did you ask for/receive compensation?
4 … your luggage ever been lost or sent to the wrong destination? Did you get it back? How?

Use of English 2:
lexical cloze

▶▶ **exam strategy**

Paper 3, Part 1 ▶ p.13

1 1 Look at the question in the title to the exam task. How would you answer it?

2 Now read the text all the way through, ignoring the gaps for the moment. Compare your answer with the text.

2 Now complete the exam task. Read the gapped sentences very carefully. Remember, to help you choose the right word, you should:

- pay careful attention to meaning.
- be aware of grammatical patterns such as prepositions after verbs and adjectives.
- make sure that linking words fit the meaning of the text.

Use these clues to help you with the task.

Question:

1 Only one verb makes sense in the sentence.
3 Only one verb can be followed by the preposition *with*.
5 *Not* introduces a contrast with the previous statement. Which linking word do you need here?
7 Only one verb collocates with *an effect on*.

Read the text below and decide which answer A, B, C or D best fits each space. There is an example at the beginning (0).

0 A fastest B grandest C widest D longest

TOURISM – GOOD OR BAD?

In many countries, tourism is one of the (0) *A*. growing industries and, of course, tourism can (1) ..... enormous advantages to countries, especially poorer ones. Tourists (2) ..... money on local goods and services and so (3) ..... a proportion of the local population with work, and thereby a (4) ..... of income. Not all the effects of tourism are so positive, (5) ...... If the development is uncontrolled, unplanned or (6) ..... too quickly, it can pose a threat to the natural environment and so may (7) ..... a bad effect on a country's wildlife. One way of (8) ..... some of the environmental dangers associated with tourism is to make the tourists themselves more (9) ..... of the problem. If tourists are encouraged to buy locally-grown food, for example, (10) ..... of imports, then the local economy is less likely to change as a result of new developments. This is because local farmers, with a good market for their products, will be less likely to (11) ..... the traditional patterns of land use that wildlife has adapted to. (12) ..... that, nature reserves need to be (13) ..... and tourists encouraged to visit them. If these reserves can actually become a tourist (14) ....., then the tourist industry will be more (15) ..... in making sure that the wildlife survives.

1	A do	B bring	C send	D make
2	A pay	B buy	C spend	D cost
3	A employ	B provide	C produce	D ensure
4	A place	B root	C base	D source
5	A meanwhile	B although	C moreover	D however
6	A reaches	B exists	C happens	D goes
7	A cause	B have	C lead	D get
8	A distracting	B lacking	C avoiding	D missing
9	A aware	B sensitive	C wise	D worried
10	A instead	B rather	C whereas	D except
11	A deny	B abandon	C withdraw	D resign
12	A As well as	B What's more	C In spite of	D Apart from
13	A discovered	B composed	C created	D invented
14	A invitation	B temptation	C attraction	D fascination
15	A ready	B concerned	C keen	D interested

3 Highlight all the verb / noun / adjective + preposition combinations in the text. Add them to your vocabulary notebook under the preposition. Write an example sentence to help you remember the meaning and the combination.

Example:
pose (a threat) to
Population growth is posing a threat to our wildlife.

Writing: *discursive composition*

In **Paper 2**, **Part 2**, you may be asked to write a discursive composition. This kind of composition must have a definite point of view. You may want to:
- argue in favour of something.
- argue against something.
- give both sides of the argument.

Whichever you choose, your opinion and your arguments must be very clear.

▶▶ *exam strategy*

Make sure you:
- 'brainstorm' your ideas on paper.
- organise your ideas by grouping similar points together.
- make a paragraph plan before you start to write.
- develop points by giving examples or explaining what you mean.
- use linking words to list points in your argument and introduce examples.
- write a clear introduction and conclusion.

1 Read the writing task below.

1 Underline all the points you must cover in your composition.

Your class has recently been discussing the positive and negative aspects of mass tourism. Your teacher has now asked you to write a composition giving your opinion on the following statement:

There is nothing wrong with mass tourism. Do you agree?

Write your **composition in 120–180 words in an appropriate style.**

2 Who is going to read your composition? What style should you use, informal, neutral or formal?

Focus on brainstorming and planning

2 **1 First, brainstorm ideas and useful vocabulary related to the topic. Write down as many points as you can think of under these headings.**

Positive aspects of tourism
brings money to the area

Negative aspects of tourism
beaches ruined

2 Tick (✓) the two or three most important positive aspects and the two or three most important negative aspects from your lists.

3 Decide on the outline of your composition and make a paragraph plan. Which of these plans would <u>not</u> help the student to write a good composition? Why?

Plan A

Para. 1 = positive effects of tourism
- brings money to the area

Para. 2 = positive and negative effects of tourism
- pollution
- can benefit wildlife
- tourists disturb wildlife
- forces authorities to clean up polluted places

Para. 3 = more negative effects
- places are spoiled by too much development

Para. 4 = conclusion

Plan B

Para. 1 = introduction

Para. 2 = positive effects of tourism
- brings money to the area
- forces authorities to clean up polluted places
- can benefit wildlife

Para. 3 = negative effects of tourism
- places are spoiled by too much development
- tourists disturb wildlife
- pollution

Para. 4 = conclusion

3 **Read the composition one student wrote in answer to the task.**

1 Answer these questions.

1 Underline the topic sentences in paragraphs 2 and 3. What methods of organising points has the writer used?
2 Underline examples of linking words used to <u>list</u> points in the argument.
3 When you are writing points for or against a certain topic you should develop each point by giving an example or explanation. Find examples of this in the sample composition and underline them. What linking expression is used to introduce them?

2 The introduction to the sample composition is not very well-developed. Can you write a more appropriate introduction? What should it include?

I don't agree with the statement. I think there are a lot of problems.

First, let's look at the positive side. Tourism often brings in money which helps the economy. Also, it can force the authorities to do something about problems like pollution as tourists don't like dirty places, for example oil on beaches. Another point is that tourism can benefit wildlife. Governments are keener to protect animals and plants if tourists come on holiday to see them.

Now let's look at the bad side. Beautiful places are often spoiled because of tourism. In my country, huge, ugly hotels have been built near the turtle beaches. The government ought never to have allowed this. A second problem is that tourists often disturb wildlife. They interfere and harm it when they should have left it alone. For example, they take coral from the sea, or pick rare flowers that will never grow back. Pollution is a problem too. Tourists should be taught to clean up their rubbish.

We must be careful not to spoil the places that attract tourists. Otherwise mass tourism will be seen as a really bad thing.

Focus on grammar ▶ p.182

4 **1 Circle all the modal verbs in the sample composition above. How many did you find? Match them to the uses in the grammar file.**

grammar files 16, 17

Present/future	**Past**
A Obligation / necessity / criticism	**A Criticism of past actions**
1 We **must do** more to protect the environment.	1 We **should have done** more to protect the environment.
2 We **don't have to/need to build** so many huge hotels.	2 We **needn't have built** so many huge hotels.
3 The authorities **should do** more to regulate development.	3 The authorities **should have done** more to regulate development.
4 We **ought not to allow** resorts to be over-developed.	4 We **ought not to have allowed** resorts to be over-developed.
B Ability	**B Missed opportunity**
We **can do** more to protect wildlife.	We **could have done** more to protect wildlife.

2 Complete the second sentence in each pair so it has a similar meaning to the first. Use an appropriate modal verb in the correct form from the grammar file.

1 I was offered the opportunity to visit a zoo last week but I turned it down.
   I .... a zoo last week but I turned the opportunity down.
2 I don't think it's a good idea to keep animals in zoos.
   I don't think animals .... in zoos.
3 It's imperative that we close down zoos that treat animals cruelly.
   We .... zoos that treat animals cruelly.
4 It was wrong to keep animals confined in small cages, as we did in the past.
   We .... animals confined in small cages in the past.
5 I think it may be necessary to keep some zoos so that we can save endangered species.
   We may .... so that we can save endangered species.
6 It wasn't necessary to take so many animals from the wild but we did this in the past.
   We .... so many animals from the wild in the past.

Over to you

5 **Write your answer to the following task in 120–180 words in an appropriate style.**

Your class has had a discussion about the advantages and disadvantages of zoos. Your teacher has now asked you to write a composition giving your opinion on the following question.

Zoos are unnecessary. They should all be closed down.

Write your composition.

Follow the advice in the exam strategy box. Remember to:

- divide your composition into clear paragraphs.
- check your writing for errors when you have finished.

Progress test 2

1 Lexical cloze

For questions 1–15, read the text below and decide which answer A, B, C or D best fits each space. There is an example at the beginning (0).

0 A landed **B** dropped **C** beached **D** sailed

THE FAIREST LAND

In 1492, Christopher Columbus (0) *A.* in what is now the Dominican Republic. He looked around him and (1) ....., 'This is the fairest land human eyes have ever seen.' This is not surprising as the country (2) ..... from a thousand miles of beautiful coastline, the highest mountains in the Caribbean and spectacular national parks which (3) ..... sparkling rivers and deep canyons.

The Dominican Republic lies on the island (4) ..... as Hispaniola, the second largest in the Caribbean, which it (5) ..... with its neighbour, Haiti. The island is accessible to tourists as there are (6) ..... flights from many parts of the world. If you arrive as an independent holidaymaker, you should (7) ..... a hire car or a taxi from the airport and (8) ..... for one of the tasteful hotels in the new (9) ..... along the coast. These developments offer incredible (10) ..... for money compared with other Caribbean islands. You can participate in sports (11) ..... sailing, snorkelling, canoeing, tennis or golf and then, when the sun goes down, (12) ..... the lively evening entertainment.

But the highlight of any (13) ..... to the island is a visit to the capital, Santo Domingo. It boasts the oldest buildings in the Americas. A cathedral, a university and a hospital, all situated within the beautifully (14) ..... Old Colonial Quarter and all (15) ..... from the early 1500s.

1	A resumed	B declared	C responded	D denied
2	A rewards	B advantages	C benefits	D favours
3	A contain	B compose	C concern	D complete
4	A meant	B known	C called	D named
5	A divides	B shares	C halves	D splits
6	A ready	B straight	C direct	D stable
7	A drive off	B get by	C take on	D pick up
8	A turn	B head	C seek	D point
9	A resources	B restorations	C refreshments	D resorts
10	A value	B saving	C bargain	D deal
11	A such as	B as for	C so as to	D as if
12	A take part	B make up	C put on	D join in
13	A jump	B travel	C trip	D stay
14	A preserved	B reversed	C conserved	D revised
15	A lasting	B ageing	C timing	D dating

2 Key word transformations

For questions 1–10, complete the second sentence so that it has a similar meaning to the first sentence, using the word given. **Do not change the word given. You must use between two and five words, including the word given.** There is an example at the beginning (0).

Example:

0 It's four months since Sally became a full-time singer. **singing**
   Sally has *been singing full-time for* four months.

1 The sports coach advised Tony to start doing weightlifting. **you**
   'If I .... up weightlifting,' the sports coach said to Tony.

2 When Pam was at school, she often forgot to do her homework. **used**
   Pam often .... her homework when she was at school.

3 Fred regrets having asked such a rude question. **shouldn't**
   Fred realises that .... such a rude question.

4 I bought a house in London in 1980 and I have lived in it ever since. **living**
   I .... own house in London since 1980.

5 Louise couldn't play the piano until she was a teenager. **able**
   Louise .... the piano until she was a teenager.

6 First she ate her lunch and then she took her dog for a walk. **once**
   She took her dog for a walk .... her lunch.

7 Graham has a lot more friends now than when he lived abroad. **fewer**
   Graham .... he lived abroad.

8 'You mustn't open the parcel until your birthday, Eric,' said his aunt. **to**
   Eric's aunt .... the parcel until his birthday.

9 'Try not to disturb Jane, she's studying.' **avoid**
   'Try .... Jane, she's studying.'

10 'I can get you some batteries when I go to the supermarket,' Mandy said to me. **offered**
    Mandy .... batteries when she went to the supermarket.

3 Error correction

For questions 1–15, read the text below and look carefully at each line. Some of the lines are correct, and some have a word which should not be there. If a line is correct, put a tick (✓) in the space by the number. If a line has a word which should not be there, write the word in the space. There are two examples at the beginning (0 and 00).

A LATE STARTER

0	✓	I never really enjoyed sports when I was a teenager at school,
00	*and*	probably because such a lot of importance was always and given
1	....	to team sports. In fact, I have had no interest in exercise at all until
2	....	I was about to sixteen, when I started lifting weights and running
3	....	in an attempt to get me fit. Then I bought a boat with a friend and
4	....	we started to water ski off the coast of North Wales near where my
5	....	home. That was the start of my love of unusual sports and I went on
6	....	to do all jet skiing, scuba diving and mountain biking by the time
7	....	I was reach twenty. But my most thrilling moments came when I
8	....	was water-ski jumping. You have to be going at a considerable
9	....	speed to get over the ramp and you hardly have time for to think
10	....	before you're launched into the air and find yourself flying with
11	....	a speedboat is doing thirty miles per hour ahead of you. Landing
12	....	on your skis is not at all an easy and it took a dozen attempts
13	....	before I succeeded it. These days, I like sports where you only
14	....	need one other person and I play squash for that reason ever. But
15	....	I'm afraid I still don't share them the national passion for football.

4 Word formation

For questions 1–10, read the text below. Use the word given in capitals at the end of each line to form a word that fits in the space in the same line. There is an example at the beginning (0).

ADVERTISING

In recent years, Britain has seen the (0) *introduction* of a series of	INTRODUCE
laws designed to control advertising, (1) ..... the promotion of certain	SPECIAL
goods to young people. For example, the (2) ..... of main meals with	REPLACE
snack foods should not be encouraged in advertisements and (3)	COMPETE
aimed at young people should not involve making an (4) ..... number of	EXCEED
purchases. Health (5) ..... for young people are also being more strictly	PRODUCE
controlled than in the past. For example, it is now (6) ..... to advertise	POSSIBLE
slimming foods which are specifically aimed at teenagers and the (7)	IMPORTANT
of medical (8) ..... in dieting has to be stressed at all times. And companies	SUPERVISE
claiming that their goods are environmentally (9) ....., which often makes	FRIEND
them more (10) ..... to young people, must be able to prove that what	ATTRACT
they say is true.	

9 Discoveries

Lead-in

1 **Talk about the photos on this page. Use words and expressions from the box below.**

> extra-terrestrial   alien creature
> the universe   galaxy   planet   Mars
> the solar system   space exploration
> to orbit (the Earth/Sun)
> to be a threat to the human race
> (unmanned) spacecraft
> radio telescope   to build space colonies
> to travel at the speed of light

2 **Read this statement. Do you agree or disagree? Justify your opinion.**

There must be intelligent life on other planets.

3 **Now read the article opposite quickly. Look for information to support the statement in Exercise 2.**

Does any of the information make you change your original opinion?

Reading 1: *multiple matching*

> ▶▶ *exam strategy* Paper 1, Part 1 ▶p.10

1 **Read the instructions for the exam task and discuss these questions.**

1 What reading skill does this type of task test?
  a) the ability to read and understand a text in detail
  b) the ability to understand the main points of a text
  c) the ability to find specific items of information in a text
2 Is it important to understand every word in the text? Why/Why not?

> ▶▶ *exam tip!*
>
> The heading sums up the main idea of a paragraph. DON'T be misled by details. DO look for words in the headings that paraphrase words and expressions in the text.

2 **1 Look at the headings in the exam task. Some of them ask questions, so the text must give answers to these questions. Look for these answers.**

Example:
Heading I asks *How has our thinking changed?* Look at the underlined linking words in paragraph 1 which introduce key sentences to answer this question.

2 Use these clues to help you do the exam task.
Heading:
B Which paragraph talks about the existence of aliens and also talks about mathematics?
E There are references to the Earth throughout the text, but which section says that the Earth may be very special?

Over to you

3 **1 Make notes on the following points using information you have found in the text. Use context clues to work out the meaning of unfamiliar words.**

- why life was able to develop on Earth
- signs of alien activity on Earth
- what scientists are doing to prove the existence of intelligent life on other planets
- how likely life is on other planets

2 Now tell a partner what you have learned.

You are going to read an article about the possibility of intelligent life elsewhere in the universe. Choose the most suitable heading from the list A–I for each part (1–7) of the article. There is one extra heading which you do not need to use. There is an example at the beginning (0).

A The truth about what really happened

B Can mathematics prove aliens exist?

C An unlikely meeting

D Have other life forms visited Earth?

E Is the Earth unique?

F Your chance to be famous

G Finding a way to communicate

H We are not alone

I How has our thinking changed?

Is there life on other planets?

Scientists are increasingly convinced of the existence of other intelligent life forms. Where should we be looking?

0 I

Ever since people realised the Earth was just a tiny part of the universe, they have wondered about the existence of other intelligent life forms. Early on, many people thought that intelligent life might be found on Mars or Venus, our two nearest planets. Now that we have sent unmanned spacecraft to these planets, we know that no intelligent life exists there.

1

The Earth's position in relation to the Sun makes it the only planet in our own solar system which is obviously capable of sustaining life. If we were nearer the Sun, there would be a thick layer of cloud around us; this would trap heat, causing the temperature to rise. Within a short time, the Earth would turn into a desert, completely unsuitable for life. If we were further away from the Sun, there would not be enough heat to prevent water from freezing. The polar ice caps would expand, and the sea level would fall. Before long, the Earth would become an Arctic wasteland.

2

Many people claim to have seen unidentified flying objects (UFOs), proving that alien life must exist. Most scientists, however, believe UFO sightings to be imaginary or to have a rational explanation. The formation of crop circles (strange patterns that appear in fields of wheat) in different parts of the world was once claimed to be evidence of alien activity.

Now these circles are thought to be either a natural phenomenon or the work of hoaxers. And scientists certainly do not believe some people's claims to have been abducted by aliens.

3

Ironically, the US government is to blame for the biggest UFO story of all. In 1947, a mysterious crash took place near a government airbase in New Mexico. For many years, the US government denied that anything strange had taken place. This led some people to conclude that the government was covering up evidence of an alien spacecraft that had crashed. Recently, more information has been released. It turns out that the wreckage was part of a top-secret aircraft and nothing to do with UFOs at all.

4

Sceptics dismiss the idea of other life forms as complete nonsense. However, Frank Drake, an astronomer, has worked out an equation to estimate the number of civilisations in our galaxy. The equation is complicated and relies on a lot of guesswork. Even so, it is taken seriously by scientists, who have calculated that there may be several billion civilisations in our galaxy alone. Telescopes have detected 1,000 million galaxies in the universe, so the probability of intelligent life becomes extremely high.

5

The best proof of life beyond Earth would be to come face to face with aliens from another planet.

But unless they visit us, this won't happen. Space travel to even the nearest star, Alpha Centauri, is at present totally impossible because of the distance. Modern spacecraft travel at about 36,000 kph. At this speed, it would take 12,000 years to reach Alpha Centauri. We might like the idea of encountering aliens, but it is unrealistic to expect it to happen.

6

So scientists are pinning their hopes on exchanging messages with alien civilisations, if they exist. They are scanning the universe for radio waves sent as signals from aliens. However, there are a number of problems with this approach. How do we know a radio wave is a signal? If it is, how do we decode what it means? Moreover, the message may have taken centuries to reach us; any reply we send will take just as long.

7

For many years, Frank Drake's Search for Extra-Terrestrial Intelligence (SETI) Institute in California has been monitoring the radio signals we receive from outer space for signs of artificial origin. When the US government cut the Institute's funding, SETI started a project involving the personal computers of people around the world, called SETI@home. To link up, you register with the SETI website, download the necessary software and a small section of the universe appears on your screen. This is monitored for signals while your computer is not in use. If your computer helps to detect extra-terrestrial life, you can be named as a co-discoverer.

Grammar: *modals* ▶ *p.182*

		Present	Past
A	**Possibility:** *may / could / might (have done)*	1 The Earth **may not be** the only planet with intelligent life. 2 Other galaxies **may/could be** home to intelligent life forms. 3 We **may / could / might make** contact with aliens in the near future.	1 Aliens **may / could / might have visited** Earth in the past. 2 People **may (not) have been telling** the truth about seeing 'flying saucers'. 3 **Could** aliens **have built** the pyramids?
B	**Assumption/ deduction:** *must/can't (have done)*	1 There **must be** life on other planets. 2 The Earth **can't be** the only planet where life exists. 3 Aliens **can't be trying** to contact us. We've received no signals from them so far.	1 Fossils show that primitive forms of life on Earth **must have evolved** billions of years ago. 2 Aliens **can't have visited** Earth because space travel takes too long. 3 People **must have been imagining** things when they claim they saw aliens.

1 **The pyramids in Egypt are one of the wonders of the ancient world. Who built them? Match the sentence halves to make true statements.**

1 The Egyptian pharaohs were buried in rich tombs. Not all of these have been discovered,
2 It's hard to believe that a structure as complex as a pyramid
3 If humans built the pyramids,
4 The workmen who built them may have believed
5 Many of those workmen
6 Some people believe that the pyramids
7 They are convinced that extra-terrestrials
8 They think this alien civilisation

a) they must have been highly skilled craftsmen.
b) couldn't have been built with the technology available then.
c) could have been wiped out by a natural disaster.
d) so more treasures could be lying buried in the sands.
e) must have landed on Earth and built them.
f) must have been injured in the course of their work.
g) could have been built in the lifetime of one pharaoh.
h) that they were ensuring their own afterlife by building the pyramids.

2 **Sightings of mysterious large animals have been reported in Britain. Look at the photos of 'The beast of Bodmin Moor' and a skull that was found in southwest England. Big cats do not live wild in Great Britain. How can you explain the photos?**

3 1 Now complete this dialogue using modal verbs from the grammar file and the verbs in brackets.

A: Hey, stop the car! There's a huge animal in that field. It looks like a puma!

B: Don't be ridiculous. I can't see anything. You (1) .... (see) a puma anyway – they aren't found in Britain. It (2) .... (be) something else.

A: Well, it (3) .... (be) a puma exactly but it was definitely some kind of big cat.

B: Let's get out and have a look. I don't suppose it (4) .... (go) far.

A: OK. It was over by that rock.

B: Wow, I can see it! It's huge – it (5) .... (weigh) as much as a big dog!

A: What's that beside it? Ugh! It (6) .... (kill) a sheep or something!

B: Yes, but I wonder where it came from.

A: (7) .... it .... (escape) from a zoo?

B: What zoo? We're miles from anywhere!

A: What shall we do? If we tell the police, they'll say we (8) .... (imagine) it!

2 What would you have done?

Over to you

4 Discuss these questions.

1 Do you know anything about:
a) the Loch Ness Monster?
b) the yeti?

Do you think they could be real? If not, how do you explain people's claims that they have seen them?

2 Are there similar mysteries in your country?

Use of English 1: *structural cloze*

▶▶ *exam strategy*   Paper 3, Part 2 ▶ p.57

1 1 Read the text below all the way through, ignoring the gaps. What does the title refer to?

2 Retell the story in your own words to a partner.

3 What do you think could have happened to Thomas Beale?

2 Now read the text again and fill in the gaps. Which of the following types of word are missing from the text? Tick (✓) them. Which word types occurred most often?

- prepositions
- linking words
- determiners
- possessive adjectives
- auxiliary verbs
- adverbs
- relative pronouns
- pronouns

! *substituting words*

We can use the verb *do* to stand in for another verb, for example: *He promised to return but he never **did**.* (= he never returned)

What does *do* replace in these sentences?

1 Aliens must have built the pyramids. Humans could never have **done so**.

2 'Why don't we send a spacecraft to Mars?' 'We have **done**.'

Read the text below and think of the word which best fits each space. Use only one word in each space. There is an example at the beginning (0).

CRACKING THE CODE

In 1845, in Virginia, USA, a hotel owner named Robert Morris decided to break open a locked box that (0) *had* been given to him for safekeeping by a guest named Thomas Beale. Twenty years (1) ...., Beale had stayed at the hotel for two months and then vanished, (2) .... to be seen again. His box contained three sheets of paper written in different codes, all numbers. There was a note in English saying that Beale had found a large amount of gold, (3) .... he had hidden in a secret location. Unfortunately, there was (4) .... key to the code.

Morris worked on the codes without success, before handing them over to (5) .... else in 1860. This person, (6) .... identity remains unknown, managed to crack the second code, which was based (7) .... a sentence in the American Declaration of Independence. The decoded message revealed further clues to the location of the treasure and made possible an estimation of (8) .... value ($20 million (9) .... today's prices). However, the first and the third codes, which (10) .... believed to contain more details, remain unsolved.

(11) .... who is interested in the Beale papers can read them because they (12) .... published as long ago as 1885. (13) .... then, some of the world's finest analysts have worked on the codes but, (14) .... the promise of hidden treasure, no one has managed to crack them. Whoever (15) .... this will become fabulously wealthy.

Listening: *sentence completion*

1 Look at the illustration. What do you know about the mystery of the Bermuda Triangle?

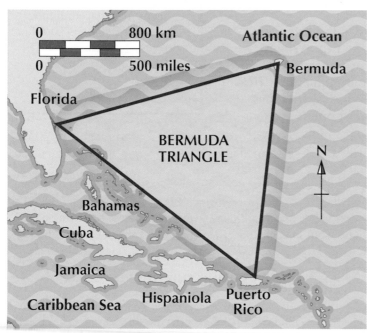

2 Read through the exam task below. What information does it tell you about this area?

3 Look at the gaps in the task.

What kind of information is missing? For example, Question 1 needs a number.

▶▶ *exam tip!*
If the answer is a number, you can write it in words or as a figure, e.g. *two hundred* or *200*. ◀◀

4 ▭ Listen to the recording twice and complete the exam task.

5 ▭ The words you need to write are on the recording, but the sentences in the task often express the information in a different way. Listen to four extracts from the recording. How are the following ideas in the questions expressed on the recording?

Question:
5 stopped working
8 lack of fuel led to ...
9 the US Navy ... said that ... was the real cause
10 was caused by

Over to you

6 Discuss.
Several different explanations are mentioned in the recording for the many strange events that have occurred in the Bermuda Triangle. Which explanation do you think is most likely?

You will hear part of a talk about an area called the Bermuda Triangle. For questions 1–10, complete the sentences.

Over a 500-year period, as many as [___1___] strange things have happened in the Bermuda Triangle.

The name 'Bermuda Triangle' was first used in a [___2___] in the 1960s.

The purpose of Flight 19 was to give trainee pilots practice in [___3___] flying.

Lieutenant Charles Taylor, commander of Flight 19, was a [___4___] with the US Navy.

Charles Taylor first became worried when his [___5___] stopped working.

Officers working in the [___6___] at Fort Lauderdale soon realised that Flight 19 had lost its way.

The navy sent a [___7___] to try and help Flight 19.

It is thought that lack of [___8___] led to the final disappearance of Flight 19.

The US Navy originally said that [___9___] was the real cause of the tragedy.

The speaker thinks the loss of Flight 19 was actually caused by [___10___] and the weather.

Speaking: *individual long turn*

▶▶ *exam strategy* Paper 5, Part 2 ▶ p.21/59

1 **Work in groups of three.**

Student 1: You are the examiner. Give the candidates the instructions on page 205. Time each candidate. If necessary, interrupt Candidate A after one minute. Don't give Candidate B more than about 20 seconds to comment.

Student 2: You are Candidate A. Compare and contrast the two photos on this page, according to the examiner's instructions. You have one minute.

> archaeologist   a tomb
> an archaeological dig
> They must be somewhere like (Egypt).
> to find something by chance
> buried treasure/coins   statue
> a metal detector
> to plough   to dig   to excavate
> to feel elated / excited / amazed / puzzled

▶ **Functions files 1 and 3 p.200**

▶▶ *exam tip!*

You will improve your performance if you compare and contrast the photos and go on to talk about the theme in a more general way, according to the focus given in the examiner's instructions. ◀◀

Student 3: You are Candidate B. The examiner will ask you to comment on the two photos briefly after Candidate A has finished. You should take about 20 seconds for this.

2 **Turn to the photos on page 205. Work in groups of three as in Exercise 1. The examiner should give the instructions on page 207.**

▶ **Functions files 1 and 3 p.200**

9 Discovering the past

Lead-in

Look at the pictures on this page, which show how our ancestors probably lived thousands of years ago. Compare what their way of life must have been like with life today. Talk about:

- clothes
- food
- travel
- health

Reading 2: *gapped text (paragraphs)*

exam file

In previous units, you have practised inserting sentences into a gapped text. Another task in **Paper 1**, **Part 3** asks you to insert **paragraphs** into the text.

1 **Read the instructions for the exam task opposite and the title of the text. Discuss these questions.**

1 What is the text about?
2 What do you know about this topic? Have you heard of other, similar discoveries?
3 What do you think the text will tell you? Make a list of questions.

Example:
Where was the ancient man discovered?

2 **Read the whole of the base text once, including the example answer, to find out the answers to your questions in Exercise 1. (Ignore the extracted paragraphs for now.) Discuss what you have learned with the class.**

3 **Read the first paragraph and the example answer (H) again.**

1 What is the main point of each paragraph?

The first paragraph describes how important the hunter's find was. Paragraph H …

2 Underline the words that connect the two paragraphs.

Examples:

Link	Para. 1	Question 0 (H)
linking words:	*What they discovered could change what we know about …*	*For, …* (= explanation)
parallel words/ expressions:	*three modern-day hunters*	*the trio*

4 **Read the rest of the base text section by section. Identify the main point of each paragraph in the base text and try to predict how the ideas in the text will develop.**

1 Tick (✓) the most likely option below.
Will the missing paragraph tell you more about:

Gap:

1 a) the area of the Yukon?
  b) the body?
2 a) a similar discovery elsewhere?
  b) what was found with the man?
3 a) the ice man Otze?
  b) how valuable the new find is?
4 a) the experts' opinions?
  b) how the body was found?

2 Now you continue.

Gap:

5/6 The missing paragraph will probably tell me …

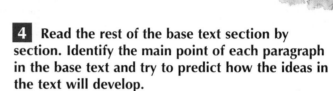

5 **Now read the extracted paragraphs and look for the paragraph that fits each gap. Remember to check for language links to be sure your answers are right.**

Vocabulary: *using context*

6 **Explain the meaning of the words in bold in the text (1–13). Use context clues to help you work it out. Decide if you should add them to your vocabulary notebook. How useful are they?**

Over to you

7 **1 What have you learned about the life of ancient man from this article? Make notes.**

2 Did anything surprise you at all?

The ice man

In the depths of an Arctic wilderness, three modern-day hunters were tracking wild sheep like their ancestors before them. But that is not what they found. What they discovered instead could change what we know about our most ancient **predecessors**[1].

0 **H**

Dressed in a cloak sewn from the skins of small animals, and with his own skin preserved by the cold, the body of the frozen hunter was found at a height of 6,500 feet in a **remote**[2] area of northern Canada. It is a place where little has changed in more than 2,000 years. What modern developments there are, are to be found in Whitehorse, the largest human settlement in the Yukon territory, where the body is in cold storage.

1

The frozen hunter was found above the tree line some distance from Whitehorse, however, on a tundra plateau. At his side was a stout walking stick, a spear, a woven hat and what looked like tools made of bone.

2

Scientists are comparing the find to that of the prehistoric hunter found in a European glacier in 1991. That ice man – discovered in the Alps and nicknamed Otze – was 5,000 years old. He became the subject of intense research, and provoked many **heated**[3] discussions in the scientific community concerning his diet and health.

3

He described the academic value of the body as enormous. 'We have the **potential**[4] to learn what he had been eating, what his health history was, and where he had been travelling,' he said.

4

One of the hunters, Bill Hanlon, described how the body was found. 'We went up on the ice and started to pick up pieces of wood, which seemed kind of strange given the height we were at,' he said. 'We noticed carvings in the pieces of wood, and they were notched. There was also what looked like a backpack. You could see the actual threading and the holes where it had been sewn together.'

5

Announcement of the discovery was delayed while the archaeologists consulted the elders of the Champagne and Aishihik First Nations – a 1,140-member Indian tribe that controls **artefacts**[5] found in the area, which is their ancestral home.

6

According to stories passed down through the generations, they have been in the Yukon since **time immemorial**[6]. 'It was a time when animals could speak to people,' he added.

A The team are quietly confident that the remains could have lain frozen in the blue ice for thousands of years. None of his belongings were of the European variety first brought to the area by Russian traders 250 years ago.

B It is more than five millennia since he tended his flock of sheep. Yet scientists have been able to discover the age, occupation, medical **ailments**[7] and even the last meal of a mummified stone-age man found in the ice.

C They turned out to be in favour of scientific study of the body. Their heritage resource officer explained how they were convinced that the ancient man caught in the ice was an ancestor.

D One man's experience highlight's the **inhospitable**[8] character of the area. Surgeons at the local hospital were operating on someone who had been attacked by a grizzly bear not far from the town.

E His colleague, Warren Ward, pulled out his binoculars to look at the body through the half-melted ice. 'It looked like the sort of picture we'd been seeing in the National Geographic magazine for years,' he said, 'I could see a lot of **tattered**[9] leather and pieces of a fringe.'

F There was also a leather **pouch**[10] containing what was intended to be his next meal: **edible**[11] leaves and the remains of a fish. That was before he slipped down a crevice and **succumbed to**[12] the biting cold, however, because he never got to eat it.

G He too was carrying tools, and the bones of a mountain goat lay next to him. The two situations were comparable in a number of ways, said Al Mackie, the leading archaeologist of a team from Vancouver which has descended on Whitehorse. But for the time being, Mackie and his team are being careful to refer to the latest find only as an 'ancient man'.

H For, according to archaeologists, the body which the trio came across in a melting glacier in one of North America's roughest and most unforgiving **terrains**[13] may be as many as 5,000 years old.

Vocabulary

1 Choosing the right word

Read each sentence carefully and fill in the gap with the best word in the correct form.

1 *invention/discovery*
a The ...... of the first dinosaur skeleton must have amazed archaeologists.
b Experts say the ...... of the wheel was one of the most significant points in human history.

2 *legend/rumour*
a There's a ...... going round the village about the local castle. People say it's haunted by the ghost of a young woman.
b Some modern books are based on the characters in Greek ....

3 *hoax/fake*
a A man said he had found the body of an alien creature but it turned out to be a ....
b The photo of the ghost wasn't genuine; it was a ...... which had been altered on a computer.

4 *deny/refuse*
a I ...... to believe that there is life on other planets.
b The reporter ...... just ...... everything he told the public about the UFO sighting.

5 *prove/try*
a His theory is interesting but he needs ...... that what he claims is true.
b Scientists will ...... find more evidence of prehistoric life in the area.

2 Expressions with *bring / make / take / come*

These verbs are often used to form phrasal verbs and fixed expressions. Read the following text. Then use the correct form of *bring, make, take* or *come* to fill in the gaps. Underline the complete expression.

Bones of crocodile-like creature confirm Arctic was once a hot spot!

We should never (1) _take_ anything for granted as far as science is concerned. Every now and then scientists (2) .... a discovery that amazes us and changes what we believe.

A fossil found recently in the Arctic has (3) .... to light some amazing facts. A student (4) .... across the fossil while examining some shale, or ancient mud, in the Canadian Arctic. He was (5) .... part in some geological research, led by Professor Tarduno of the University of Rochester in New York.

When the student realised the importance of his discovery, it must have (6) .... his breath away. For it didn't (7) .... long to see that this was a bone from a crocodile-like beast whose nearest relatives live in tropical climes.

What did scientists (8) .... of this find, which suggested that the Arctic was once tropical? They have (9) .... to the conclusion that the Arctic must once have had a climate like that of modern Florida: hot and humid.

3 Spelling: words ending in -e

1 Add the suffixes given to make new words:
arrive + -al, fame + -ous, advertise + -ing, advertise + -ment, care + -ful

2 Complete the spelling rule by underlining the correct word in *italics*.

> When you add a suffix to a word that ends in -e, you must *keep/drop* the -e if the suffix starts with a vowel and *keep/drop* the -e if it begins with a consonant.

3 Make nouns from these verbs:
explore, behave, starve, agree

4 Complete the spelling rule by underlining the correct word in *italics*.

> When you add a suffix to a word that ends in -ee you *keep/drop* the second -e.

4 **Spelling:** words ending in -y

1 Make nouns and adverbs from these adjectives: *lazy, happy, nasty*

2 Now make adjectives from these nouns: *mystery, history, glory*

3 Complete the spelling rule.

> When you add a suffix to a word that ends in -y, you must …

5 **Spelling:** less predictable changes

In the exam, you may be asked to make an internal change in a word, e.g. *choose* (verb) – *choice* (noun), or form a word which does not fit in with general word-building patterns, e.g. *complain* (verb) – *complaint* (noun). Complete the tables below.

Verb	Noun		Adjective	Noun
receive	....		poor	....
fail	....		warm	....
know	....		high	....
fly	....		broad	....
lose	....		beautiful	....
laugh	....		proud	....

Use of English 2: *word formation*

▶▶ *exam strategy*　　　　Paper 3, Part 5 ▶ p.49

1 Read the text below to find the answers to these questions.
1 What is Hadrian's Wall?
2 Where is it?
3 Who built it? When?

2 Do the exam task. Pay careful attention to meaning and look out for:
● plural forms of nouns.　　● negative forms.
Remember to check your spelling when you have finished.

3 Discuss these questions.
1 How important do you think it is to preserve the past?
2 What are the most important historical monuments in your country?
3 Imagine a visitor wants some information about them. How much can you tell the visitor about their origin?

Read the text below. Use the word given in capitals underneath to form a word that fits in the space in the text. There is an example at the beginning (0).

HADRIAN'S WALL

Hadrian's wall is a 117 km long (0) *defensive* barrier which ran from coast to coast along what was (1) ..... the border between England and Scotland. It was an (2) ..... piece of military engineering and (3) ..... the biggest stone structure the Romans, or indeed anyone, ever built in Ancient Britain. It must have been an amazing (4) ..... in its day, but for most of its 2,000-year (5) ..... the wall stood abandoned and largely forgotten, known only as a (6) ..... ruin.

Thanks to the efforts of (7) ..... and archaeologists, what remains of the wall has now been preserved. The wall makes a great (8) ..... on visitors, because of its (9) ..... lonely setting. Even without much (10) ..... you can believe yourself back in ancient times. Since 1987, it has been a World Heritage site.

(0) DEFEND	(3) EASY	(6) MYSTERY	(9) WONDER
(1) FORMER	(4) SEE	(7) HISTORY	(10) IMAGE
(2) CREDIBLE	(5) EXIST	(8) IMPRESS	

Writing: *story (last line)*

exam file

In **Paper 2**, **Part 2**, you may be asked to
write a story for a magazine or a
competition, using a given sentence. In
Unit 6, you wrote a story **beginning** with
the given sentence. In this section, you write
a story that **ends** with the given sentence.

▶▶ **exam strategy**

Make sure you:

● write the story from the point of view
  you have been given in the exam task.
  This may be first or third person.
● use the given sentence in the correct
  position. DON'T change it.
● use vivid vocabulary to make your
  story interesting and dramatic.
● vary the way you begin sentences
  and paragraphs.

1 Read the writing task below and
answer these questions.

1 Who is going to read your story? Where
  will it be published?
2 How must your story end?
3 Will you tell your story in the first or
  third person?

A student magazine is publishing
a series of short stories about
strange and unusual experiences.
You have been offered a fee of £50
for your story. The story must end
with the sentence:

*It was the strangest experience of
my life.*

Write your **story** in 120–180 words
in an appropriate style.

4 What sort of story could you write
  – a ghost story, a story about a
  coincidence, another type of story?
5 What tenses will you need to use most
  when telling your story?
  a) present tenses?
  b) narrative tenses?
  c) present perfect?

2 1 Read the first part of the story one student wrote. How
do you think it will end?

One summer, my brother and I went to stay at my
grandfather's isolated farm. Being city kids, we were
desperate to explore the countryside around us.

In the second week, I fell ill and had to stay indoors
while my brother went exploring. Sitting on my bed in the
evening, he described his adventures. He'd found tall trees
to climb and a wonderful lake to swim in.

One day, while resting on the sofa, I heard a noise at the
window. Looking up, I saw a scruffy dog barking furiously
at me. Where could it have come from? It ran towards the
forest, looking back anxiously. I got dressed and followed it.

The dog led me straight to my brother. He was lying
there unconscious, having fallen from a tree. Without
medical attention, he might die. I raced for help and,
thankfully, my brother was soon safe in hospital.

2 With a partner, work out a suitable ending for the sample
story. Remember to use the last line given in the task.

3 Compare your ending with the ending the student wrote.
Which do you prefer?

When I returned home, I hunted for the dog but it
had vanished. I never saw it again. Later, in my
grandfather's drawer, I found a photo of a dog he'd had as
a boy. My blood ran cold when I realised it was identical to
the dog I had seen! Was it just a coincidence? It was the
strangest experience of my life.

Focus on vivid vocabulary

4 **1** **A really good story should include interesting vocabulary. Find words and phrases in the story in Exercises 2 and 3 with a similar meaning to the words below.**

1 a long way from any others
2 very keen
3 nice
4 dirty and untidy
5 loudly
6 went quickly
7 looked for
8 gone
9 I was shocked

2 **The following phrases are often used in mystery or suspense stories. Using your imagination, finish each sentence so that the meaning of the phrase is clear, as in the example.**

1 His heart sank when *he realised that he was alone in the house.*
2 She turned pale when …
3 He froze in terror when …
4 She gazed in horror when …
5 She stared in amazement when …

Focus on grammar ▶ p.185

5 **1** **Read the information in the grammar file. Then find and underline all the examples of participle clauses in the sample story.**

2 **Use a participle clause to join these pairs of sentences. Make any necessary changes.**

Example:

John accepted a dare from his friends. He spent the night in the haunted house.
Having accepted a dare from his friends, John spent the night in the haunted house.

1 He climbed through a window. Then he started to explore.
2 He shone a torch into a large room. He was surprised to see that everything was clean and polished.
3 Then he heard a noise. It was coming from one of the rooms upstairs.
4 He shook with fear. He hid under the table.
5 When he looked up, he saw a man. The man was standing in the doorway.
6 John didn't want the man to see him. John held his breath and kept very still.
7 The stranger pointed a finger towards John. He gave a bloodcurdling cry.

---

grammar file 25

A **We can use present and perfect participles:**

● **to replace clauses beginning with** *as / because / since*
1 ***Being forced*** to spend the day indoors, I explored the old house. (= Because I was forced …)
2 ***Not knowing*** where I was, my friends began to search for me. (= Because they didn't know …)
3 ***Never/Not having been*** to the house before, they didn't realise that there was a secret room. (= As they had never/not been …)

● **for actions that happen at the same time or in sequence**
4 A man stood by the window, ***staring*** straight at me.
5 ***Trembling*** with fear, I ran from the room.
6 ***Having reached*** the safety of the street, I looked up at the window. (= After I had reached …)

● **after some time conjunctions and prepositions:** ***before, after, when, while; despite, on***
7 ***After meeting*** the stranger, I decided never to go in that house again. (= After I had met …)
8 ***Despite being*** scared, I was keen to investigate what had happened. (= Although I was scared …)

B **We can use present participles:**

● **to shorten some relative clauses**
Had the man ***waiting*** in the secret room been a ghost? (= who had been waiting)

Over to you

6 **Write your answer to the following task in 120–180 words in an appropriate style.**

A student magazine is running a writing competition. The prize is a mystery weekend in Paris. Readers are invited to send in short stories for a series entitled 'Stranger than Fiction'. Your story must end with the sentence:

When John got into bed that night, he could hardly believe what had happened that day.

Write your story.

Follow the advice in the exam strategy box. Use the questions in Unit 6, Exercise 2, page 76 to help you work out a plot. Remember to:

● make a plan before you start to write, and keep it simple.
● start your story in an interesting way.
● divide your story into clear paragraphs.
● use a good range of narrative tenses.
● check your writing for errors when you have finished.

10 Technology

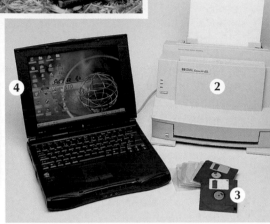

Lead-in

1 **Look at the photos. Can you label the numbered items using words and expressions from the box below?**

desktop computer   monitor
keyboard   mouse   printer
floppy disk   CD drive
disk drive   lap-top computer
screen   hard disk
hand-held positioning device

2 **The computer is part of our everyday lives.**

1 List as many areas as you can think of where computers are used.

Examples:
In offices for typing and storing documents.
By travel agents to check the availability of flights, hotels, etc.

2 Discuss what life would be like without computers and computer technology.

Examples:
If we didn't have computers, …
  we wouldn't be able to surf the Internet.
  communication wouldn't be as easy as it is now.

Reading 1: *multiple-choice questions*

▶▶ *exam strategy*   Paper 1, Part 2 ▶ p.22

1 **Look at the exam task opposite.**

1 Read the instructions, the title and the first paragraph.

1 What does the title refer to?
2 What kind of products do you think the rest of the article will talk about?

2 Read the rest of the text quite quickly to find out:

1 what products are mentioned.
2 what applications they have.

3 Discuss.

1 What kind of publication do you think this text was written for?
2 Do you read this kind of publication? Why/Why not?

2 **Now answer the multiple-choice questions, using the exam strategy you have learned. Be prepared to justify your answers to the class.**

▶▶ *exam tip!*

Look for the **best** answer to the multiple-choice questions according to what is in the text. You will not always find three options that are obviously wrong. ◀◀

3 **Discuss these questions about the task.**

1 Which questions in the exam task focused on:
  a) detailed comprehension?
  b) understanding meaning in context?
  c) understanding grammatical links?
  d) identifying the writer's point of view?

2 Which questions did you find most difficult?

3 Were there any unfamiliar words you needed to understand in order to answer a question? If so, how did you deal with them?

Over to you

4 **Work in pairs or groups.**

1 Discuss how each of the devices mentioned in the article could improve your life. Decide which one would be your favourite.

2 Think of another 'smart' device that you would find useful. Describe what it would look like and what it would do. Then find out what other students have decided. Whose idea for a smart device seems to be the best?

SMART STUFF

INCREASINGLY over the last few years, we have become familiar with the range of small electronic gadgets that come under the heading 'smart' accessories. Joggers, for example, run with heart-rate monitors, and shop assistants carry pocket-sized computers. But these are just the first examples of a whole range of new products that promises to change our lives in all sorts of surprising ways.

As a scientist at Massachusetts Institute of Technology's Media Lab, Rosalind Picard tries out all kinds of smart accessories before they go on the market. One of these was the so-called 'frown headband'. It came as a shock to Rosalind to realise just how often she frowned. Stuck in a traffic jam recently, waiting for the cars to move forward, Rosalind kept hearing the sounds of the tiny sensor inside the band worn around her forehead – each time she frowned in frustration, the sensor gave out a signal.

Headbands that check facial expressions are just one of the things she and her colleagues have designed. **Their** aim is to make ready-to-wear items that both look good and give the wearer useful feedback. Body sensors, like those in Rosalind's headband, can detect physical changes that the wearer might not otherwise be aware of. Hidden inside watches, rings or shoes, these sensors can check for signs of stress, give information and offer advice.

Another computer scientist, Steven Feiner, is working on a pair of glasses that will do more than help you to see. Imagine you want to try a restaurant in a foreign city but you're not familiar with the dishes on the menu. If you are wearing a pair of Steven's glasses, all you have to do is **glance** above the restaurant's doorway and your glasses will immediately become windows to the Internet, offering you full details of the meals served inside. Are you one of those people who lack confidence when giving a talk to an audience?

Look to the right and the glasses will flash your notes in front of your eyes. They could also prove useful for cooks who want to check a recipe without leaving sticky fingermarks all over their cookery books.

At the moment, Steven's invention looks more like a pair of ski goggles than a pair of glasses. It's a headset connected to a hand-held computer and a Global Positioning System (GPS) receiver, which tracks the wearer's position. Students who don't mind being stared at have tried out the *Star Trek*-like device on campus. But Steven says that these head-worn displays will eventually get smaller, lighter and smarter as technology improves. As they will be relatively cheap, he foresees them replacing the notebooks and manuals that workers have to carry. He predicts that they will be useful to surgeons, giving them instant access to a patient's medical notes while carrying out operations.

And, of course, this new technology has a fashionable as well as a useful application. A chemical engineer named Robert Langer has invented a new microchip that, if put inside a ring, can give off different scents according to a person's mood. That, of course, may or may not appeal to you. And, in the end, it is shoppers, not scientists, who will determine which of these smart accessories will succeed as fashionable items and which are destined to join history's long list of crazy inventions. Steven Feiner, concerned that vanity may prevent some people from wearing his glasses, is already working on the idea of contact lenses with the same features.

It is clear, however, that as small computer displays get brighter and cheaper, they will pop up in all sorts of easily-wearable accessories, even in the buttons on your coat. What's more, this is something that's going to happen a lot sooner than we all expect.

Star Trek: a science fiction programme on TV

1 When Rosalind wore the headband, she was surprised at
   A how well the sensor worked.
   B how affected she was by the traffic.
   C how strong the signal was.
   D how comfortable it was to wear.

2 What does 'Their' in line 28 refer to?
   A facial expressions
   B headbands
   C colleagues
   D ready-to-wear items

3 'glance' in line 45 describes a way of
   A wearing something
   B looking at something
   C pointing to something
   D finding something

4 Steven's glasses will help people who are giving a talk by
   A telling them if they forget to say things.
   B checking how nervous they're feeling.
   C signalling if they make a mistake.
   D helping them to remember things.

5 What is the current problem with Steven's glasses?
   A where they are worn
   B how much they cost
   C what they look like
   D the way they've been tested

6 What is the writer's view of Robert Langer's invention?
   A It is unlikely to work successfully.
   B It is a bad use of new technology.
   C He is sure people will laugh at it.
   D He is uncertain whether people will buy it.

7 In general, what does the writer think about 'smart' accessories?
   A They will soon be widely available.
   B Much more research is needed into them.
   C Only a few of them will prove to be useful.
   D They will only affect the lives of certain people.

Grammar:
future forms ▶ *p.178*

grammar file 5

A Future simple
1 *I think I'll buy myself a pocket computer.* (= decision made at this moment)
2 *Science will revolutionise our lives in the next few years.* (= prediction)

B Future continuous
1 *In twenty years' time, we will / may / could be taking holiday trips to the moon.* (= future action in progress)
2 *Will you be studying technology next year?* (= planned future action)
3 *I'll be working this morning as usual.* (= routine/normal activity)
4 *I won't be coming to the technology exhibition with you.*

C Future perfect
1 *By the time our children grow up, the world will / may / could have changed completely.* (= action completed before another future action)
2 *In ten years' time, solutions will / may / could have been found for many of the world's problems.*
3 *By the time/When the project is completed, they will have been working on it for six whole years!*

D be (due) to
Scientists are (due) to meet next week to discuss ways of prolonging human life. (= fixed arrangement)

---

1 Underline the correct form of the verb in each pair. Then tick (✓) the sentences you think are true.

1 By the middle of this century, cures will already *have been discovered/be discovered* for many common illnesses.
2 By that time, we will all *live/be living* much longer as a matter of course.
3 Governments *will have to/are due to* make some important medical decisions in the next few years.

2 **1** Look at the survey below and fill in the gaps in the questions with a future form. You can read the explanation of the results on page 199.

What weird things will happen in the next 50 years?

By the year 2050, ...	YES	NO
1 .... extra-terrestrials have judged us advanced enough to make contact?	61%	39%
2 .... women .... overtaken men as the dominant sex?	42%	58%
3 .... extra senses such as ESP* have .... accepted as fact?	89%	11%
4 .... we .... allowed to design our own children?	74%	26%
5 Will a computer .... elected Prime Minister/ President?	9%	91%

* extra-sensory perception = the ability to know what will happen in the future, or to know what another person is thinking

2 Use the following prompts to make more questions. Use the future continuous, future perfect or future simple tense. Sometimes more than one tense is possible. Add two more questions yourself.

6 we / manage to contact life in another galaxy by the year 2050?
7 we / still / drive the sort of cars we have now in 50 years' time?
8 scientists / discover how to prolong human life by the middle of this century?
9 people / live until they are 150 by the end of this century?
10 time travel / already / become a reality 20 years from now?
11 in 10 years' time, robots / do most of the jobs that humans do now?
12 we / ever / learn how to recreate extinct animals like dinosaurs?
13 ....
14 ....

3 Carry out a class survey, using questions 1–14. Write a report of the results. (See Unit 8, page 92 for help.)

Over to you

3 **Ask and answer in pairs.**

1 Where do you think you will be living in five years' time? Are you going to leave home when you start work?

2 What do you think we will all be wearing in 50 years' time?

3 Do you think you will have had any children in 10 years' time? How many will you have?

4 What job do you think you will be doing in 20 years' time? How much do you think you will be earning?

5 What will you be doing this time next week?

6 How long will you have been learning English by the time you take the First Certificate exam?

7 Will you still be learning English this time next year? Are you going to do the Proficiency exam?

8 Will you have finished this book by the end of term?

Use of English 1: *error correction*

▶▶ *exam strategy*   Paper 3, Part 4 ▶ p.69

1 **Read the title of the text below.**

How would you answer this question?

2 **Read the text all the way through.**

1 How does the writer answer the question in the title?

2 Do you agree or disagree with the writer?

3 **Now do the exam task. What types of errors will you look for? Add to this list.**

Unnecessary:
- prepositions and particles
- pronouns

Read the text below and look carefully at each line. Some of the lines are correct, and some have a word which should not be there. If a line is correct, put a tick (✓) in the space by the number. If a line has a word which should not be there, write the word in the space. There are two examples at the beginning (0 and 00).

IS TECHNOLOGY ALWAYS BEST?

0	...*as*	In my opinion, technological advances are not always as such a great
00	...✓	advantage. It is true that new forms of communication bring benefits,
1	....	especially if you have some research even to do for a school assignment,
2	....	or if you need to get in touch them with someone urgently. I am not so
3	....	convinced, however, that they are actually have such a positive effect on
4	....	people of my generation. Like so many the teenagers in this country, I find
5	....	that I use my mobile phone a great deal, and if I do write to someone,
6	....	it's usually a quick e-mail. It was when my girlfriend actually took up the
7	....	trouble to write me a long letter that I stopped to think about it what I
8	....	was doing. She said a lot of nice things in that letter. It was written on
9	....	classy paper and she had taken there a lot of care about her handwriting.
10	....	Although I'm not a great romantic, I'm sure it's something I'm always
11	....	going to treasure. But she also said a few of hard things which made me
12	....	to think. Can it be true that I'm more interested in chatting with complete
13	....	strangers online than I am in talking to her face to face? And she was
14	....	exaggerating when she said we never get rather more than five minutes alone
15	....	together without that one of my gadgets buzzing or bleeping, wasn't she?

Listening: *multiple matching*

▶▶ *exam strategy*   Paper 4, Part 3 ▶ p.71

1 Read the instructions for the exam task opposite and the options A–F.

1 Discuss these questions, using expressions from the box below.

1 What can each piece of technology A–F be used for?
2 What jobs do you think someone employed by a recording studio might do?
3 Why might they find the pieces of technology A–F useful?

> to stay/keep in touch   to play/listen to music
> to type reports   to calculate percentages
> to store/access information   to do calculations
> to add up / subtract / divide / multiply
> to send / receive / leave messages (electronically)

2 Explain to a partner how each device works. Use expressions from the box below to help you.

> to plug something in   to speak after the tone
> to play back   to press the right key
> to run on electricity/batteries   to switch on/off
> to tap the right numbers   to press the 'send' button
> to check your message box

2   **Listen to the recording twice and complete the exam task.**

▶▶ *exam tip!*

Sometimes a word in the options is mentioned by more than one speaker. Don't let this mislead you. Check your answers carefully on the second listening. ◀◀

3 Compare your answers with the class.

You will hear five different people who work for a record company talking about a piece of technology they couldn't do without. For questions 1–5, choose from the list A–F the thing each person is talking about. Use the letters only once. There is one extra letter which you do not need to use.

A	lap-top computer	Speaker 1	1
B	pocket calculator	Speaker 2	2
C	mobile phone	Speaker 3	3
D	e-mail	Speaker 4	4
E	CD player	Speaker 5	5
F	voice mail		

Speaking: *collaborative task and discussion*

▶▶ **exam strategy**
Paper 5, Part 3 ▶ p.33/82/94

1 Part 3 task

Work in groups of three.

Student 1: You are the examiner. Give Students 2 and 3 the instructions on page 207. Time them and interrupt if necessary after three minutes.

Students 2 and 3: Listen to the examiner carefully and do the task.

▶ **Functions files 5, 9, 12 and 13 p.200–201**

▶▶ *exam tip!*

You don't have to agree with your partner, but remember to disagree politely.

▶▶ **exam strategy**
Paper 5, Part 4 ▶ p.45/82

2 Part 4 discussion

The examiner should now join in the discussion.

Student 3: You are the examiner. Ask Students 1 and 2 the questions below to develop the topic further. Stop the discussion after four minutes. (Don't worry if you don't manage to ask all the questions.)

Students 1 and 2: Discuss the examiner's questions.

1 Can you think of any other inventions that are important in our everyday lives?
2 What is the most important invention in your home?
3 Which inventions would you find it most difficult to live without?
4 Are there any drawbacks to using these inventions?
5 If you were an inventor, what device would you develop to improve people's lives?

to make life easier/more convenient
to give people more leisure time
to make your own entertainment
to rely on technology
to make people lazy/dependent
labour-saving devices
household chores
a fast/slow pace of life

10 Crime prevention

Lead-in

Look at the photos, which show the British police working to reduce crime. Compare and contrast the photos, saying how technology has changed the way the police work today. Use words and expressions from the box.

closed circuit television (CCTV)
a network of cameras   to monitor the public
to scan a crowd   to improve security
officers on the beat   to patrol an area
a patrol car   better communications
basic/sophisticated equipment
to respond quickly

CCTV main control room

The old Information Room at Police Headquarters in London

Reading 2: *gapped text (paragraphs)*

►► **exam strategy**   Paper 1, Part 3

- Read the base text and the example paragraph for general understanding, and identify the main idea of each paragraph.
- Read the paragraph before and after the gap carefully.
- Think about the development of ideas in the text. Ask yourself what kind of information would link the paragraphs logically.
- Read the extracted paragraphs and look for topic links with the paragraphs in the base text. Are there any associated expressions or paraphrases?
- Pay attention to linking words that show the relationship between ideas.

1 Read the instructions for the exam task opposite, the title of the text and the sub-heading.

1 What is the article about?
2 What do you already know about the topic?
3 What words and expressions do you expect to come across in the text? Make a list.

2 Read the base text and example (H), highlighting the main points. Then discuss with the class what you have learned.

3 Think about the way the writer develops his ideas in the first three paragraphs.

Paragraph 1   introduces the idea of a more advanced technology than CCTV.
Paragraph 2   (extract H) names the new technology.
Paragraph 3   …

Underline the words used to refer to the new technology in each of the three paragraphs. What sentences do they appear in? (Paragraph 1 has been done for you.)

4 Follow the exam strategy to complete the task. Pay special attention to the first and last sentence in each paragraph. Use these clues to help you.

Question:

1 The paragraph before the gap describes the new Virtual Interactive (VIP) Policing system. The paragraph after the gap talks about prototype systems used in court. Which extracted paragraph links the two? Look for associated words.

2 The paragraphs before and after the gap both contain quotes by the same person. Which extracted paragraph links the two?

6 The paragraph before the gap talks about other areas the police are investigating apart from video. Which extracted paragraph gives another example?

Over to you

5 1 Read the text again and make notes about:

- how VIP works
- the benefits of VIP
- the potential drawbacks

2 Use your notes to explain the new system to a partner.

3 Add any useful new words to your vocabulary notebook.

Someone to watch over you

Video cameras that can read your numberplate or identify your face are just two of the systems the police are investigating for the 21st century.

Cities using closed circuit television cameras (CCTV) in public places have reported massive drops in crimes such as street theft. The public is impressed and the Government has provided extra funding to help towns buy the equipment. Despite this, CCTV could soon be overtaken by <u>more advanced technology.</u>

0   **H**

The new system uses computer software linked to video cameras to enable police officers to scan a crowd or street and automatically match the faces to a database of offenders. A variety of factors, such as the distance between the chin and the eyes, are analysed, providing accurate matches within seconds.

1

Prototype systems are being used, but only by getting expert witnesses to confirm their accuracy. 'It's difficult if the courts are faced with pictures of a robbery and the person accused claims that the photo is not of him,' says Barry Irving, director of the Police Foundation. 'So we have launched an initiative to gain validation for these systems.'

2

'There are thousands of photos in police hands, plus a huge database from security cameras. As town centre cameras are used more and more, the information builds up,' says Irving. Linking private systems and police records will make it possible to search for an individual's involvement in thousands of crimes.

3

To the police, such technology is a big advantage. It gives them the ability to patrol without being physically present, which saves money. 'There is a constant conflict between limited police resources and widespread public demand for improved crime control,' says Irving. But for people concerned about their civil rights there are worrying implications.

4

Nevertheless, once the VIP system has proved itself, the applications for it are endless. One important development is for identifying criminals entering the country via Customs and Immigration. Future possibilities include linking it to software that could artificially age photos of wanted criminals when up-to-date pictures are not available.

5

The greater use of video is only one of the areas police are investigating. A large investment is being made in the Police National Computer (PNC), which gives all the country's police forces access to information on serious crimes. PNC links are currently only available in police stations but could be made available to officers patrolling in cars.

6

Within a few years, when all these different systems could be working with each other, the familiar face of the 'bobby on the beat' could have been replaced by a camera mounted on a pole.

A   His team is also involved in a project to bring together police records and databases of images from other sources, including images from security cameras in shops and banks.

B   Another use for image analysis software is to read and recognise car numberplates using a hidden video camera. It takes only 0.25 seconds from the moment a car enters its field of vision for the software to come up with details of the car and its owner.

C   The researchers at the university's computer-science department hope to perfect the system within two years. By then, officers will be able to recreate a three-dimensional crime scene on computer in a couple of hours.

D   The introduction of 'Personal Digital Assistants' (PDAs) to replace the traditional notebook is also being considered by some police forces. PDAs can be loaded with the most up-to-date information on suspects, stolen cars and burglaries.

E   'Of course, the police must have all the tools they need in the fight against crime, but we are concerned about the question of freedom,' said a spokesman for Liberty, an organisation that defends the freedom of the individual citizen. 'A balance must be found.'

F   Although such facial recognition systems are highly reliable, their results are not yet acceptable in a trial in the same way that fingerprints or DNA analyses are.

G   The system can also look for multiple appearances by the same person, as the date, time and location of each appearance are recorded. 'This information makes it possible to gather criminal intelligence about someone even if we don't know who they are,' says Irving.

H   The equipment in use today needs an operator, which means it is expensive. More importantly, the faces on the screen are not clear enough to be identified easily. Virtual Interactive Policing (VIP), a highly sophisticated system now in development, could change all that.

Vocabulary

1 Crimes and criminals

1 Look at the groups of crimes below. Can you complete the missing definitions?

A	B	C	D
1 shoplifting – *stealing from a shop* 2 mugging – 3 pickpocketing –	1 smuggling – *taking goods from one country to another illegally* 2 fraud – 3 forgery –	1 drink-driving – *driving when under the influence of alcohol* 2 joyriding – 3 speeding –	1 arson – *setting fire to property in order to cause damage* 2 burglary – 3 hijacking –

2 Now complete the table below with the correct form of the words above. For one crime there is no noun form for the person.

Person	Verb
shoplifter	to shoplift
mugger	....
....	....

3 Match a verb in Column A to a noun in Column B.

A	B
1 rob	a) a wallet
2 hold	b) a ransom
3 burgle	c) someone hostage
4 pay	d) a bank
5 catch	e) a house
6 steal	f) a thief

4 Decide which crime in each group (A–D) in Exercise 1.1 is the most serious. Then compare your opinions with other students. Explain your choice.

5 Read what happened to John Brown. Put the events in the correct order.

- [1] John Brown was suspected of committing a crime.
- [ ] He was charged.
- [ ] He appealed.
- [ ] He was found guilty by the jury.
- [ ] He was handcuffed and taken into custody.
- [ ] He was arrested.
- [ ] He was pardoned.
- [ ] He was questioned and his fingerprints were taken.
- [ ] He was sentenced.
- [ ] He was imprisoned.
- [ ] He was set free.
- [ ] He was sent for trial.

2 Choosing the right word

Underline the correct word in each group. Then ask and answer the questions in pairs.

1 Have you ever sat in a law *court / trial / house* to see how the justice system works?
2 How big a *fine / penalty / fee* do you think a motorist should pay if he/she is caught speeding?
3 In your opinion, should a burglar always be sent to prison if he/she *robs / burgles / steals* a house?
4 Do you think men are more likely to *do / commit / execute* a crime than women? If so, why?
5 Do you think everyone suspected of shoplifting should be *accused / tried / convicted* in an open court?
6 How comfortable should a typical prison *cage / ward / cell* be?
7 Have you ever been a *lookout / viewer / witness* to a crime?
8 What punishment do you think hijackers should receive if they eventually free their *innocents / captors / hostages*?
9 If someone is found *accused / guilty / responsible* of murder, what punishment do you think they should receive?
10 Are you in favour of the death *punishment / sentence / penalty*?

3 Phrasal verbs

Fill in the gaps in the sentences with the correct form of the phrasal verbs in the box. Add a pronoun or reflexive pronoun where necessary. Use each verb once.

> make off with   get away   get off with   let someone off
> give yourself up   break into   get up to   give yourself away

1 Masked men robbed a bank in the city centre today and .... $10,000.
2 An aunt of mine was stopped for speeding, but they .... with a caution.
3 The hijackers .... when they realised there was no hope of escape.
4 The shoplifter .... by dropping the goods he had stolen as he left the store!
5 'How did the burglar .... the house?' the police officer asked. 'He broke a window.'
6 Those boys are always .... some kind of mischief or other!
7 'Stop thief! Don't let him .... !'
8 A boy in my class was caught painting graffiti on a wall but, luckily for him, he .... just a warning.

Use of English 2: *lexical cloze*

▶▶ *exam strategy*

Paper 3, Part 1 ▶ p.13

1 **1 Read the title and the first paragraph of the text opposite. What will the text be about?**

2 Now read the text all the way through, ignoring the gaps for the moment.

What do you learn about *the way it was*?

2 **Now complete the exam task. Read the gapped sentences very carefully.**

Remember, to help you choose the right word, you should:

● pay careful attention to meaning.
● be aware of grammatical patterns such as prepositions after verbs and adjectives.
● make sure that linking words fit the meaning of the text.

3 **Highlight all examples in the text of a noun followed by the preposition *of*. Add them to your vocabulary notebook. Write an example sentence to help you remember the meaning and the combination.**

Example:
to make use of

Read the text below and decide which answer **A, B, C** or **D** best fits each space. There is an example at the beginning (0).

0　　A make　　B bring　　C hold　　D find

THE WAY IT WAS

Today the police are able to (0) *A.* use of all kinds of scientific and technological aids in their (1) ..... against crime. This was not always the (2) ....., however.

In the early days of the British police force, during the nineteenth century, the police officer's whistle was his (3) ..... way of calling for help if he got into (4) ..... . Gradually, in the twentieth century, things (5) ..... to improve. Those police officers lucky enough to be (6) ..... a patrol car rather than a bicycle could also take (7) ..... of radio communications.

In 1903, a new system for identifying people by their fingerprints was discovered. (8) ..... it soon proved to be one of the most significant developments in crime investigation, a (9) ..... of the national fingerprint collection could (10) ..... days, if not weeks, until computers were introduced in the 1970s.

A similar problem (11) ..... any police officer who got the registration number of a car used in a midnight robbery and needed urgently to (12) ..... who owned it. The only way of doing this out of office (13) ..... was to phone up Police Headquarters in London. They would send an officer to wake up the caretaker at County Hall, where the records were (14) ..... . The two would then have to go (15) ..... an enormous card index system in the basement. Today, police officers can identify the owner of a vehicle in seconds, via the Police National Computer.

1	A charge	B fight	C duty	D match
2	A instance	B event	C case	D condition
3	A mere	B whole	C main	D pure
4	A complaint	B anxiety	C concern	D difficulty
5	A believed	B began	C became	D belonged
6	A thought	B given	C thrown	D caught
7	A advantage	B profit	C benefit	D service
8	A Although	B Whether	C Despite	D Moreover
9	A hunt	B look	C seek	D search
10	A pass	B stand	C take	D spend
11	A approached	B posed	C solved	D faced
12	A ask after	B find out	C check in	D come across
13	A hours	B place	C doors	D date
14	A wrapped	B stocked	C looked after	D kept
15	A across	B through	C about	D round

Writing: *report (recommending)*

exam file

In **Paper 2**, **Part 2**, you may be asked to write a report which includes recommendations.

▶▶ *exam strategy*

Make sure you:
- don't include too many points in your report: select three or four major points and develop them fully.
- make it easy for the reader to skim through.
  - state what the report is about in the introduction.
  - set out your report clearly: group similar points under headings.
  - state your conclusion and summarise your recommendations in the last section.
  - avoid sentences that are too long and complex.
- make your report impersonal: you can use the passive to achieve this.
- don't use informal language.

1 Read the writing task and answer the questions below.

> There is a high level of crime amongst young people in the area where you live. The community police would like to make the area safer. As a member of your school council, you have been asked to write a report for the community police officer, suggesting reasons why there is so much youth crime in the area and making some recommendations.
>
> Write your **report** in **120–180** words in an appropriate style.

1 Who is going to read your report?
   What style will be appropriate?
2 Why are you writing the report? What information does your reader want? Underline all the points you must cover in your report.

2 Work with a partner to brainstorm ideas and useful vocabulary.

1 Note down as many reasons as you can why there might be a lot of youth crime in a particular area.

2 Now choose the three most important items in your list that you could mention in your report.

3 What recommendations could you make to solve the problems you have selected?
Example:

Reasons for youth crime	*Recommendation*
1 *Not enough police officers on duty*	*Have more police officers on patrol*

3 Read the report one student wrote in answer to the task. Ignore any errors in style or register for the moment. Discuss the questions that follow the report.

To: The Community Police Officer
From: Alicia Herrera
Date: 16 June 20—
Subject: Youth crime

Dear Sir,

Introduction
The purpose of this report is to suggest reasons why there is youth crime in this area and to give you some tips.

1 Lack of amenities
There are no youth clubs in the area and the other facilities are too pricey. Some teenagers get frustrated because there is nothing to do.

Recommendation: Activities like free sports coaching, games, and summer camps should be arranged. It would be a good idea to have a youth club built in the area.

2 Lighting and security
You wouldn't believe the state of the lights in the area! This makes it easier for thieves to escape detection.

Recommendation: You've really got to fix the broken lights. I would also recommend having security systems installed, such as closed circuit TV.

3 Education
Some young people don't have a clue about the effect on victims when they are burgled or if they have their car broken into.

Recommendation: The community police should help run the youth club and start classes to help young people understand the consequences of crime.

Conclusion
Youth crime is a big problem in this area. However, I believe we can tackle it by following the recommendations in this report.

---

1 How many reasons for youth crime does the writer give?
2 Compare the writer's ideas with your own notes. How similar or different are they? Are the writer's recommendations relevant and suitable?
3 Has the writer set out the sample report clearly so that it is easy for the reader to follow? If so, how has she done this?
4 What mistake has the writer made in the format of the report?

Focus on style and register

4 **Underline five words or phrases in the report that are too informal. Rewrite them in a more formal way.**

Focus on grammar ▶ *p.184*

5 **1 Read the information in the grammar file. Then find examples in the sample report in Exercise 3.**

grammar file 22

A *have/get* + object + past participle
We use this structure to show that we are arranging for someone else to do a job for us. Notice the word order!

1 *'Are you going to fit that car alarm yourself?'*
  *'No, I'm going to **have** it **fitted** by the experts.'*
2 *Why **don't** we **have** a burglar alarm **installed**?*
3 *I **must get** my watch **insured** in case it is stolen.*
4 *The police advised us **to have** door security systems **installed**.*
5 *They recommended **having** security catches **fitted** on our windows too.*

Note: *have* is more formal than *get* in British English.

B *have* + object + past participle
We use *have* (but not *get*) when something unpleasant happens.

1 *My sister **had** her purse **stolen** yesterday.*
2 ***Have** you ever **had** your house **broken into**?*

2 Fill in the gaps in these sentences, using the structures from the grammar file and the verbs in the box. Be careful of tense!

put up	steal	build	break into	install (2)

1 There's a lot of crime in our town. A lot of people .... their cars .... recently.
2 Only last week my friend .... his wallet .... from his pocket while he was shopping.
3 The town council should .... a youth centre .... so that teenagers have somewhere to meet.
4 It would be a good idea to .... alarms .... to deter burglars from breaking into houses at night.
5 Why not .... a closed circuit television .... in the shopping centre? It will deter criminals because they know they will be recognised.
6 We ought to .... notices .... everywhere warning people about pickpockets.

Over to you

6 **Write your answer to the following task in 120–180 words in an appropriate style.**

There has been an increase in crimes such as shoplifting, mugging, and house burglary in your town. You have been asked to represent residents of the town, young and old. The Crime Prevention Officer has asked you to write a report saying why you think criminals target the area and what measures should be taken to make houses, shops, etc. more crime-proof.

Write your report.

Follow the advice in the exam strategy box. Remember to:
- read the question carefully and include all the relevant points.
- brainstorm ideas and select the ones that you can develop best in your report.
- make a plan before you start to write.
- check your writing for errors when you have finished.

11 The environment

Lead-in

Look at the photos. Use words and expressions from the box to answer these questions.

1 What animals can you see in the photos?
2 What are they doing?
3 What common theme do the photographs have?
4 Make a list of things that make humans different from animals.

> a chimpanzee   a squirrel   a rat
> to solve problems   to imitate   to use tools
> to work things out   to show intelligence
> to learn tricks   to think for themselves

Reading 1: *gapped text (paragraphs)*

> ▶▶ *exam strategy*   Paper 1, Part 3 ▶ p.122

1 Read the instructions for the exam task opposite, the title of the text and the first paragraph.

1 What is the article about?
2 Why might people laugh at the idea of animals having 'culture'?
3 Turn the underlined sentence in paragraph 1 into a question:
   What have thirty years of research ... ?
4 Can you suggest any answers yourself? Think of anything you have read, heard or discussed.

2 1 Read the base text and the example (H). As you read, decide what key point is being made in each paragraph.

2 Discuss what you have found out.
What examples are mentioned in the text that prove that chimpanzees
a) are intelligent?   b) can learn from each other?

3 Complete the exam task. Pay special attention to:

- the first and last sentence in each paragraph. These usually contain ideas that point forward to the next paragraph and back to the previous paragraph.
- linking words that a) introduce an example b) add extra points c) introduce contrasts.
  These will help you follow the development of ideas through the text.
- associated words and parallel expressions.
- pronoun links.

>  ▶▶ *exam tip!*
> Be prepared to spend longer on the middle questions in a gapped text. These are usually the ones which cause most problems.
> ◀◀

Vocabulary: *using context*

4 Explain the meaning of the words in bold in the text (1–11). Decide what words you want to add to your vocabulary notebook.

Over to you

5 Now you have read the whole text, note down all the examples that support the argument that chimpanzees and other animals may have 'culture'. Decide if you agree or disagree.

6 Do you think it is right or wrong to:
- use animals in scientific research?
- keep animals as pets?

The social life of chimpanzees

The idea of animals having something which could be described as 'culture' once seemed laughable. But thirty years of research have uncovered surprising intellectual and social riches in the life of chimpanzees.

0   H

Andrew Whitton, who led the project, describes it as 'just the beginning' of research into social **diversity**[1] amongst chimpanzees. Many differences, such as voice dialects, were left out of the report because there was too little evidence to draw any clear conclusions.

1

One example is 'ant dipping'. Some groups of chimpanzees fish for ants with short sticks, eating the insects off the stick one by one, whilst others have a better technique; catching many ants on a long stick in one hand and then **sweeping**[2] them off into the mouth with the other.

2

But is this like human culture? It is a bit like asking if chickens can fly. Compared with an eagle, perhaps they can't, but they do use their wings and they can get up into trees. Compared with human culture, which is very advanced, other animals seem **nowhere in sight**[3]. But what if we look at them in a different way and don't measure them by our standards?

3

A clever young individual started cleaning the vegetables in water before eating them. Her mother followed the example and soon the habit **spread**[4] through the entire population. Although the original individuals are now dead, their descendants carry on the tradition.

4

As well as the **fieldwork**[5] with wild chimpanzees, there is research with captive animals, those kept in zoos and elsewhere. This has given scientists a higher opinion of their intelligence than used to be the case.

We know, for example, that they can add and subtract numbers up to nine. Language is a more **controversial**[6] area. Chimpanzees cannot imitate human speech, and vocal communication among wild chimps has hardly been studied.

5

Another mark of intelligence is **self-awareness**[7]. A chimpanzee can recognise itself in a mirror or in a photograph. This sort of self-recognition in a mirror is limited to humans and chimpanzees; monkeys cannot do it.

6

Another problem is whether chimpanzees are sufficiently like us to be protected by human rights legislation. A sad story illustrates the chimpanzee's position. Vicky, a chimpanzee who grew up in a human family, was sorting photographs of people and animals into two piles. She put a photo of herself into the human pile, but one of her chimpanzee father went into the animal pile.

A Another such activity is the 'rain dance' with which some groups celebrate a heavy shower. These things are regarded as 'culture' because chimpanzees learn them from each other, in contrast to things they do naturally, or by **instinct**[8].

B At the time, Western scientists didn't agree with Imanishi's idea that because a single type of behaviour spread amongst monkeys, this meant they had 'culture'. But the recent evidence for this amongst chimpanzees is very strong. We can only say that chimpanzees don't have culture if we change our definition of the word.

C Apart from chimpanzees, scientists regard whales as the other species that might well fall into this second category. Whale songs show **distinct**[9] dialects and some populations show other differences, for example in hunting techniques.

D But the international team did find thirty-nine examples of behaviour, including the use of tools, keeping clean and the forming of relationships, that are passed on from generation to generation in some groups, but are **absent**[10] in others.

E The discovery that chimpanzees may possess 'culture' raises an urgent conservation issue. The wild population, estimated at 200,000, faces attack from people who like to eat 'bushmeat', as chimpanzee meat is called.

F Chimpanzees kept in captivity can be taught simple sign language, however. Although few scientists believe they use sign language as a deaf person would, hidden cameras have shown them using signs learned from humans, even when the humans weren't there.

G The first scientist to propose such a change in how we regard animals was Kinja Imanishi in Japan. He observed the spread of potato washing amongst monkeys on the island of Koshima in the 1950s.

H In a recently published study, a group of scientists compared the behaviour of seven separate groups of chimpanzees living in the wild in tropical Africa. They found **extensive**[11] 'cultural variation' between these groups.

Use of English 1: *structural cloze*

▶▶ exam strategy   Paper 3, Part 2 ▶ p.57

1 Read the exam task below, ignoring the gaps for the moment. Ask yourself these questions as you read:

1 How many people are in the story?
2 Where did it take place?
3 Why were the people there?
4 What happened?
5 What is the message of the story?

2 Retell the main points of the story to a partner.

3 Now read the text again and fill in the gaps.

4 Compare your answers with a partner. What kinds of words did you put in the gaps?

Over to you

5 How many ways can you think of in which animals help or provide services for people?

Examples:
*guide dogs for the blind – help blind people to live a normal life
domestic pets – provide companionship*

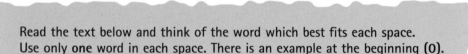

Read the text below and think of the word which best fits each space. Use only **one** word in each space. There is an example at the beginning (0).

SAVED BY DOLPHINS

Attacked by a shark (0) ..*off*.. the coast of Australia, a tourist thought his life was over. But then, miraculously, three dolphins came to (1) .... rescue. They were the same dolphins he (2) .... been playing with a few minutes prior to the shark attack.

Friends on a boat saw exactly (3) .... was happening but could do (4) .... to help. One of them said afterwards, 'If the dolphins hadn't arrived on the scene, it would (5) .... been the end for Tom. We saw him trying to punch the shark to keep it away, but it was hopeless.' The dolphins then turned up (6) .... swam in circles around Tom, keeping the shark (7) .... a distance. They also made a lot of noise (8) .... slapping the water with their fins and tails. This scared the shark off and prevented (9) .... from returning. According to experts, dolphins behave in the (10) .... way when their young (11) .... being attacked.

The dolphins continued to circle (12) .... Tom's friends were able to pull him into the boat. They raced to the shore, where Tom (13) .... given first aid, and then drove him to a local hospital, where he was able to recover from his wounds.

This is just one of many reported cases of dolphins helping humans (14) .... get into trouble in the sea. They seem to regard us (15) .... one of their family.

Grammar: *conditionals*
▶ *pp.182–3*

1 Read the grammar file and complete the example sentences.

grammar files 18, 19

A Real or likely conditions: present/future time

- *If/Unless* + present + present / *may* / *might* / *could* + bare infinitive / imperative OR
- *If/Unless* + present + *will* / modal verb + bare infinitive

1 *If you .... swimming off the Great Barrier Reef, you .... see sharks.* (= possible)

2 *Sharks .... attack people unless they mistake them for seals or dolphins.* (= fact)

B Unlikely/unreal conditions: present/ future time

- *If* + past + *would* / *could* / *might* + bare infinitive

1 *If you knew there .... be sharks, would you go into the sea?* (= hypothetical)

2 *If you .... attacked by a shark, what .... you do?*

C Unreal conditions: past time

- *If* + past perfect + *would* / *could* / *might* + *have* + past participle

1 *If the dolphins .... not defended Tom from the shark attack, he might .... been killed.* (but they did defend him)

2 *If Tom hadn't .... playing with the dolphins earlier, they might .... helped him.*

D Omitting *if*

Had the dolphins not protected Tom, anything could have happened. (= formal)
If the dolphins ....

E Mixed conditionals

1 *If the dolphins hadn't come to the rescue* (= unreal past), *Tom might not be here now* (present).

2 *If Tom weren't a good swimmer* (= unreal present), *he wouldn't have been swimming in the ocean alone* (= unreal past).

3 *If dolphins .... regard humans as friends* (= unreal present), *they .... helped Tom* (= past).

2 **1** Read the following story. Then combine the pairs of sentences using unreal past conditionals. Begin with the word given in brackets.

Last winter, Hans had a very lucky escape …

1 One morning, Hans quarrelled with his friends. They went off for the day without him. (If …)

2 Hans was feeling bored. He decided to go up the mountain, snowboarding. (If …)

3 He didn't listen to the weather warning. He didn't know there was danger of an avalanche in that area. (Had …)

4 He ignored the rumbling noise above him. He continued snowboarding. (If …)

5 He didn't take shelter. He was caught in the avalanche. (Had …)

6 Back at the chalet, his dog sensed something was wrong. He set off to search for Hans. (If …)

7 The dog found Hans's body buried in the snow and dug a hole. Hans had enough air to breathe. (If …)

8 The dog ran off and returned with help. Hans was rescued. (If …)

9 The dog acted intelligently. Hans did not die. (Had …)

2 Now complete this sentence in your own words:

If I had been in the same situation as Hans, I …

3 Have you heard of any similar stories in which animals have helped or rescued people? If so, tell the class.

4 Read the following sentences 1–7, which form a continuous text. Then fill in the gaps with the correct form of the verbs in brackets. You will need to use a variety of conditionals.

1 If you .... (compare) animal with human intelligence, you will find that humans are far superior.

2 A century ago, if you .... (suggest) that animals were intelligent, people .... (think) you were mad.

3 But if you .... (look) more carefully, you .... (discover) that animals' minds are capable of amazing acts.

4 Many animals use tools. They .... (not/be able) to do this if they .... (not/have) some kind of intelligence.

5 If a sea otter .... (want) to open a shell, it .... (dive) to the seabed and returns with a stone. It balances this on its chest and uses it as a tool.

6 This behaviour is not instinctive; scientists tell us that sea otters .... (not/be able) to do this unless they .... (learn) the skill as babies, usually from their mothers.

7 If you study the behaviour of whales and dolphins, you .... (find) that they are highly intelligent, too. If dolphins .... (not/be) so intelligent, the navy .... (not/use) them in the past to hunt for mines underwater.

Listening: *sentence completion*

▶▶ **exam strategy**   Paper 4, Part 2 ▶ p.108

1 Look at the exam task below. Read the instructions and the gapped sentences and answer these questions.

1 How much do you find out about the new scheme?
2 What kind of information is missing in each sentence?

2 📼 Listen to the recording twice and complete the exam task.

You will hear a woman called Anna Fordham talking about a new scheme to reduce car dependence. For questions 1–10, complete the sentences.

Anna is talking about a project called the [_____ 1]

Anna says that people find [_____ 2] is not good enough for their needs.

Anna points out that concerns about [_____ 3] discourage many people from cycling.

A major factor preventing more people from cycling in cities is [_____ 4]

The new project will benefit both commuters and those interested in [_____ 5] cycling.

As many as [_____ 6] people could have easy access to the new routes.

Many cycle ways will follow existing routes such as disused [_____ 7]

Anna reminds us that cycling is recommended by the [_____ 8]

The new routes will be good for young mothers and people who use [_____ 9] as well as cyclists.

It is hoped that the cycle routes will also lead to the development of [_____ 10] and jobs.

Over to you

3 Discuss these questions.

1 What are the key benefits of the scheme you have just heard about?
2 Are there any similar schemes in your country? If not, do you think a scheme like this should be introduced?
3 Are there any drawbacks to the scheme?

4 Using information from the talk, prepare a short speech to persuade your local council to introduce a cycle path scheme in your town.

Speaking:
collaborative task and discussion

▶▶ **exam strategy**
Paper 5, Parts 3 and 4 ▶ p.33/45/82/94

1 Look at the leaflet and the photographs opposite.

1 Describe what you can see in each photo.
2 Think of one benefit and one drawback for each suggestion.

Examples:

If everyone left their car at home, the air would be much less polluted. On the other hand, it would take much longer to get to school and work.

If we grew our own fruit and vegetables, we would be healthier, because it would be pesticide-free. On the other hand, farmers would suffer.

a health risk   toxic waste   recycling facilities
chemical residues in food   water conservation
exhaust fumes   to improve air quality
to reduce the danger of accidents

2 Part 3 task

Work in groups of three.

Student 1: You are the examiner. Give Students 2 and 3 the instructions on page 207. Time them and interrupt if necessary after three minutes.

Students 2 and 3: Listen to the examiner carefully and do the task.

▶ **Functions files 5, 8, 12 and 13 pp.200–201**

> ▶▶ *exam tip!*
>
> Listen carefully to the examiner's instructions. In this task, you should try to agree on two choices that you believe are both practical and effective. ◀◀

3 Part 4 discussion

The examiner should now join in the discussion.

Student 3: You are the examiner. Ask Students 1 and 2 the questions below to develop the topic further. Stop the discussion after four minutes. (Don't worry if you don't manage to ask all the questions.)

Students 1 and 2: Discuss the examiner's questions.

1 Does your family have a car? How often do you use it, and for what purpose?
2 How good is public transport where you live? What improvements can be made, in your opinion?
3 What recycling facilities are there in your town or city?
4 What could you do personally to protect the local environment?
5 What do you think the world will be like in 100 years if we do not change our ways?

A BRIGHT NEW FUTURE FOR PEOPLE, ANIMALS AND THE ENVIRONMENT!

Don't waste water! Collect rainwater for the garden!

Give wildlife a chance! Support local wildlife reserves!

Walking Bus

Reduce traffic congestion around schools! Start a walking bus!

Don't contaminate the earth! Use biodegradable cleaning materials!

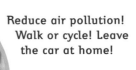

Reduce air pollution! Walk or cycle! Leave the car at home!

No more pesticides! Grow your own fruit and vegetables organically!

Don't waste resources! Recycle everything!

Be kind to animals! Become a vegetarian!

11 | The weather

Lead-in

Look at the words and phrases in the box, which describe different weather conditions.

1 Which weather conditions are illustrated in the photographs on this page?

2 Group the expressions according to the time of year these conditions are most likely to occur in your country. Which types of weather rarely or never occur?

> heavy snowfalls   dense fog   strong winds
> thunder and lightning   freezing cold   scorching sun
> a heatwave   severe floods   soaring temperatures
> violent storms   high humidity   light showers
> pleasant breezes   torrential rain   tornado

Reading 2: *multiple matching*

▶▶ **exam strategy**   Paper 1, Part 1 ▶ p.10

1 Read the instructions for the exam task opposite. Then read the first paragraph.

1 Which of these questions do you think the text will answer? Tick (✓) them.

1 What kinds of weather conditions are especially threatening?
2 How and why do they happen?
3 How do scientists predict these conditions?
4 How accurate are the predictions at the moment?
5 Why is it difficult to make accurate predictions?
6 How much warning do people need?
7 What should people do to prevent damage and loss of life?
8 What kinds of weather conditions are beneficial?

2 Read the text quickly to check your predictions and find the answers.

2 Now do the exam task.

3 Compare your answers with other students. What words helped you to identify the right headings?

> ▶▶ **exam tip!**
>
> If you have problems finding a particular answer, this may mean that you have already used the heading you need for an earlier paragraph. Always be prepared to go back and check.
>
> ◀◀

Vocabulary: *word formation*

4 **1 Complete this table with words from the text. Then fill in the remaining gaps, using your knowledge of word formation rules or a dictionary to help you.**

Verb	Noun	Adjective
threaten	....	....
warn	....	—
....	....	terrified / ....
....	rotation	....
....	prediction	(un)predictable
....	evacuation	—
....	deceit	....
....	trick	....
—	catastrophe	....
—	turbulence	....
—	disaster	....

2 What nouns related to weather conditions can be described by the adjectives you have listed?

Example: *terrifying storms*

Over to you

5 **Read the text again and make a note of three facts that you found especially interesting. Compare your facts with other students.**

You are going to read an extract from a book about extreme weather conditions. Choose the most suitable heading from the list **A–I** for each part (1–7) of the article. There is one extra heading which you do not need to use. There is an example at the beginning (0).

A A dangerous mission
B Further consequences
C A difficult decision
D A terrifying prediction
E A means of identification
F At greatest risk
G Traditional wisdom
H Mysterious origins
I Continuing research

The coiled serpent

0 I

Bad weather often disrupts our well-ordered plans, but occasionally it can become so extreme and violent that it threatens our homes, possessions and even our lives. That is why scientists are always 5 studying threatening weather conditions in the hope of finding better ways to predict more accurately where and when they might occur, so that timely warnings can be given and appropriate action taken to avoid damage and loss of life.

1

10 One of the worst weather hazards faced by people in tropical areas is the storm known as a hurricane or cyclone. This is a rotating storm about 800 kilometres across. Around one hundred of these storms form across the world's oceans each year, 15 causing an enormous amount of damage when they hit land. They are so frequent in the Atlantic that each one is given the name of a person, starting with the letter A at the beginning of the year and then working through the alphabet.

2

20 The process by which an ordinary rainstorm changes into a hurricane involves so many unknown factors that meteorologists can only identify what they think happens. In the Atlantic, the starting point for many such storms is a calm area known as 25 the Doldrums. The calm is, however, deceptive because from time to time the stillness of the Doldrums is broken by violent thunderstorms. Most of these storms travel thousands of miles westwards and just die out, but occasionally, for 30 reasons that are unclear, one will develop into an extremely dangerous cyclone.

3

The movement and characteristics of these tropical hurricanes are closely monitored by satellites and radar as well as by aircraft, whose pilots fly bravely 35 into the turbulent clouds of the hurricane to record wind speeds and air pressure. However, even with such detailed information, predicting the course of a hurricane remains extremely difficult.

4

It is nonetheless important for forecasts to be 40 accurate, because the question of when and how to best prepare for a hurricane is a tricky one. If the alarm is raised, whole communities may be forced to abandon their homes. If there are too many false alarms, people may decide not to bother leaving 45 next time, with disastrous consequences. Obviously a short-term warning of, say, twelve hours is more likely to be accurate, but the time needed for evacuation is often considerably longer than that.

5

Perhaps coastal residents should follow the example 50 of the Seminole Indians of Florida and observe the behaviour of birds, rats, wolves and even alligators to know whether a hurricane is going to strike. In one year, Florida was the target of two hurricanes. The Seminoles left the area as the first storm 55 threatened, whereas the National Weather Bureau forecast it would miss Florida. For the second hurricane, the Seminoles stayed put, while the Weather Bureau issued an evacuation warning. The Seminoles were correct both times.

6

60 The threat to island and coastal communities from tropical cyclones comes from a combination of enormous wind speeds, high seas and heavy rainfall. A measure of the potential violence of a hurricane is the air pressure in the centre of the storm. The 65 lower the pressure, the stronger the wind speeds, the higher the seas, and the heavier the rainfall. In affected areas, low-lying coastal communities with high population densities are always working to be prepared for the worst.

7

70 Once they reach land, hurricanes begin to die, cut off from their source of energy, but they can give rise to tornadoes. These are black, twisting clouds that suddenly appear from nowhere, travel at terrifying speed, move in unpredictable ways and 75 cause catastrophic damage in seconds. Their small size and brief duration makes forecasting when and where they are likely to strike extremely difficult.

Vocabulary

1 What is the greenhouse effect?

Look at the diagram of the greenhouse effect. Write the correct number from Box A to label the diagram. Then complete the summary with the words from Box B in the correct form.

A
1 cutting down trees
2 vehicle exhausts
3 burning of fossil fuels
4 power stations

B
balance   give off
forests   coal   trap

How the greenhouse effect works

Energy from the Sun

Heat trapped by carbon dioxide in the atmosphere

Heat

Gases like (1) *carbon dioxide* are important for the Earth's temperature. They let heat from the Sun reach the ground, and keep it there. In this way, they help to keep the Earth's temperature at the ideal level. However, human activities are destroying the natural (2) .... of these gases. When we burn fossil fuels like (3) ...., oil and gas, we produce too much carbon dioxide (CO_2). This CO_2 collects in the atmosphere and (4) .... too much heat. We make the problem worse when we cut down (5) .... Living trees absorb carbon dioxide and (6) .... oxygen, but when we cut trees down we release carbon dioxide back into the atmosphere.

2 Phrasal verbs

Replace the words in *italics* with a phrasal verb from the box in the correct form. There are two verbs that you won't need.

give in to   cut down on   use up
give up   face up to   run out of
do away with

1 Our planet is in great danger. We all need to *accept and deal with* the challenges if we are to avoid disaster.
2 We will probably *no longer have enough* oil in the next 60 years, so we need to develop renewable energy sources such as wind power.
3 Natural resources like wood and coal are being *finished* at an ever-increasing rate.
4 We ought to *reduce* the amount of energy we use; for example, we should switch off lights when we leave a room.
5 We ought to *stop* using cars for unnecessary journeys and use public transport instead.

3 Choosing the right word

Underline the correct word in each pair. Then answer the questions with a partner.

1 How many *species/forms* of birds can you name in English?
2 Which animals may become *vanished/extinct* in the near future?
3 What kinds of crops are *grown/grown up* in your country?
4 What do scientists mean by *soil/earth* erosion and what causes it? Is it a problem in your country?
5 What sort of animals and fish live off the *coast/beach* of your country, e.g. whales, dolphins?
6 What happens to wildlife if oil tankers *dump/drop* oil in the seas?
7 Have you had any wildlife *catastrophes/misfortunes* related to pollution in your country recently?

Use of English 2: *lexical cloze*

▶▶ *exam strategy*   Paper 3, Part 1 ▶ p.13

1 **Read the text opposite all the way through, ignoring the gaps for the moment.**

1 What information does it give about the causes and effects of global warming?

2 According to the text, what will happen if we don't do something about it now?

2 **Now complete the exam task. Read the gapped sentences very carefully. Remember, to help you choose the right word, you should:**

- pay careful attention to meaning.
- be aware of grammatical patterns such as prepositions after nouns and verbs, and infinitives after verbs.
- look out for collocations and fixed phrases.
- make sure that linking words fit the meaning of the text.

3 **Read the whole text again and find:**

1 four examples of verb + particle or preposition

2 two collocations with *take*

3 one collocation with *have*

Have you already got these items in your vocabulary notebook? If not, add them, and write an example sentence to help you remember the meaning.

Read the text below and decide which answer **A, B, C** or **D** best fits each space. There is an example at the beginning (**0**).

0   A recognised   B regarded   C registered   D represented

GLOBAL WARMING

The Earth's climate is a very complicated system. What's more, it is now widely (**0**) *A* that human activity is having an effect on it. The pollution which (**1**) ..... from the use of oil and coal in industry, (**2**) ..... the increased use of private cars, is causing significant changes in temperature in many parts of the world. These changes often have a knock-on effect on other aspects of the climate, (**3**) ..... to things like extreme weather (**4**) ..... and rising sea levels. Studying the changes which are taking (**5**) ..... and predicting those that are (**6**) ..... to happen in the future is now a major area of scientific research. The information which the scientists (**7**) ..... is very useful in helping governments to (**8**) ..... the effects of climate change and so be better prepared to (**9**) ..... with them.

A much more (**10**) ..... problem, however, is how to prevent the situation from (**11**) ..... worse. This depends on how quickly, and to what extent, the (**12**) ..... of pollution in the atmosphere increases. Although many countries have now agreed to try and limit the pollution they create, much more (**13**) ..... to be done. If no further action is (**14**) ....., then temperatures are set to rise by about 0.2% per decade (**15**) ..... the 21st century. Such a rate of warming is greater than anything that has occurred over the last ten thousand years.

1	A recovers	B concludes	C results	D happens
2	A as far as	B as soon as	C as long as	D as well as
3	A leading	B causing	C finishing	D producing
4	A examples	B conditions	C cases	D instances
5	A point	B part	C path	D place
6	A surely	B probably	C likely	D possibly
7	A provide	B progress	C prove	D propose
8	A prevent	B pretend	C predict	D prefer
9	A handle	B face	C manage	D cope
10	A serious	B determined	C thoughtful	D anxious
11	A going	B giving	C getting	D gaining
12	A addition	B amount	C average	D account
13	A needs	B wants	C wishes	D hopes
14	A held	B taken	C made	D carried
15	A already	B during	C while	D still

Writing: *discursive composition*

exam file

In **Paper 2**, **Part 2**, you may be asked to write a discursive composition in which you offer solutions to a problem.

▶▶ *exam strategy*

Make sure you:

- don't try to include too many points. Three or four will usually be enough.
- support the points you make with explanations and/or examples.
- organise your points into clear paragraphs and use linking words to show the connection between your ideas.

1 Read the writing task below.

1 Underline the key words in the task.

> Your class has recently had a discussion on global warming. Your teacher has now asked you to write a composition giving your opinion on the following question:
>
> *What should we all do to help reduce global warming?*
>
> Write your composition in 120–180 words in an appropriate style.

2 Should the style of your composition be formal, neutral or informal?

2 Work with a partner.

1 Brainstorm ideas and useful vocabulary for the writing task.

2 Tick (✓) three or four points which you feel you can develop in your composition. Decide in what order you will deal with them, and number them, as in the example below.

Problems	Solutions
1 deforestation	*recycle waste*
traffic	*1 plant trees*
	use public transport

3 Decide how many paragraphs you will need and make a paragraph plan. (See Unit 8, Exercise 2 page 100.)

3 Which of the following would provide the best introduction to the sample composition below? Why? What is wrong with the others?

1 *We are all worried about global warming but we don't do enough about it.*

2 *Global warming is known to be damaging our planet. Weather patterns are changing and it is feared that the ice caps are melting. It is not too late to halt the process but we all need to play our part.*

3 *What can we do to solve the problem of pollution? Everywhere we see signs that our environment is being poisoned. It is time to act.*

Introduction

....

Body

    There are many ways we can help. The use of fossil fuels is said to be one of the main factors affecting the atmosphere. We should persuade our governments to use alternative sources of energy, like solar power. Traffic pollution adds to global warming so we should use public transport more. If bus and train services aren't good, we should make our governments improve them. We should stop buying things with a lot of packaging because it contains materials that damage the atmosphere. Moreover, old refrigerators that still contain CFC coolants should be disposed of safely and not left in the streets. We must stop cutting down trees. They are said to be 'the lungs of the Earth' because they absorb carbon dioxide and produce oxygen, so we should think about planting trees wherever and whenever we can.

Conclusion

    I believe we can all do something about global warming, and we must. If we ignore the problem, the consequences will be disastrous.

Focus on organisation

4 Answer these questions about the sample composition.

1 How many main points does the writer make? What solutions does he suggest? Put them in two columns.

2 The writer should have divided the body of the composition into more paragraphs. Mark where you think paragraph breaks could come.

3 The composition would be much easier to read (and get a better mark) if the writer had used linking words to list the points in his argument. Choose an appropriate expression from each group below and mark where you think it should go.

1 A At first,	B In the beginning,	C First of all,
2 A Secondly,	B In second place,	C In second,
3 A Beside,	B Thirdly,	C As well,
4 A Finally,	B In the end,	C At the conclusion,
5 A At the end,	B To sum up,	C Last but not least,

Focus on grammar ▶ *p.184*

5 **1** Read the examples of impersonal passive constructions in the grammar file. Then read the sample composition in Exercise 3 again. How many examples can you find in it?

grammar file 21

The following reporting verbs are often used in the impersonal patterns below: *allege, believe, claim, expect, fear, know, report, say, think, understand.*

1 *People* **say** *that the recent extreme weather* **is** *due to global warming.*
   ➔ **It is said** *that the recent extreme weather is due to global warming.*
   The recent extreme weather **is said to be** *due to global warming.*

2 *Scientists* **think** *that the polar ice caps* **are melting**.
   ➔ **It is thought** *that the polar ice caps* **are melting**.
   The polar ice caps **are thought to be melting**.

3 *They* **expect** *that sea levels* **will rise** *by 20–40 cm in the 21st century.*
   ➔ **It is expected** *that sea levels will rise by 20–40 cm in the 21st century.*
   Sea levels **are expected to rise** *by 20–40 cm in the 21st century.*

4 *Naturalists* **believe** *that many species of animals* **have become extinct**.
   ➔ **It is believed** *that many species of animals* **have become extinct**.
   Many species of animals **are believed to have become extinct**.

2 Rewrite these sentences as in the example.

Example:

It is **said** that the Earth is in danger.
The Earth *is said to be in danger*.

1 It is **claimed** that pollution from factories and cars is poisoning our planet.
Pollution from ....

2 It is **thought** that a third of the world's rainforests have been destroyed.
A third ....

3 It is **expected** that we will have run out of oil by the end of the century.
We are ....

4 Cutting down trees is **believed** to have caused the recent severe floods in many parts of the world.
It is ....

5 Temperatures are **expected** to continue rising by about 0.2% per decade.
It is ....

Over to you

6 Write your answer to the following task in 120–180 words in an appropriate style. Follow the advice in the exam strategy box. Remember to:

- make a plan before you start to write.
- divide your composition into clear paragraphs.
- write a suitable introduction and conclusion for your composition; avoid repeating points that you have already made in your conclusion.
- check your writing for errors when you have finished.

Your class has been doing a project on animals in danger. As part of this project, your teacher has asked you to write a composition giving your opinion on the following question.

What can be done to save endangered animals?

Write your composition.

12 Careers

Lead-in

Look at the photos of people doing different jobs. Compare and contrast the jobs. Talk about these points:

1 What skills and qualifications do you need for each job?
2 What do you think each job involves? For example:
   • working on your own/with others   • a lot of travel
   • working indoors/outdoors   • lots of variety
   • working under pressure
3 What personal qualities does each job require?

> drive   commitment   patience   initiative   maturity
> imagination   resourcefulness   a sense of humour

Reading 1: *multiple matching*

▶▶ *exam strategy*   Paper 1, Part 4 ▶ p.46

1 Read the instructions for the exam task opposite and discuss these questions.

1 What do you have to do?
2 Does this type of task test your ability to:
   a) read and understand a text in detail?
   b) understand the writer's main message?
   c) find specific items of information in a text?
3 What will you read first, the text or the questions?
4 Do you need to understand every word in the text in order to answer the questions? Why/Why not?

2 Do the multiple-matching task.

3 Compare your answers with the class. What phrases helped you to find the answers?

Example:
Question 0: *keep up-to-date* with the latest developments
Text A: *stay abreast of* what's going on

Over to you

4 1 Read the article again. Choose which job you would most/least like to do and say why.

2 Add any useful vocabulary related to jobs to your vocabulary notebook.

5 Think about other students in the class. What jobs do you think they will be doing in 10 years' time? Justify your ideas.

You are going to read an article about five people and the careers they have chosen. Answer the questions by choosing from the people A–E. The people may be chosen more than once. When more than one answer is required, these may be given in any order. There is an example at the beginning (0).

Write: **A** = Andrew   **C** = Carl   **E** = Eric
        B = Barbara   **D** = Diane

Which of Colin's classmates

says his/her job involves keeping up-to-date with the latest developments?	**0 A**
wasn't paid for the work he/she did at first?	**1**
has already been promoted to a more responsible position?	**2**
feels there were some pros and cons of the course he/she took?	**3**
finds the unpredictable nature of the job exciting?	**4**
feels that people may have the wrong idea about his/her job?	**5**
is involved in planning activities for other people?	**6**
has plans to branch out into another line of business?	**7**
is optimistic about his/her future career prospects?	**8**
says he/she worked with a more experienced colleague at first?	**9** **10**
explains how his/her job can be physically demanding?	**11**
has to try and raise money to support the work he/she does?	**12**
failed to complete a course of study?	**13** **14**
says that he/she has to work with some difficult people?	**15**

Class of 2000

Do you ever wonder what will become of your classmates? Can you spot who's going to become famous, travel the world or get a really interesting job? Colin Bacon decided to look up some people he'd known at secondary school to find out just that.

The first person I found was **Andrew**. He'd always wanted to work in the music industry. He reminded me, 'As a student, I used to do DJ work at the weekends. The academic side of university wasn't my main priority. After graduation, I did temporary jobs before getting into a record  company as assistant to the marketing manager. I learned a lot from him and progressed quickly. I'm now in charge of signing new bands. A typical week involves meetings with artists and producers, and I have to stay abreast of what's going on in the music world. No two days are ever the same in this job and an average day can change in an instant if you hear a new band and you realise you're on to something big. The thrill of that makes all the dull days worthwhile.'

Barbara was much more of a shock. She was always rather quiet at school. She explained, 'After school I got a place at Art College to do a four-year degree, but after a year I had a change of heart and swapped to a Geography degree which I thought was more interesting. On that course, I met up with some people who were thinking of joining the army. I suddenly realised it was just the thing for me too. After graduation, I spent a year doing officer training and then shadowed another officer for two months before getting my own first commission.' She now has fifty-five soldiers under her command. 'Promotion depends on performance and time served, but I hope to have been promoted to the rank of captain in two years' time.'

Carl was always a patient sort, so I wasn't surprised to find him still in the classroom. He told me,

'In my last year at school, I considered teaching as a career, but I ended up doing two years of a medical degree instead, because that was the advice I was given at the time. I never really felt committed to it, however, and after two years switched to Biology and returned to my original plan. I chose a very practical training course where I spent a lot of time in schools rather than in a lecture theatre. The advantage is that you build up a teaching style quite quickly, but you do miss out a bit on the educational theory behind it. I now work in an inner-city secondary school and the challenge is motivating the rather troublesome pupils to learn.'

Biggest shock of all was **Diane**. She was quite scruffy at school and the last person I expected to be working as a fashion model. As she explained, 'Anyone who says you become a model just because you're pretty is totally wrong. To be successful you need personality, drive, maturity as well as good looks. A model's job involves getting up early, performing miracles in front of the camera even when you feel awful, and then staying miles away from home because you've got to do it all again tomorrow. It is often exhausting. It's glamorous enough if you make it to the top, but most don't. Fortunately, I'm building up the experience necessary to start my own agency because modelling is not something you can do forever.'

And finally, I tracked down **Eric**. He works from home, but spends a lot of his time in the great outdoors. As he told me, 'I completed a degree in Zoology and because I've always been interested in the sea, I started doing voluntary work with the Marine Conservation Trust while I was looking for a job.  It wasn't long before I got taken on to the staff, however, and I'm now their education officer. This involves responding to telephone enquiries from the public and setting up courses for people who want to come and study the seashore. I also have to do things like go round companies and try to get sponsorship for our schemes.'

Grammar: *hypothetical meaning* ▶ *p.183*

grammar file 20

We use *wish/if only* to express wishes and regrets. *If only* is slightly more emphatic.

A Wishes about the present: *wish/ if only* + past simple/continuous

1 *I wish I could* find a job. (= but I can't)
2 *If only I knew* what job I'd be best at! (= but I don't)
3 *I wish I wasn't* (informal) */weren't* (formal) *starting* work so soon. (= but I am)

B Wishes/regrets about the past: *wish/if only* + past perfect

1 *I wish I hadn't given up* my university course. (= but I did)
2 *If only I had done* some practical training!* (= but I didn't)

C Wishes about the future: *wish/if only* + would/could + bare infinitive

1 *I wish I/we could work* abroad next year, but I/we can't. (NOT ~~I wish I/we would~~)
2 *My parents keep nagging me about my future career! I wish they would stop*. (= a complaint about a person)
3 *I'm going to be late for this interview. I wish/If only the train would come!* (= a wish about a situation)

grammar file 20

A *It's time to do* or *It's time you did*?

- **For statements of fact, use: *it's time* + *to*-infinitive**
  It's six o'clock. It's time (for us) to stop work.

- **For something that should be done now/very soon, or that should have been done before, use: *It's (about/high) time* + person + past simple/continuous**
  1 *Don't you think it's time you had a haircut?* (= an implied criticism)
  2 *It's midnight! It's (about) time you were going home.* (= you should go home now)

B *would rather*

- **To express personal preferences, use: *would rather* + bare infinitive**
  1 *I'd rather go to university than start work straight from school.*
  2 *Would you rather be a doctor or a lawyer?*

- **To say what we would prefer other people (not) to do, use: *would rather* + person + past simple/past perfect**
  1 *I'd rather the meeting started a little earlier.* (= present time)
  2 *Don't phone me at work. I'd rather you phoned me at home this evening.* (= future time)
  3 *I'd rather you hadn't told the boss about the delay.* (= past time)

---

1 **Choose the correct form of the verb in each sentence.**

1 My sister doesn't like her job. She wishes she *stayed/had stayed* at college longer.
2 I've got to find a job as soon as I leave school but I wish I *could/would* go to college.
3 He doesn't know what career to choose when he leaves school. He wishes his teachers *will give/would give* him more advice.
4 John hates commuting every day. He wishes his workplace *is/was* a bit nearer home.
5 I'd like to study all the time. If only I *didn't need/don't need* to work at all!
6 We can't afford to go on holiday. I wish we *would earn/earned* a bit more money!
7 I'd get a better job if I could speak English well. If only I *paid/had paid* more attention when I was at school!
8 My boss never listens to me. I wish I *were/would be* a bit more assertive!

2 **Use your imagination to complete the sentences in a logical way.**

1 It's time you .... You've been working all day!
2 It's hard to find a job in this village. I wish we ....
3 I'd rather you ...... in class. It's so annoying.
4 I didn't know anything about the job vacancy. If only I ...... the advertisement sooner!
5 Don't you think it's time you ...... ? You're the only one in the family who can't!
6 I wish the job agency .... I've been waiting to hear about the job for days.
7 My boss keeps giving me extra work. I wish he ....
8 I'd rather you ...... tonight. You have a job interview tomorrow.

Over to you

3 **Tell your partner about three things:**

a) that you wish were different now
   Example: *I wish the weather was/were better.*

b) that you wish would happen/you could do in the future
   Example: *If only I could get a job in films.*

c) that you regret about the past
   Example: *I wish I hadn't broken your CD player.*

d) that should be done now
   Example: *It's time we had a party.*

Use of English 1: *error correction*

▶▶ *exam strategy*　　　Paper 3, Part 4 ▶ p.69

1 **Read the title of the text below and discuss these questions.**

1 Is it common for young people to do holiday jobs in your country?
2 What kind of holiday jobs can they do?

2 **Read the text all the way through and answer these questions.**

1 What kind of job did the writer do?
2 Was it an enjoyable experience for him/her?

▶▶ **exam tip!**

Between three and five lines will be correct. Don't leave blanks to indicate correct lines. Always put a tick (✓).

3 **Now do the exam task.**

4 **Compare your answers with a partner when you have finished. How did you score?**

5 **Which grammatical areas do you still need to work on for the exam? Make a revision table based on your answers in the exam task. Find the unit and the grammar file that deals with each area. Study the grammar file in the unit and at the end of the book. For practice, do the exercises in the relevant unit again.**

Example:

Line	Grammar point	Unit	Grammar file
0	*quantifiers*	8	2
1	*present perfect/past*	1, 2	6, 8
7	*relative clauses*	....	....

Read the text below and look carefully at each line. Some of the lines are correct, and some have a word which should not be there. If a line is correct, put a tick (✓) in the space by the number. If a line has a word which should not be there, write the word in the space. There are two examples at the beginning (**0** and **00**).

A HOLIDAY JOB

0	*of*	So you want to earn some of extra money during the summer
00	✓	holidays? I can tell you one job that I'd certainly avoid if I were
1	......	you. Last year, I have heard that an easy way to make some extra
2	......	cash was to go on fruit picking. You don't need any special skills
3	......	and you spend all day outside in the sunshine. I wish I had known
4	......	what I was letting it myself in for! Basically, you have to fill up
5	......	baskets with strawberries which are then weighed and then you
6	......	get paid according to how much you have and picked. Of course,
7	......	they don't pay you anything for the ones what you eat, but after a
8	......	few days in the fields, I never been wanted to see another strawberry
9	......	again in my life! My hands were permanently red and sticky and my
10	......	back ached from so much all bending down. And what's more, where
11	......	there's fruit, there's bound to be wasps. I spent a fortune on both insect
12	......	repellent and still got stung twice! The best way to make it fun is if only
13	......	a crowd of mates do it together, but the farmers are not always so keen
14	......	on this because they think as you're going to fool around and not get on
15	......	with the work. Given that it was so much boring, they were absolutely right!

Listening: yes/no *answers*

1 **Read the instructions for the exam task opposite and answer the questions.**

1 What is the subject of the radio programme you are going to hear?
2 Why do you think some young people decide to do this? What kind of things do you think they do during this year?

2 **Read the statements 1–7 and underline key words. What do you need to listen for?**

3 📼 **Listen to the recording twice and complete the exam task.**

▶▶ *exam tip!*

If you are not sure what the answer is first time, don't worry. Go on to the next question. You can check your answers on the second listening. ◀◀

4 📼 **Compare your answers. If you have different answers, listen to the recording again, and listen out for the parts that give the answers.**

Over to you

5 **Discuss these questions.**

1 After hearing the recording, do you think you would like to take a year off between school and further education? What do you think would be the main benefits? For example, you can:

• become more mature and self-reliant
• broaden your skills/learn practical skills
• explore your interests before making a decision
• learn to work with other people in a team
• see a range of things you wouldn't otherwise see
• meet new people and learn about different cultures

2 Are there any ways it could disadvantage you when you return to finish your education?
3 Do you know anyone who has done a gap year? Tell the class about it. What did they feel they gained from it?

You will hear part of a radio programme about the value of a 'gap year', where young people take a year off between school and further education. For questions 1–7, decide which views are expressed by any of the speakers and which are not. In the boxes provided write YES next to those views which are expressed and NO next to those views which are not expressed.

1	You may be asked to justify your choice of gap year activity.	1
2	My parents were opposed to the idea of a gap year.	2
3	I appreciated the opportunity to work independently.	3
4	I feel guilty about leaving my original job.	4
5	I changed my plans to fit in with my friends.	5
6	I am grateful for the help I got from an agency.	6
7	My long-term plans were realised.	7

Volunteers at a summer camp for children in the USA

Speaking: *individual long turn*

▶▶ *exam strategy*

Paper 5, Part 2 ▶ p.21/59

1 **Work in groups of three.**

Student 1: You are the examiner. Give the candidates the instructions on page 206. Time each candidate. If necessary, interrupt Candidate A after one minute. Don't give Candidate B more than about 20 seconds to comment.

Student 2: You are Candidate A. Compare and contrast the two photos on this page, according to the examiner's instructions. You have one minute.

> to get work experience
> a classroom assistant
> to take responsibility for others
> to do voluntary work   to dig a well
> a bucket   conservation work
> to work as a team

▶ **Functions files 1 and 5 p.200**

Student 3: You are Candidate B. The examiner will ask you to comment on the two photos briefly after Candidate A has finished. You should take about 20 seconds for this.

2 **Turn to the photos on page 206. Work in groups of three as in Exercise 1. The examiner should give the instructions on page 207.**

▶ **Functions files 1 and 8 p.200**

Lead-in

1 Look at the photos on this page.
Compare and contrast the photos, using words and expressions from the box. Say how much satisfaction the young people are getting from what they are doing.

to play the violin / cello / drums / flute / keyboards
a steel band   modern dance   to train   to rehearse
to put on a play   to have fun

2 Discuss these questions.
1 Do schools do enough to encourage students to develop their talents in the arts?
2 What more could they do?

Reading 2: *multiple-choice questions*

▶▶ *exam strategy*   Paper 1, Part 2 ▶ p.22

1 Do the exam task, using the strategy you have learned.

You are going to read a newspaper article about a musician. For each of the questions, choose the answer (A, B, C or D) which you think fits best according to the text.

Rising star

At the age of 18, Hilary Hahn has the focus and self-possession to promise a bright career as an international soloist.

Hilary Hahn is one of the best young solo violinists to emerge in the world of classical music. With tied-back hair and china-doll features, Hilary seems
much younger than her years, but in fact she is quite mature enough to face up to the
5 competitive demands of the concert hall.

Brought up in the US city of Baltimore, Hilary first reached for the violin when she was three. Shortly before her fourth birthday, she joined a class of pre-school children all keen to learn to play the instrument. She quickly gained an understanding of her own progress. 'There were always children ahead of me and children behind me, so it helped to see that with time
10 and practice, I could really become a better player,' she recalls. It wasn't long before she was making her first public performance and winning her first competition. Then, at the age of just ten, she got a place at the prestigious Curtis Institute of Music in Philadelphia.

Now, when she is not touring, Hilary's time is divided between her family home in Baltimore and her flat near the Curtis Institute's classrooms in Philadelphia. She spends
15 much of her time with her father, who has joined her in Philadelphia to take on the role of full-time assistant and touring companion. Her mother, Anne, lives and works as a tax accountant in Baltimore. Although both parents share a casual interest in music, neither could have anticipated the outcome of Hilary's brilliant playing. 'Dad keeps me company, goes out, gets food and answers the phone when I'm practising,' says Hilary.
20 There is always the danger that such prodigious talent can fall into the wrong hands. But Hilary has been lucky enough to gain further support from the team of teachers and colleagues who surround her. David Zinman, a violinist with the Baltimore Orchestra, first heard Hilary when she was rehearsing for a competition at the Baltimore Symphony Hall. Since then he has monitored her progress, helping her in the transition from enthusiast

2 **Compare your answers with the class.**

Over to you

3 **Read the text again.**

1 What aspects of Hilary's life would you find a) most appealing?
   b) hardest to cope with?
2 What special qualities do you think are necessary for someone
   to make a successful career as a professional musician or artist?

25 to professional. Together with her teachers, David has kept a **watchful eye** on
her progress.

   David advised Hilary not to commit herself to too many concerts too soon. 'He
always told me to keep performing, but not to make it my whole life,' she recalls.
Although Hilary spends up to six hours a day in the Curtis Institute's practice rooms,
30 she is keen to maintain a life beyond her studies. 'Some people could say I do
nothing other than study music, that I haven't had much of a life. But that's not true
because I've always had a lot of friends, and still have some very good ones actually.
Some kids focus on sports, some on academic study and I'm the same, except that
my focus is on music.'

35   As Hilary recounts her childhood, you can't help feeling that even she is
surprised by her success. 'The last seven years have gone like a blur, I feel like I've just
been carried along by **it all**.' She has shown, however, that she is more than capable
of making her own decisions about what music she plays. On her highly praised first
recording, released last year, she played a selection of Bach sonatas which are
40 difficult enough to challenge people twice her age.

   But Hilary is in no hurry to take to the road full-time. Although the world of
international concert tours is available to her, she will for the moment continue with
her studies in Philadelphia and look forward to each new performance that comes
her way. 'Staying at school gives me the time to think,' says Hahn. She is determined
45 not to burn out before reaching musical maturity as so many child prodigies do.
'I want to continue doing the same as I have done up until now. I've achieved a lot
already, but there is so much that I have yet to do.'

1 When Hilary first went to violin
  lessons she was

  A aware of how good she was.
  B jealous of more able children.
  C impatient with less able children.
  D worried about her rate of progress.

2 How do Hilary's parents feel about
  her success?

  A They are not really interested in it.
  B It is the fulfilment of their dreams.
  C They regret the disruption to
    their lives.
  D It took them very much by surprise.

3 David Zinman first recognised Hilary's
  talent when she

  A was playing in an orchestra.
  B was taking part in a competition.
  C was practising for a performance.
  D was having a violin lesson.

4 What does the expression 'watchful
  eye' in line 25 tell us about David's
  attitude to Hilary?

  A He doesn't trust her.
  B He wants to help her.
  C He is ambitious for her.
  D He is aware of her weaknesses.

5 How does Hilary feel about her way
  of life?

  A She'd like to see more of her
    friends.
  B She'd like to develop other
    interests.
  C She thinks she's similar to other
    teenagers.
  D She thinks she's spent too long
    studying music.

6 What does 'it all' in line 37 refer to?
  A her childhood
  B her success
  C her surprise
  D her material

7 From what we learn in the article,
  how can Hilary best be described?

  A She's committed to what she does.
  B She enjoys being the centre of
    attention.
  C She has a wide range of abilities.
  D She's keen to take advantage of
    all opportunities.

Vocabulary

1 Choosing the right word

Underline the correct word in each pair. Then ask and answer the questions with a partner.

1 Have you ever *filled in/filled up* an application form for a job? If so, what sort of job was it? Did you get it?

2 Would you prefer a job where you could work *overtime/flexitime* and start and finish when you liked?

3 What sort of salary are you hoping to *earn/win* in your career?

4 What careers do you think offer the best opportunities of *promotion/progression* to the top posts?

5 Do you think your teacher would give you a good character *reference/testimonial* if you needed one for a job?

6 Do you know how many people are *without work/out of work* in your country?

7 Have you done any work *experience/practice*? If so, where?

8 At what age can people *resign/retire* in your country? In Britain, it's 65.

2 Prepositions and prepositional phrases

Complete the sentences with a preposition from the list. (You will need to use some of the prepositions more than once.) Then ask and answer the questions with a partner.

for / at / on / about / out of / in / with / of / from

1 What sort of career do you think would be suitable .... your best friend?

2 What sort of job would *you* prefer? Would you be more successful .... business or the arts?

3 Are you ambitious? Will you be satisfied .... a junior position or do you want to get to the top of your career?

4 Do you think you would get tired .... doing the same job every day?

5 Do you enjoy working in a team or do you prefer doing things .... your own way?

6 What do you think you will be good .... in your job?

7 Would you enjoy working .... the financial field? How would you feel .... being responsible .... the firm's finances?

8 Would you resign .... your job if the boss asked you to do something you didn't want to do?

9 Do you believe workers should be legally entitled to go .... strike?

10 Can you use a keyboard? If so, can you type fast or are you .... practice?

3 What's important in a job?

1 What is most important for you in a job? Choose the five most important features from this list and put them in order of importance for you (most important = number 1).

- [ ] variety
- [ ] doing something useful for other people
- [ ] good prospects of promotion
- [ ] job security
- [ ] working in a team
- [ ] a good salary
- [ ] flexible working hours
- [ ] job satisfaction
- [ ] convenient location
- [ ] pleasant surroundings
- [ ] overtime possibilities
- [ ] perks (e.g. a company car, free health insurance)
- [ ] independence
- [ ] age of retirement
- [ ] a good pension
- [ ] plenty of time for other things outside work

2 What else do you look for in a job? Can you add items to the list?

4 Word formation

1 Complete these sentences with the right form of the word in capitals.

1 Some young people feel rather .... about the future of work. WORRY

2 As a result of .... advances, traditional patterns of work are changing rapidly. TECHNOLOGY

3 The number of .... jobs available, such as routine assembly work in factories, is falling. SKILL

4 Fortunately, for those with determination and .... , the future should hold no fears. IMAGINE

5 In the past, people often worked for the same company all their lives, but this is changing, so more .... will be required from the workforce. FLEXIBLE

6 There will be more part-time or temporary contracts, but these can benefit the .... as well as the employer. EMPLOY

7 The full-time worker may feel .... to do unpaid overtime to finish a piece of work, whereas a part-time worker would not. OBLIGE

8 Self-investment in expertise, skills and personal qualities is .... essential if a young person is to succeed in the 21st-century job market. ABSOLUTE

2 What's your opinion? Do you feel optimistic about the future of work or not?

Use of English 2: *word formation*

▶▶ *exam strategy*   Paper 3, Part 5 ▶ p.49

1 Do the exam task below, using the strategy you have learned.

Read the text below. Use the word given in capitals at the end of each line to form a word that fits in the space in the same line. There is an example at the beginning (0).

SUCCESS AT LAST

After leaving university, Martin couldn't find any kind of (0) *employment*,	EMPLOY
no matter how hard he tried. But finally he found a (1) ..... to his	SOLVE
problem. His friends found his idea completely (2) ..... . In fact,	BELIEVE
some of them said it was absolutely (3) ..... and told him he had	COMIC
no hope of success. However, Martin now runs a (4) ..... business	GLOBE
and his (5) ..... are truly astounding. He employs hundreds of	ACHIEVE
people all over the world and is now a (6) ..... . Martin says,	MILLION
'I didn't ever think I would live in (7) ..... but I am surprised	POOR
at how rich I have become.' Martin is the (8) ..... of a system	CREATE
which can improve your memory. 'I learned how to (9) ..... long	MEMORY
lists of almost anything and I'm very (10) ..... that I have been	PRIDE
able to develop my skill into a business.	

2 Adjectives from nouns and verbs

1 Make adjectives from the words in the box and put them in the correct column in the table. Be careful of spelling!

help	fun	achieve	critic	compete	predict	music	create
success	sleep	hope	optimist	suit	imagination	memory
profession	product	luck	tradition	photograph

-able	-al	-ful	-ic	-ive	-y
believable	*technological*	*skilful*	*pessimistic*	....	....
....	....	....	....	....	....
....	....	....	....	....	
....	....	....			
....	....				

2 Which of the adjectives in the table can you make negative using a prefix or suffix?

Over to you

3 Work in groups. Look at the headlines below. Can you think of any other real-life examples of simple ideas that were developed into successful businesses? Then try to come up with an idea of your own.

EX-PUPIL WHOSE MATHS PROJECT GREW INTO A COMPUTER FIRM

New range launched

– clothes designed by teenagers for teenagers

Writing: *transactional letter*

exam file

In **Paper 2**, **Part 1**, you may be asked to write a letter, formal or informal, summarising information contained in maps, diagrams or timetables.

►► *exam strategy*

Make sure you summarise the key information you need to give. If you try to include too many details, your letter will be too long.

1 **Read the writing task below.**

1 Think about these questions and underline the points you must include in your letter.

1 Who is going to read your letter?
2 Where are they now? Where are you?
3 When are they coming to Britain? Why? What are all three of you planning to do?
4 What information do your friends need from you? What else do they expect from you besides information?

2 What style will be appropriate for your letter: formal, neutral or informal? Why?

2 **1 In this type of question, it is important to analyse the key information before you start to write. Work out the answers to these questions.**

1 How long does the journey take by train and by plane? Would travelling by car be faster or slower, do you think?
2 What form of transport would allow a) maximum time in Glasgow b) maximum flexibility?
3 Which is the cheapest way to travel and on which day?

2 Work with a partner and discuss the advantages and disadvantages of each way of travelling. Then note what you think are the most important advantages and disadvantages in the table.

	Advantages	*Disadvantages*
1 *Car*		
2 *Plane*		
3 *Train*		

3 Decide which way of travelling you think is best and why.

4 Use the table to help you select the information you need to send to your friends. (Remember you will have to summarise the key points, or your letter will be too long.) Make a plan for your letter. How many paragraphs will you need to write?

You are doing work experience in London and two English-speaking friends who live in your country are planning to visit you next month. During their visit, all three of you want to go to the Scottish city of Glasgow. They have asked you for information on the best way to get there. You have the following information from a travel agent. Read it carefully, then write a letter to your friends, giving them information about the three different ways of travelling to Glasgow. Suggest which you think is the best way, and explain why.

TRAINS

London dep.	Glasgow arr.
7.00	12.33
8.35	14.00
9.00	14.33

Standard class return fare: £75.25 (Fridays and Saturdays), £66.25 (other days)

CAR
London to Glasgow – 641 km
Car hire: £40 per day plus petrol

FLIGHTS

London dep.	Glasgow arr.
7.15	8.30
8.15	9.35
9.15	10.30
10.20	11.35

Return flight: £123.20 (weekdays), £95.00 (Saturdays and Sundays)

N

• Glasgow

641 km

London

Write a letter of between **120** and **180** words in an appropriate style. Do not write any postal addresses.

Focus on linking words

3 **1 Read the information in the box. Then do the exercise that follows.**

Linking words and expressions

A Listing points

First of all, / Firstly, Secondly, Thirdly, The first option / The second/next option
Finally, / The last possibility

Examples:
1 **The first option** is to go by car.
2 **The final possibility** is to go by plane.

B Expressing contrast

although, whereas, while
even though/even if
Despite .../In spite of ...
However, ... Nevertheless, ...

Examples:
1 **Although** the roads are good, it's a long drive to Scotland.
2 It'll take seven hours to get there, **even if** we don't stop for lunch.
3 **While** the train is cheaper than the plane, it's also slower.
4 The train journey takes five and a half hours, **whereas** the flight is just over an hour.
5 **Despite/In spite of** the cost, going by plane would be a good idea.
6 I think we should take the plane **even though** it's expensive.
7 Flying is the most expensive option. **Nevertheless**, it's the one I'd recommend.

C Comparing

either/or, neither/nor, both/and

Examples:
1 I suggest you take **either** the train **or** the plane.
2 **Neither** the train **nor** the plane is/are very cheap.
3 **Both** the plane **and** the train are expensive.

D Summarising

In conclusion, On the whole,

Examples:
1 **In conclusion**, I would say that the plane is probably your best option.
2 **On the whole**, I think you'd better get the train.

---

2 Combine these sentences using appropriate expressions from Sections B and C of the box. Try not to use the same expression more than once.

1 The plane is comfortable. It costs more.
2 The train is fast. It isn't as fast as the plane.
3 The weekday flights are quite expensive. The weekend flights are quite expensive too.
4 The train is expensive. I think we should take it.
5 I'd like to take you in my car. I'm afraid I won't be able to.
6 The motorway isn't very good. The smaller roads aren't very good.

Focus on editing

4 **1 Read part of a letter which a student wrote in answer to the writing task. The writer did not edit her work. Find and correct the errors she has made in these areas:**

- layout
- style
- organisation: paragraphing
- accuracy: grammar, spelling and punctuation

Hi Daniel and Susana!

I'm so pleased you will come to see me in London. I planned a fantastic day sightseeing for you. More later! There are three ways for us to get to Glasgow We could travel by car; it's 641 kilometres and car hire costs £40 per day plus petrol. We could take the train. There are regular services each morning and the journey takes about five and a half hours It's £75.25 on Fridays and Saturdays or £66.25 all other day. We could take a plane. there are flites every hour and it costs £123.20 weekdays or £95.00 at weekends. I suggest to go by plane. It may seem expensive. But there are advantages. the train journey would be quite tiring as you will already have been travelling. The plane would get us there in just over an hour and would cost only £20 more than the train if we go at the weekend. While the car is not a bad option, the plane would get us there more quickly and confortably.

Anyway, let me to know what you think and I'm going to book the tickets.

Yours sincerely,

Ana

---

2 Improve the range of sentence patterns the writer has used by adding linking words where appropriate.

Over to you

5 **Write your own answer to the exam task in Exercise 1. Follow the advice in the exam strategy box. Use the plan you made in Exercise 2. Remember to:**

- use the correct layout and style.
- check your writing for errors when you have finished.

Progress test 3

1 Structural cloze

For questions 1–15, read the text below and think of the word which best fits each space. Use only **one** word in each space. There is an example at the beginning (0).

CONFESSIONS

Media publicity about the work of the police often helps them in the fight (0) ..*against*.. crime. Some television programmes actually give viewers details about the crimes committed in their area. The idea is (1) .... members of the public are reminded (2) .... things they may have seen or heard and then come forward with new information that can (3) .... to an arrest.

(4) .... other occasions, however, media coverage of crime can (5) .... in false confessions which can be very annoying for the police. Some of these confessions come from innocent people (6) .... are confessing in order to protect the guilty person, possibly a loved (7) .... or a criminal colleague. It (8) .... thought that others confess simply because they enjoy the attention that this brings. They become famous for (9) .... short while, possibly seeing themselves on the television news. Sometimes such people even manage to convince themselves that they must (10) .... committed the crime, until the police can prove that this is not the case.

(11) .... as to avoid wasting too (12) .... time on these false confessions, the police are always careful to hold back at (13) .... one piece of important information relating to each big case. After (14) ...., if they have found a footprint or a fingerprint, only the true criminal (15) .... have the shoe or finger that matches it.

2 Key word transformations

For questions 1–10, complete the second sentence so that it has a similar meaning to the first sentence, using the word given. **Do not change the word given.** You must use between two and five words, including the word given. There is an example at the beginning (0).

Example:

0 Cooking is something that Martha has always found difficult.
good
Martha has never ......*been good at*........ cooking.

1 According to the timetable, the bus will leave at 10 o'clock.
due
The bus .... 10 o'clock according to the timetable.

2 Mark regrets not continuing with his guitar lessons.
wishes
Mark .... his guitar lessons.

3 It's a shame you can't stay longer than one night at the seaside.
able
I wish .... longer than one night at the seaside.

4 Rachel didn't enjoy someone painting her portrait.
having
Rachel didn't .... painted.

5 Although the weather was wet, they still enjoyed their holiday.
despite
They enjoyed .... weather.

6 'There's a chance that I left my passport on the plane,' said Norma.
might
Norma said that she .... passport on the plane.

7 People say that the film star has signed a new contract.
said
The film star .... a new contract.

8 She can't have told the truth when she talked to the police.
lying
She .... when she talked to the police.

9 It was only lack of money that prevented Lois from buying the dress.
would
Lois .... if she'd had enough money.

10 My hair is getting in my eyes, it needs cutting.
have
I need .... because it's getting in my eyes.

3 Error correction

For questions 1–15, read the text below and look carefully at each line. Some of the lines are correct, and some have a word which should not be there. If a line is correct, put a tick (✓) in the space by the number. If a line has a word which should not be there, write the word in the space. There are two examples at the beginning (0 and 00).

BECOMING A WRITER

0 ...✓.... When I left school last year, I decided that I was going to become

00 ..the.. a writer. I realised that self-discipline was going to be the one of my

1 .... greatest problems and so I am decided that I would need to try and

2 .... work the same sort of hours as people in other jobs. I go upstairs to

3 .... my study at 9.00 a.m., a journey so that takes me thirty seconds. I take

4 .... an hour for have lunch, and work until 6.30 in the evening. In this

5 .... way, I am able to pretend that my life is actually much more organised

6 .... than it really is. The most creative part of my day it is the first hour,

7 .... and my wastepaper basket gets quickly fills up with my unsuccessful

8 .... attempts at first lines, first paragraphs and even first pages. After

9 .... that a while, though, I begin to get bored. The afternoon is terrible and,

10 .... once or twice, I have actually fallen to asleep. I spend a lot of time

11 .... thinking about what it will be like when I'm a such famous novelist, and

12 .... looking out of the window in search of ideas. I usually spend up the

13 .... evening with my girlfriend. She has always said that in order to write,

14 .... you first need to get some experience of your life. Perhaps I should

15 .... think of getting a regular job. But then, would I have time for to write?

4 Word formation

For questions 1–10, read the text below. Use the word given in capitals at the end of each line to form a word that fits in the space in the same line. There is an example at the beginning (0).

ANCIENT AND MODERN

Archaeologists in Egypt made an important (0) ..discovery.. in 1987. **DISCOVER**
They found a (1) ..... unexplored network of tombs hidden in the **PREVIOUS**
 (2) ..... area of ancient monuments known as *The Valley of the* **FAME**
Kings. The find was quite (3) ..... and the archaeologists were **EXPECT**
(4) ..... very keen to share their amazing findings with the world. **UNDERSTAND**
They found a very modern way of doing this. (5) ..... about their **INFORM**
(6) ..... find is available, along with photos taken within the tombs **LATE**
themselves, on their regularly (7) ..... website. Although the **DATE**
(8) ..... of the objects found are everyday in nature, they all have **MAJOR**
(9) ..... stories to tell. As more research is done, it is hoped that **FASCINATE**
(10) ..... might be found to many of the mysteries of the pyramids **SOLVE**
and the pharaohs. If they are, the very modern medium of the
Internet will provide a window to this ancient world.

Practice exam

PAPER 1 Reading

Part 1

You are going to read an article about a factory that makes children's rocking horses out of wood. Choose the most suitable heading from the list **A–H** for each part (**1–6**) of the article. There is one extra heading which you do not need to use. There is an example at the beginning (**0**).

A	Satisfied customers
B	Attention to detail
C	Gaining the expertise
D	Initial disappointments
E	A source of inspiration
F	Responding to clients
G	Taking the risk
H	Stimulating creativity

▶▶ *exam tip!*
You only need to understand the **main point** of each paragraph. Don't worry if you don't undestand every word. ◀◀

The Rocking Horse Factory

Angela Clay visits an English village where the art of carving wooden horses is still alive.

0	H

Surrounded by exquisitely carved rocking horses in a workshop in the English village of Bethersden, Marc Stevenson said, 'When you're on one of these you have to use your imagination – you're about to jump the Grand Canyon to escape from the cowboys who are chasing you. It's good for children to make things up, but many toys children get today don't encourage that.'

1	

Marc and his twin brother Tony make wonderful rocking horses, the classic children's toy of the pre-electronic age. Rocking horses have been at the centre of the Stevenson family for more than fifty years. Uncle James Bosworchick, known as 'the rocking horse man' locally, started it all and encouraged Marc and Tony to follow in his footsteps.

2	

Marc was working at a sports company in London and Tony for an oil company when they told Uncle James they'd like to make rocking horses. 'He told us we were absolutely mad and that there wasn't a market anymore,' said Marc. The brothers persisted, however, and in the end their uncle said, 'If you're really serious, I'll charge £1,000 to train one of you.' They tossed a coin and it was Tony who went on to do the apprenticeship, while Marc worked and saved towards the business which they started in 1982.

3	

Their first workshop was a borrowed shed on their sister's farm. 'We lived in the farmhouse and worked eighteen hours a day,' said Marc. 'People said we were stupid to give up proper jobs to make rocking horses, but we wouldn't let anyone put us off, because we thought there was a good chance of success.'

4	

Eighteen years and a lot of experience later, Marc is proud of the fact that Stevenson Brothers have achieved their original goals of re-introducing the rocking horse as a toy of today, and being the best rocking horse makers in the world. Their impressive client list is surely testament to this. The Sultan of Brunei recently commissioned a 12-horse carousel, and a life-sized stallion is a permanent feature of Harrods department store in London.

5	

All the horses start as a shipment of timber, but looking at these lifeless blocks of wood on the workshop bench when they first arrive, it takes real imagination to visualise the proud creatures they will become. In the workshop each horse takes shape slowly, and at one stage, when the different sections are being glued together, the animal looks surprisingly futuristic, with clamps sticking out from a square body. It's fascinating to watch the creative skill of the carvers as they delicately sculpt perfectly-formed ears, nostrils and mouth, and a very lifelike face begins to appear from the wood.

6	

'We have a lot of grown-ups buying a horse for themselves because they always wanted one as a child,' said Marc. 'And a lot of customers ask us to make a horse to look like one of their real-life favourites. They send us photographs and we copy things like the colouring on and around the face.' Imagine the excitement when your very own carved wooden horse emerges bit by bit from the wrappings and you realise there isn't another exactly like it anywhere in the world. Stevenson's horses are numbered, and the brothers were up to number 3,554 when this article was written.

Part 2

You are going to read an article about a trip to the Arctic. For Questions **7–14**, choose the answer (**A**, **B**, **C** or **D**) which you think fits best according to the text.

Arctic Passion

Cruising over the pack-ice with our heavy snowmobiles, my guide, Arne, and I looked out across the dazzling expanse of snow. We had come to the tiny, remote island of Svalbard, northeast of Greenland, to photograph polar bears, but now we were exhausted with searching. The day had been particularly frustrating, as every bear we'd slowly approached had run away from us. Fed up and hungry, we decided to abandon our search for the afternoon and stop for a snack beside one of the many tall, blue icebergs.

As always, a good meal was followed by an intense desire to sleep, and we decided to give in to it, even though the temperature was down to -30° C. Sleeping at the same time would be unwise with our furry friends around, so we decided to take it in turns. As Arne slept, I scanned the snow with my binoculars, looking for anything moving. An hour passed. I was just about to wake my companion, when I noticed a dot on the horizon. I wiped the *line 27* lens, but **it** was still there. I began to make out the typical mayonnaise colour and the striding walk – it was a polar bear, and it was coming our way.

I awoke Arne instantly and he confirmed that it was a bear and it was indeed heading in our direction. For the next thirty minutes, the bear continued on its direct course towards us, which was strange because the wind was blowing our scent straight towards him, so he must have been aware of our presence.

When he was a couple of hundred metres away, I decided to lie down in the snow so as to get a better photograph. 'You realise you look just like seal like that, don't you?' warned Arne, for once sounding a bit worried. Seals are what polar bears like to have for dinner. Onwards the bear came, and by now I could hear the crunching sound of his feet on the ice. It struck me that this was a big bear, travelling at some speed. I turned to speak to Arne, and saw him pulling a gun from his bag. Polar bears are incredibly unpredictable animals, and to be in their environment without protection is foolish. But Arne had strict instructions from me only to use the gun to frighten the bear away, and then only if necessary.

By now the animal was only 25 metres away and the atmosphere had changed. Arne sat up on the snowmobile calmly awaiting the bear's next move, while I struggled to change the film in my camera with my cold, shaking hands. Then, just as I was thinking that there was no escape, as I tensed myself for the inevitable attack, the bear **veered off** to one side and then *line 68* went straight past us. 'Look!' whispered Arne. 'Behind us!' I turned and saw a second creamy head with two black eyes peering around the corner of an iceberg a few hundred metres behind us. A female bear. Our friend's goal had clearly been in his sight the whole time, and we were the only thing between him and his beloved.

> ▶▶ *exam tip!*
> Ignore any unfamiliar words unless they are necessary to help you answer the questions. If you need to know the meaning, use **context** clues to work it out. ◀◀

7 How did the writer feel when he stopped for a meal?

A disappointed
B excited
C doubtful
D anxious

8 Why did the writer stay awake while his guide slept?

A The temperature was dangerously low.
B They might have been approached by animals.
C They needed to contact their colleagues.
D There might have been a change in the weather.

9 What does 'it' in line 27 refer to?

A the horizon
B the dot
C the lens
D the companion

10 What surprised the writer about the bear's behaviour?

A It was moving very strangely.
B It was moving against the wind.
C It didn't seem put off by them.
D It wasn't looking towards them.

11 What was Arne concerned about as the bear continued to approach them?

A the writer's safety
B the size of the bear
C the writer's courage
D the speed of the bear

12 What did the writer feel about the gun?

A He was annoyed that Arne took it out.
B He was surprised that Arne didn't use it.
C He was keen that the bear shouldn't be hurt.
D He was worried about frightening the bear.

13 How did the writer feel when the bear got very close?

A surprisingly calm
B too afraid to move
C too cold to think
D extremely nervous

14 What does 'veered off' in line 68 mean?

A changed direction
B slowed down
C stopped suddenly
D looked around

Part 3

You are going to read a newspaper article about sport. Eight sentences have been removed from the article. Choose from the sentences **A–I** the one which fits best each gap (**15–21**). There is one extra sentence which you do not need to use. There is an example at the beginning (**0**).

HOW KIDS GET THEIR KICKS

Lack of exercise means that children are much less fit than they used to be.
Leigh Childs is a sports trainer who thinks he may have the answer to this problem.

It was a Thursday evening in a very ordinary-looking gym above a pizza restaurant in the English provincial town of Swindon. This may, at first, seem an unlikely place to go in search of an answer to children's growing health problems **0** **I** Leigh Childs, a sports trainer, runs a *tae kwon do* class in the gym. When I arrived, young boys and girls, dressed in their white uniforms, were kicking and punching the air. The place was alive with determined energy, full of clapping and laughing.

15 Originating in Korea, *tae kwon do* is what is known as a martial art. In Britain it is often also called kick-boxing. Leigh told me that the younger a person starts to exercise in this way, the greater are the long-term benefits. So he's keen to get as many children involved as possible.

16 It takes children through an aerobic-style workout, alive with kicks and punches, with Leigh leading the way through a popstar-style headset. And it couldn't have come at a more opportune time. Research studies have shown that fitness levels amongst British kids have been falling in recent years, a trend that seems to have come from the other side of the Atlantic.

17 Last week, a nationwide survey showed that over one third of six- to eight-year-olds do less than an hour's physical exercise per week. Where it is provided at school, this is usually with teachers who have very little specific training and without access to good sports facilities. The government's response has been to issue a report which says that primary school children should be doing at least two hours of sport per week.

Leigh Childs, it seems, could have the answer. 'I would like to take martial arts into schools,' he says. '**18** Learning self-defence is also important these days, as is discipline and self-confidence.' Leigh, aged twenty-eight, first got involved in *tae kwon do* because he was not well-built and his grandfather thought he ought to know how to defend himself. He so enjoyed the sport that he went on to become five times national champion before going on to set up his own school. 'Kids are materialistic. They want the next pair of designer trainers,' he says. 'I teach them about dedication and hard work.'

I spoke to one of Leigh's pupils, 12-year-old Gareth Davies, a promising champion of the future. 'I started because it was fun,' he says. 'Now I know I'm good at it and it gives me more self-confidence. If you go along to a football club, half the kids there don't listen to what's going on. **19** '

But what about the experts, do they agree with Leigh Childs? I asked Professor Collins, head of sports performance at Edinburgh University. He agrees that martial arts can be superb for some children because it's a structured way of getting all-round physical training. He too approves of the self-discipline, of channelling the children's energies in a positive way. **20** 'It's the quality of the instructor that matters. And even then, it's not a sport that's going to work for everybody. Some children just don't like combat sport, they find it too aggressive.'

Leigh would agree that *tae kwon do* will not suit all children. **21** 'You get hurt in all sports, but there are fewer injuries in martial arts than in football or rugby.' He prefers to see the sport as a way of relieving stress. There's no doubt that Leigh Childs is doing his best for kids. And even the most convinced couch potato amongst them should be persuaded to watch his video.

A And not only because of the fitness benefits.

B We all know the causes: computer games, too much television, lifts to school.

C But here, you have to show respect.

D He offers a note of caution, however.

E To this end, he has just released a video for kids called *Kick-boxing Fitness*.

F He denies that it is violent, however.

G This is apparently what happens when children learn the sport.

H It's a basic human instinct to defend yourself.

I But there I met a man who's convinced he has the solution.

 exam tip!

Remember, there is **one** paragraph that doesn't fit anywhere. This paragraph will contain ideas similar to those in the rest of the text, but there will be no grammatical or lexical links with other paragraphs.

Part 4

You are going to read an article in which five people give their views on the way in which celebrities are treated. For Questions **22–35**, choose from the people **A–E**. The people may be chosen more than once. When more than one answer is required, these may be given in an order. There is an example at the beginning (**0**).

Which of the people thinks that:

it's less risky to gossip about celebrities than people you know?	**0**	A
it's all right to criticise celebrities because they are highly paid?	**22**	
people are less interested in gossiping about celebrities whose work is good?	**23**	
many people are actually jealous of celebrities?	**24**	
celebrities have chosen their way of life?	**25**	
gossiping about celebrities is something which comes naturally to us?	**26**	
everybody should expect to be gossiped about occasionally?	**27**	
to stay successful, celebrities need to attract a lot of attention?	**28**	
it's reassuring to find that celebrities have problems to deal with?	**29**	
some people may regard celebrities as their personal friend?	**30**	
it's reasonable of celebrities to expect a degree of privacy?	**31**	
it's only acceptable to criticise celebrities for the work they do?	**32**	
most celebrities know that people will discuss their private affairs?	**33**	
celebrities don't deserve to be insulted?	**34**	**35**

exam tip!
Scan to locate the right part of the text. Then read that part carefully to make sure your answer **matches** the question.

THE PRICE OF FAME

Does being famous mean losing the right to the privacy the rest of us expect – or is it time we gave celebrities a break from all the gossip? Five readers give their views.

A   Mandy Holby (19) Trainee manager

For the average celebrity, having your private life discussed in the newspapers is a fact of life and your most intimate secrets are quite likely to become public property. I think that's something the majority of them realise. But, these days, it's not unusual to see deeply personal insults about these people in the press and that side of it never really seems justified somehow. I can't say I like it. But then, if you think about it, no one forced them to become famous, did they? They wanted stardom and so they shouldn't expect to have it easy, should they? Besides if we are honest with ourselves, most of us do gossip, even if we feel guilty about it and gossiping about our friends can get us into a lot of trouble. Gossiping about famous people is safe because they're never going to hear what you've said.

B   Glenn Boyce (21) Sociology student

Famous people are obliged to take some criticism. Considering how much celebrities can earn, they shouldn't complain and should accept it as part of their job. Still, I think many people actually have a strange attitude towards these people. Imagine how we'd like to suffer the kind of criticism they do. Even though they do need the publicity to maintain their careers, I think they do have a right to a private life, too. And, according to what I've read, it seems we make a distinction between the ways in which celebrities are criticised – many people say it's OK to comment on their professional abilities, but not to subject them to personal attacks. I can't really see the difference personally.

C   Tina Smythe (22) Theatrical agent

I think that underneath, a lot of people actually resent success. There's a huge amount of envy directed at those who've had any sort of good fortune. As society becomes more and more competitive, so this feeling towards successful people increases. The public see media attention as the price celebrities pay for their success. It's almost as if they believe they really know the stars, just because they've bought their CDs or paid to see their shows. I say, sure they should be willing to accept criticism if their work is not up to standard, but I can't see what their private life has to do with it.

D   Bob Terrence (30) Psychology teacher

I've read that, in the distant past, gossip started as a way of people knowing what was going on around them and who was in control. In all situations, it's normal to gossip about powerful people; about teachers, bosses, politicians, etc. The modern world is full of images of celebrities, we see them wherever we go, and this makes us instinctively treat them like powerful individuals. Every famous figure is a potential target, but there's clearly a group who attract more attention than most. I think the public differentiates between celebrities on the basis of how their fame was acquired. Certain actors and actresses, who are thought to have genuine talent, are generally less gossiped about than others who are believed to have become famous because of their looks alone, or as a result of knowing other celebrities.

E   Mel Brighouse (25) Writer

I can't get enough celebrity gossip – I read just about every newspaper and magazine there is, because it fascinates me to discover what these people get up to. Each of us, famous or not, is gossiped about from time to time, and because famous people are in the public eye, it follows that they are going to be a topic of conversation. But I must admit that the gossip can, occasionally, become plain nasty and upsetting, and I don't really think that's fair on the individuals concerned. To a certain extent, celebrities have to realise that they are living out our dreams, that we see them as perfect. But, when we find that things go wrong in their lives, it's comforting to realise that the people who seem to have it all are, in reality, the same as, or even worse off, than ourselves.

PAPER 2 Writing

Part 1

You **must** answer this question.

1   You are staying in Scotland and next weekend you are going hillwalking with your friends, Darren and Pauline. Below is a letter which Darren has sent you about the trip. You have found some information about the area, which includes a map and an advertisement for a restaurant.

Read Darren's letter, on which you have made some notes, and the information below it. Then write a suitable reply, answering his questions and making suggestions about where to have lunch.

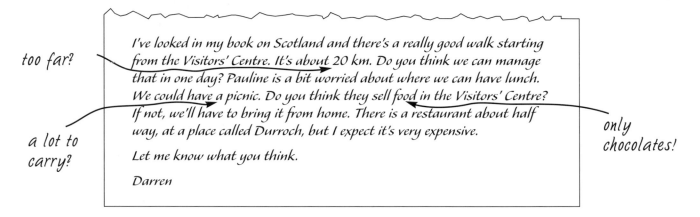

too far?

I've looked in my book on Scotland and there's a really good walk starting from the Visitors' Centre. It's about 20 km. Do you think we can manage that in one day? Pauline is a bit worried about where we can have lunch. We could have a picnic. Do you think they sell food in the Visitors' Centre? If not, we'll have to bring it from home. There is a restaurant about half way, at a place called Durroch, but I expect it's very expensive.

Let me know what you think.

Darren

a lot to carry?

only chocolates!

The Hill View Inn, Durroch.

Small family-run restaurant serving evening meals and lunchtime snacks. Tourist economy menu available.

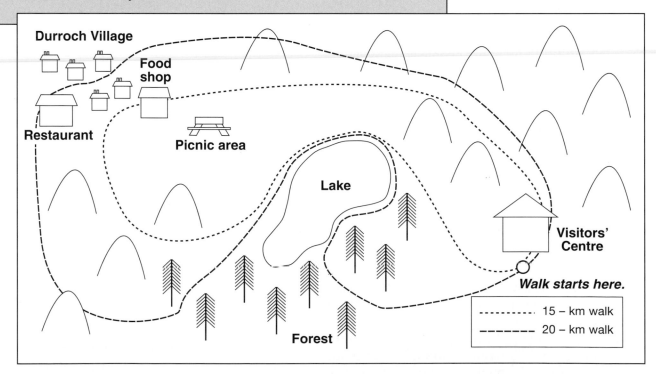

Write a **letter** to Darren of between **120** and **180** words in an appropriate style. Do not write any postal addresses.

Part 2

Write an answer to **one** of the Questions **2–4** in this part. Write your answer in **120–180** words in an appropriate style.

2   You see this notice in an international magazine.

The Best Way to Keep Fit on a Budget

We are looking for articles on the following question:

What can young people do to keep fit in their free time without spending too much money?

The best article will be published in next month's magazine.

Write your **article**.

3   A good friend of yours recently had an eighteenth-birthday party to which many different people were invited. One friend, who lives abroad, was unable to come to the party. Write a letter to your friend, describing the party and include some details about the people who came and what happened to them. Do not write any postal addresses.

Write your **letter**.

4   Your school has a large entrance area that is sometimes used for educational exhibitions. You have been asked to write a report suggesting the type of exhibition which should be put on there next term. You should describe the different things which it will be possible to see in the exhibition and say why you think the school students would enjoy it.

Write your **report**.

 *exam tip!*
Always **make a plan** before you start. Write down the points you need to cover and put them in a logical order. Group points together in paragraphs, or under headings in a report.

PAPER 3 Use of English

Part 1

For Questions **1–15**, read the text below and decide which answer **A**, **B**, **C** or **D** best fits each space. There is an example at the beginning (**0**).

| 0 | **A** announced | **B** declared | **C** informed | **D** claimed |

THE INTERNET HOUSE

A leading British building and design company has just (**0**) .*A*. their plans for the home of the future. The new design, (**1**) ..... as the 'Internet House', has five bedrooms, plenty of bathrooms and a double garage. But these are not the main selling (**2**) ....., for it is the £25,000 (**3**) ..... of automation that makes this house really different.

It will be (**4**) ..... for people who have plenty of money, but not a great (**5**) ..... of time; young professionals in other words. They are likely to be (**6**) ..... to the idea of a microwave that provides easy-to-cook (**7**) ..... via the Internet and a cooker that switches itself on or off at a command received via e-mail.

All the electrical appliances in the house, (**8**) ..... the heating and lighting controls, are linked together by (**9**) ..... of a gadget called a 'router'. Using what's called a 'Webpad', a kind of portable lap-top computer, the owners of the house tap in commands from (**10**) ..... they may be. The Webpad (**11**) ..... a signal to the router, which (**12**) ..... the message and then activates the necessary controls. On the way home at night, for example, the owners can switch on the lights or (**13**) ..... the central heating working, and so (**14**) ..... sure that they have a nice warm welcome when they (**15**) ..... into their home.

1	**A** entitled	**B** known	**C** referred	**D** named
2	**A** points	**B** plots	**C** plans	**D** paths
3	**A** value	**B** price	**C** cost	**D** worth
4	**A** accurate	**B** model	**C** precise	**D** ideal
5	**A** length	**B** lot	**C** deal	**D** extent
6	**A** excited	**B** attracted	**C** appealed	**D** interested
7	**A** recipes	**B** receipts	**C** prescriptions	**D** instructors
8	**A** as long as	**B** as well as	**C** as soon as	**D** as far as
9	**A** account	**B** regards	**C** order	**D** means
10	**A** whatever	**B** however	**C** wherever	**D** whichever
11	**A** draws	**B** speaks	**C** sends	**D** hears
12	**A** decodes	**B** discounts	**C** decides	**D** dissolves
13	**A** lead	**B** get	**C** have	**D** put
14	**A** come	**B** make	**C** keep	**D** hold
15	**A** step	**B** stay	**C** stand	**D** start

Part 2

For Questions **16–30**, read the text below and think of the word which best fits each space. Use only **one** word in each space. There is an example at the beginning (**0**).

Example: | **0** | *from* |

FASHION

You can tell a great deal about people (**0**) *..from..* the clothes they wear. Basically, most people fall into one of three groups. Firstly, there are those who feel they must wear whatever 'look' is currently fashionable, whether it suits them or (**16**) .... These people rush to the shops to buy whatever is being promoted (**17**) .... the large fashion houses and retail chains. They would never (**18**) .... seen in last year's styles or colours, because they spend quite (**19**) .... large proportion of their income (**20**) .... clothes and accessories, and devote a lot of time to looking through fashion magazines.

On (**21**) .... other hand, there are people who do not feel they (**22**) .... to follow the trend. They are content to wear the same colours and designs year after year and they have little (**23**) .... no interest in the ever-changing world of fashion. They prefer to buy (**24**) .... is cheap, comfortable or long-lasting. And then there is a third group, (**25**) .... up of people who actually take great pride (**26**) .... being different. These people (**27**) .... to great lengths to wear clothes that are not only unfashionable, (**28**) .... also rather shocking. There is always a danger, however, that such trends can become (**29**) .... popular that the unconventional clothes of the rebels actually turn (**30**) .... the latest fashion, as happened with the punk and grunge styles of the late twentieth century.

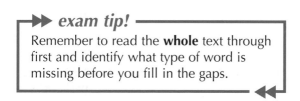

➤➤ *exam tip!*
Remember to read the **whole** text through first and identify what type of word is missing before you fill in the gaps.

Part 3

For Questions **31–40**, complete the second sentence so that it has a similar meaning to the first sentence, using the word given. **Do not change the word given**. You must use between two and five words, including the word given. Here is an example (**0**).

Example:

0   You must do exactly what your teacher tells you.

   carry

   You must .... instructions exactly.

The gap can be filled by the words 'carry out your teacher's' so you write:

0	*carry out your teacher's*

---

31   Thomas didn't ask permission before borrowing his brother's bicycle.

   without

   Thomas borrowed his .... permission first.

32   Laura usually ignores her mother's advice.
   take

   Laura doesn't usually .... her mother's advice.

33   'I'm sorry that I arrived late for the meeting', said Joe.

   apologised

   Joe .... arrival at the meeting.

34   Sue has a very good relationship with her boss.

   gets

   Sue .... her boss.

35   I regret not buying that guidebook in London last week.

   wish

   I .... that guidebook in London last week.

> **▶▶ exam tip!**
> **Be careful** when you copy the words
> onto the answer sheet in the exam. Always
> write something because you will get
> a mark if your answer is partly correct.
> ◀◀

36   The police are looking into a number of recent car thefts.

   investigated

   A number of recent car thefts .... the police.

37   Kate said we'd miss the start of the film if we didn't hurry.

   unless

   Kate said, '.. miss the start of the film.'

38   There's no diving board at the swimming pool because it's too shallow.

   enough

   The swimming pool .... to have a diving board.

39   David's keyboard skills have improved steadily over the last two years.

   improvement

   There .... in David's keyboard skills over the last two years.

40   Leo had no intention of missing his favourite TV programme.

   intend

   Leo .... his favourite TV programme.

Part 4

For Questions **41–55**, read the text below and look carefully at each line. Some of the lines are correct and some have a word which should not be there.

If a line is correct, put a tick (✓) in the space by the number. If a line has a word which should not be there, write the word in the space. There are two examples at the beginning (**0** and **00**).

Examples:

0	✓
00	*about*

THE FRUITARIAN

0	.....	You have no doubt heard of vegetarians, people who prefer not to
00	.....	eat meat. Some of them are very strict about and only eat vegetables,
41	.....	whilst others avoid meat, but still eat things they like milk, cheese
42	.....	and eggs. Well, I am what is called a fruitarian and which means
43	.....	I have a very restricted diet. Every one meal that I eat is what is
44	.....	called a 'monomeal'. I have never combine two different types
45	.....	of food in one meal and most often of the time, I have either
46	.....	Brazil nuts, coconuts or oranges, although occasionally I might
47	.....	have some cabbage or an apple for make a change. All the
48	.....	food I eat is uncooked because I believe that cooking takes all
49	.....	the goodness out of food and makes it all so taste the same. The
50	.....	question which people always ask me is whether I get bored
51	.....	with my diet. The answer is that this is not the in case at all and
52	.....	if I really enjoy the food I eat. In fact, every time I eat a coconut
53	.....	or an orange, it's like the first time I've ever tasted of one; it is
54	.....	delicious. What's more, I am never hungry. Many people eat more
55	.....	than it is good for them, but just three 'monomeals' a day keep me healthy.

> 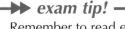 *exam tip!*
> Remember to read each complete **sentence**
> to help you understand the context, but
> only look for **one** extra word in each **line**.

Part 5

For Questions **56–65**, read the text below. Use the word given in capitals at the end of each line to form a word that fits in the space in the same line. There is an example at the beginning (**0**).

Example: | **0** | *incredible*

THE WILL TO FLY

It is (**0**) ...*incredible*... to think that as recently as 1903, many of the world's   **CREDIBLE**

leading (**56**) ..... were still absolutely certain that people would   **SCIENCE**

never fly. An (**57**) ..... US professor declared in that year that a   **INFLUENCE**

flying machine was an (**58**) ..... because something which was   **POSSIBLE**

(**59**) ..... than the air itself could not take off. But just a few weeks   **HEAVY**

later, came the surprise (**60**) ..... that two brothers from Ohio   **ANNOUNCE**

named Wright had built just such a machine.

The media remained so (**61**) ..... by their claims, however, that neither   **CONVINCE**

reporters nor (**62**) ..... were sent along to witness any of their test   **PHOTOGRAPH**

(**63**) ..... . The brothers, somewhat discouraged, then offered their   **FLY**

(**64**) ..... to the US army, who showed no interest. It was only when   **INVENT**

a French company began to take them (**65**) ..... that the brothers   **SERIOUS**

had the opportunity to prove the experts wrong.

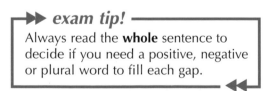

> ▶▶ *exam tip!*
> Always read the **whole** sentence to
> decide if you need a positive, negative
> or plural word to fill each gap. ◀◀

PAPER 4 Listening

Part 1

You will hear people talking in eight different situations. For Questions **1–8**, choose the best answer, **A**, **B** or **C**.

1   You hear a mother talking about her teenage son.
    How does she feel about him?
    A   She understands his behaviour.
    B   She is hurt by his attitude.
    C   She appreciates his efforts.

	1

2   You hear part of a radio programme about people who live in strange places.
    How do Adam's friends regard his tree house?
    A   They're impressed by his achievement.
    B   They're concerned about his safety.
    C   They cannot see the attraction.

	2

3   You hear a woman talking about her work.
    What industry does she work in?
    A   transport
    B   construction
    C   agriculture

	3

4   On a train, you overhear a man talking into his mobile phone.
    Who is he talking to?
    A   his boss
    B   his secretary
    C   his wife

	4

5   You hear part of a play on the radio.
    Where is this part of the play taking place?
    A   in a theatre
    B   in a concert hall
    C   in a restaurant

	5

6   You hear a boy talking about the sport he plays.
    What point is he making about the sport?
    A   It can be dangerous.
    B   Discipline is important.
    C   There are too many rules.

	6

7   You hear the weather forecast on the radio.
    What is the weather going to be like today?
    A   getting wetter
    B   getting cloudier
    C   getting windier

	7

8   You hear a young woman talking about music.
    How does she feel about the music in the supermarket?
    A   She'd rather listen to the radio.
    B   She feels it's badly produced.
    C   She hardly notices it anymore.

	8

Part 2

You will hear an interview with the crime writer, Lynda Norton. For Questions **9–18**, complete the sentences.

The title of Lynda's latest novel is [_____ **9**]

Lynda says that the character Anna should not be described as a [_____ **10**]

Most of Lynda's latest novel is set in [_____ **11**]

Certain events in the novel are based on stories told by Lynda's [_____ **12**]

Lynda's first novels were of the type known as [_____ **13**]

Lynda became a crime writer after entering a [_____ **14**] in a competition.

Lynda describes writing the television screenplay as [_____ **15**]

Lynda feels that the actor who played Inspector Benson should have been [_____ **16**]

Lynda's next book is going to be a [_____ **17**] novel.

The next Inspector Benson novel should be finished by [_____ **18**]

> ▶▶ *exam tip!*
> Part 2 isn't a dictation. Don't try to write down everything you hear. The answer is usually between **one** and **three** words.
> ◀◀

Part 3

You will hear five members of a pop group talking about the things they take with them when they are travelling abroad on tour. For Questions **19–23**, choose which of the statements **A–F** refers to each speaker. Use the letters only once. There is one extra letter which you do not need to use.

Which speaker says

A I no longer carry unnecessary things.

Speaker 1	**19**

B I ought to start getting ready earlier.

Speaker 2	**20**

C I wish I could take more things with me.

Speaker 3	**21**

D I pay little attention to my luggage.

Speaker 4	**22**

E I like to organise my things carefully.

Speaker 5	**23**

F I find it hard to limit what I take.

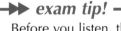
exam tip!
Before you listen, think about the topics and vocabulary you might hear. During the talk, listen for **clues** to help you. Don't leave any blanks on the answer sheet – guess if necessary.

Part 4

You will hear an interview with the young British actress, Kate Brompton. For Questions **24–30**, choose the best answer, **A**, **B** or **C**.

---

24   What does Kate say about her latest film?

    A   She was dissatisfied with her performance.

    B   She was able to draw on her personal experiences

    C   She had little in common with the character she plays.

24

25   How does Kate regard actors who spend a lot of time at parties?

    A   They should concentrate more on their work.

    B   They must have more energy than she has.

    C   They can't really enjoy themselves very much.

25

26   What does Kate dislike about 'celebrity' parties?

    A   They are not much fun.

    B   The people are unfriendly.

    C   There are too many photographers.

26

27   What does Kate say about her boyfriend?

    A   She's sorry that he's an actor.

    B   She wishes they could work together.

    C   She regrets not seeing him more often.

27

28   How does Kate feel now about her parents' advice?

    A   They didn't really understand acting.

    B   They failed to realise how committed she was.

    C   They were right to warn her about certain things.

28

29   What does Kate say about New York?

    A   She feels at ease when she's there.

    B   She feels like a foreigner there.

    C   She'd like to go and live there.

29

30   What is Kate's attitude towards her work?

    A   She enjoys being well-known.

    B   She likes to feel she is doing her job well.

    C   She would like to be better paid.

30

PAPER 5 Speaking

Part 1 (3 minutes)

Answer these questions:

What type of magazines do you like best? Why?

Is there any type of magazine that you particularly dislike? Why?

How often do you buy magazines?

Has your taste in magazines changed over the years? Why/Why not?

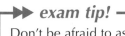 *exam tip!*
Don't be afraid to ask the examiner to **repeat** if you didn't hear properly or didn't understand.

Part 2 (4 minutes)

Candidate A photos

Look at photographs 1 and 2 below. They show people concentrating.

Candidate A: Compare and contrast these photographs, and say why each person needs to concentrate. You have about one minute to do this.

1

2

Candidate B: Where do you go when you want to concentrate?

Candidate B photos

Look at photographs 3 and 4 below. They show people pointing.

3

4

Candidate B: Compare and contrast these photographs, and say what you think the people are looking at. You have about one minute to do this.

Candidate A: What type of food do you prefer?

➤➤ exam tip!
You only have about **20 seconds** to comment on your partner's photos. It is perfectly acceptable to give a brief answer to the examiner's question.

Part 3 (3 minutes)

Look at the photographs below. They show water being used in different ways.

Candidates A and B: Imagine that you have to give a talk to young children about the importance of clean water in our lives. How important is clean water in each of these activities? Which things would you talk about with a group of young children?

Part 4 (4 minutes)

Answer these questions:

- Do you use much water in your daily life?
- Do you think that people waste water nowadays?
- What can people do to avoid wasting water?
- What should we be doing to stop water pollution?
- How important is it for children to learn about the environment?
- What other subjects is it important for children to discuss at school?

> **▶▶ exam tip!**
> Remember that Parts 3 and 4 are **interactive**. Do express your own opinions but also listen to your partner and the examiner and try to develop the topic. ◀◀

Grammar file

File 1: Articles

1 Definite article: *the*

We use the definite article:
- for something which is unique: **The Earth** is round.
- for somebody or something when it is clear who or what we are referring to: **The postman** has arrived.
- for somebody or something that we have already mentioned: *I bought a shirt and a coat.* **The shirt** was quite cheap but **the coat** cost a lot.
- with superlatives: *It's* **the best country** in the world.
- before newspapers: **the** *Mirror*; hotels and restaurants: **the** *Hilton*, **the** *Hard Rock Café*; theatres: **the** *National Theatre*; cinemas: **the** *Odeon*; galleries: **the** *Tate Gallery*; areas: **the** *southwest* of Spain; rivers: **the** *River Thames*; seas and oceans: **the** *Aegean*, **the** *Atlantic*; mountain ranges: **the** *Pyrenees*; groups of islands: **the** *Seychelles*; deserts: **the** *Sahara*
- before types of entertainment: *We went to* **the theatre**; musical instruments: *He plays* **the piano**.
- before some countries: **the** *USA*, **the** *UK*; national groups: **the** *English* and nationalities ending in *-sh*, *-ch*, or *-ese*: **the** *Japanese*
- with parts of the body after prepositions: *The ball hit him on* **the arm**. (= his arm)

2 Indefinite article: *a/an*

We use the indefinite article:
- for singular countable nouns mentioned for the first time or when we are not referring to one in particular: *I want to buy* **a** *car*.
- for singular jobs and other groups that people belong to: *I'm* **an** *engineer.* / *She's* **a** *vegetarian.*
- before certain numbers: **a hundred** *people* / **a thousand** *kilometres* / **a million** *dollars*
- with expressions of frequency: *once* **a** *week*

3 Zero article (no article)

We use the zero article:
- for plural countable nouns when we are talking in general: **Teenagers** *are sometimes moody.*
- for uncountable nouns when we are talking in general: **Health** *is more important than money.*
- before continents: *Africa*; countries: *Argentina*; cities: *Athens*; towns: *Bournemouth*; most streets and roads: *Bond Street, Fifth Avenue*; mountains: *Mount Everest*; lakes: *Lake Ontario*
- before illnesses: *I've got* **flu**. (BUT *I've got* **a** *headache*.)
- to refer to certain institutions like hospitals and prisons: *He had an accident so he was taken to* **hospital**. BUT Use the definite article to refer to the building itself: *She went to* **the hospital** *to visit her son*.
- with these expressions:
  to / at / from school / university / college / work
  in / to class
  to / in from church
  to / in / into / out of bed / hospital / prison (as a prisoner)
  go home
  for / at / to breakfast / lunch / dinner
  by car / bus / plane / boat / ferry / taxi / bicycle
  on foot

File 2: Countable/uncountable nouns and determiners

1 Countable/uncountable nouns

- Countable nouns can be singular or plural: *one* **student**/ *two* **students**, *one* **child**/*two* **children**
- Uncountable nouns have no plural. We can never use *a/an* with them: *I need* ~~an~~ **some** *advice*.
- The following common nouns are usually uncountable:

accommodation, advice, behaviour, bread, furniture, food, health, information, knowledge, luggage, money, news, progress, research, scenery, traffic, travel, trouble, water, weather, work

- Some nouns can be both countable and uncountable:
  - things we think of as single things or substances: *I've bought* **a chicken** *for lunch.* / *Would you like* **chicken** *or fish?* ● drinks: *I love* **coffee**. / *I'll have* **two coffees**, *please.* (= two cups of coffee) ● nouns like *time, room, space, place* with a change in meaning. Compare:
  1 *We had* **a great time** *last night.*
  2 *I haven't got* **time** *to stop.*

2 Determiners and quantifiers

● **Determiners with countable/uncountable nouns**

some/any (of)
Some people went to the beach but **some of us** *stayed near the pool.* (affirmative statements; *some of* before a pronoun)
It'll take **some** *time to reach the hotel.* (*some* + certain uncountable nouns = a large amount of sth)
Did you see **any** *interesting sights? No, we didn't go on* **any** *trips.* (questions and negative statements)
There was **hardly any** *time left.* (*any* with words of negative meaning like *hardly*)

all/none (of)
All *the students passed the exam.*
None of *the information was helpful.* (+ affirmative verb)

plenty of, a lot of/lots of
We've got **plenty of** *time.*
There were **a lot of/lots of** *people in town.*

more/most (of)
We spend **more** *time abroad.* (implied comparison = than we did before)
Most *students study very hard.*

● **Determiners with countable nouns**

many, a few/few
How **many** *countries have you been to?*
I've got **a few** *ideas.*
Very **few** *people can afford a Rolls Royce.* (= not many)

each (of)/every
Each of *the guests received a gift.*
Each *talk was interesting.* (+ singular countable nouns only)
I enjoyed **every** *minute of the holiday.* (+ singular countable nouns only)

several (of)/a large number of
I've made **several** visits to France this year.
He has **a large number of** friends.

both / either of / neither (of)
I can see **both** sides of the argument. (+ plural countable nouns only)
Saturday or Sunday, **either** day is fine with me. (+ singular countable noun)
Neither option was acceptable. (+ singular countable noun)
I don't know **either of** his parents. (*either of* + *his, these, the,* etc. + plural countable noun)
Neither of the brothers live/lives in England. (*neither of* + *his, these, the,* etc. + plural countable noun; *neither of* + singular or plural verb, singular verb = formal)

- **Determiners with uncountable nouns**

much, little/a little
I haven't got **much** money.
She's got **little** time for her family. (= not much)
Can you give me **a little** rice, please?

a great deal of/a large amount of
I've got **a great deal of** respect for that teacher.
Don't eat **a large amount of** food before exercising.

File 3: Comparison of adjectives/adverbs

1 Comparatives and superlatives

- We add *-er* and *-est* to form the comparative and superlative of regular one-syllable adjectives, two-syllable adjectives ending in *-y*, and adverbs with the same form as adjectives. Be careful of spelling changes: *Is Paris ~~hoter~~ hotter than Dublin in summer? / Athens is the ~~busyest~~ busiest city I have ever visited. / Please drive **faster**! / Who arrived the **earliest** at your party?*
- We use *more* and *most* to form the comparative and superlative of regular adjectives with two or more syllables. We also use *more* and *most* with most adverbs: *Is Tokyo **more expensive than** Berlin? / I think Prague is **the most beautiful city** in the world. / You'll get round London **most easily** by bus.*

2 Irregular adjectives and adverbs

Adjectives

Adjective	Comparative	Superlative
good	better	(the) best
bad	worse	(the) worst
little	less	(the) least
much/many	more	(the) most
far	farther/further	(the) farthest/furthest

Adverbs

Adverb	Comparative	Superlative
well	better	(the) best
badly	worse	(the) worst
late	later	(the) last
much/a lot	more	(the) most
little	less	(the) least

3 (not) as … as/less … than

- We use *as* + adjective/adverb + *as* to say two things are similar or equal in some way. The negative is *not as … as*: *The traffic in the country is **not as bad as** in the city.*
- We use *less … than* as the opposite of *more … than*: *Life in my village is **less exciting than** in a city.*

4 Modifying comparisons

We can use *a bit, a little, even, rather, slightly, far, (very) much* and *a lot* with comparatives: *London is **much older than** New York.*

5 Repeating comparatives

- We use *the (more) … the (more)* to show that two comparisons change at the same time: **The older** the children get, **the more independent** they become.
- We use comparative adjective + *and* + comparative adjective to say something is changing all the time: *It's getting **colder and colder**.*

6 too, very, enough

- We use *too* in front of an adjective or adverb to describe something that is 'more than reasonable': *I was home **too late** to see the film. It had already finished.*
- *Very* means 'a lot'. Compare:
  1 *I was **too late** for the meeting.* (= The meeting had already finished.)
  2 *I was **very late** for the meeting.* (= I attended the meeting but missed a lot of it.)
- We use *enough* <u>after</u> an adjective or adverb to mean 'sufficient': *I'm not ~~enough rich~~ rich enough to buy a new flat.*

7 Order of adjectives

We do not normally put more than three adjectives in front of a noun. The most common order of adjectives is: **opinion quality/size/shape/age colour origin material purpose noun**: *a fantastic, short/new/expensive, red, Spanish, leather sports jacket*

File 4: Present tenses

1 Present simple

We use the present simple:
- for regular actions and routines, often with a time expression (see below): *We **go** abroad every year.*
- for permanent situations: *Steven Spielberg ~~is making~~ makes great films.*
- for general truths: *The sun **rises** each morning.*
- in time clauses with a future meaning after words like *when, if, after, as soon as, until,* etc.: *I'll phone you **after** the film **finishes**.*
- for fixed timetables: *The film **doesn't start** until 8 p.m.*
- in film reviews or plot summaries: *The hero **escapes** when his car **crashes** into the sea.*

> **Time expressions often used with the present simple**
> - Usually before the main verb or after auxiliary/modal verbs: *never, rarely, hardly ever, seldom, occasionally, sometimes, frequently, often, usually, always*
> - Usually at the end of the sentence: *every day / week / month / year,* etc., *in the morning/afternoon,* etc., *on Mondays/Tuesdays,* etc., *once a day / week / month,* etc.

2 Present continuous: present of *be* + *-ing*

We use the present continuous for:
- actions happening now: *Look! They're shooting a film!*
- temporary situations: *The actors are having a short break.*
- actions happening around the time of speaking: *I'm working as a film extra at the moment.*
- plans and arrangements in the future: *I'm meeting my friends outside the theatre tonight.*
- annoying or surprising habits with *always*: *I'm always losing things!*

> **Time expressions often used with the present continuous**
> - Usually after the auxilliary: *always, still, currently*
> - Usually at the end of a sentence: *at present, at the moment, now*

3 State verbs

- We do not usually use the following state verbs in the present continuous: *I am preferring prefer the theatre to the cinema.*
  be*
  appear*, look*, resemble, seem
  consist of, contain, include, have*
  know, realise, understand, think*, notice, forget, remember
  feel*, hear, see*, taste*, smell, sound
  like, love, dislike, hate, prefer
  need, want, wish, lack
  agree, disagree, believe, doubt, suppose
  belong to, own, owe, possess, depend*

- We can use the verbs marked * in the list above in the continuous, but with a change of meaning. Compare:
  1 *That book looks interesting.* (= appearance)
  2 *I'm looking in the dictionary but I can't find the word I need.* (= action)

File 5: Future tenses

1 Future simple: *will* + bare infinitive

We use the future simple:
- for predictions about the future when there is no present evidence, often with *believe, think, expect,* etc.: *What do you think life will be like in the future?*
- for decisions and offers made at the time of speaking: *Don't worry about the washing-up. I'll do it!*
- for promises, threats, offers, requests: *I won't forget, I promise. / I'll never speak to you again! / We'll help you with your homework. / Will you lend me your car?*

2 *going to*

We use *going* to:
- to predict events from present evidence: *Look at those clouds! It will It's going to rain.*
- for plans and intentions: *I will buy I'm going to buy a new computer next month.*

3 Present continuous

We use the present continuous:
- for definite future arrangements: *My brother is starting university in September. He's just received all the details.*

4 Present simple

We use the present simple:
- for timetables and scheduled events: *The train leaves at 6.25 tomorrow morning.*
- after words/phrases like *as soon as, before, until, when, while*: *I'll call you as soon as I will get home.*

5 Future continuous: *will be* + *-ing*

We use the future continuous:
- for actions in progress at a future time: *I'll be lying on a beach this time tomorrow.*
- to talk about planned future actions: *Will you be going to the meeting tomorrow?* (= polite)
- for actions which are routine: *Will you be spending your holidays at the seaside as usual this year?*

6 Future perfect: *will have* + past participle

We use the future perfect:
- for actions completed before a point in the future: *We will have finished this book by the summer.*
  ! We use the future perfect continuous (*will have been* + *-ing*) to focus on the duration of an action: *By the time I take my exam, I will have been learning English for six years.*

7 *due to*

We use *be due to* + infinitive:
- for timetabled/scheduled future events: *The plane is due to take off in 10 minutes.*

8 *be about to*

We use *be about to* + infinitive:
- for actions that will happen in the immediate future: *The train is about to leave.*

File 6: Past tenses

1 Past simple

We use the past simple:
- for events that are clearly finished or that happened at a definite past time: *The first man has landed landed on the Moon in 1969.*
- for a sequence of completed past events: *The explorers woke up, had breakfast and started out across the snow.*
- for events now finished that lasted over a period of time: *I was living lived in Japan for three years as a child.*

2 Past continuous: past of *be* + *-ing*

We use the past continuous:
- for actions in progress in the past: *I was working last night.*
- for temporary actions or situations in the past: *In May last year, we were studying for our final exams.*
- for actions in progress at the same time in the past: *I was reading while my friends were playing cards.*
- for setting the scene in a story: *This story began one day last winter. It snowed was snowing and my brother and I were sitting in the kitchen, wondering what to do.*

3 Past simple + past continuous

We use past simple + past continuous:
- for interrupted actions: *I eat was eating when the phone rang.*

4 Past perfect: *had* + past participle

We use the past perfect:

- for a past action that happened before another past action or time: *The explorers sheltered under a rock until the storm **had passed**.*
  ! We use the past perfect continuous (*had been* + *-ing*) to focus on the duration of an action: *They were tired because they ~~walked~~ **had been walking** all day.*
- with phrases *no sooner … than,* and *hardly … when*: ***No sooner had** the rain **stopped than** it began to snow.*
- after expressions *It was the first/second time … or: It was (the biggest)/(most exciting) … : John went to the USA last year. **It was the first time** he **had been** there.*

File 7: *used to/would* and *be/get used to*

- We use *used to* and *would* to refer to past actions and habits: *My brother **used to play** football at school. / As a child, I **would** always **sit** in class dreaming of romance.* (*Would* is less common than *used to*.)
- We use *used to* (not *would*) to refer to past states: *I ~~would be~~ **used to be** really thin when I was a child.*
  ! Don't confuse *used to* (= past habits) with *be/get used to* (= be/become accustomed to). Compare:
  *I **used to be** an only child.*
  *I'm **used to being** an only child.*

File 8: Present perfect

1 Present perfect simple: *has/have* + past participle

We use the present perfect simple:

- for actions that have continued from some time in the past until now: *He's **been** a teacher for five years.*
- for actions that started in the past but in a time period that is not yet finished: *I've **written** three letters today.*
- for past actions or situations which have a connection to the present: *Oh no! I've **lost** my purse!* (= I have to look for it now.)
- for actions that happened in the past but the time is not known/stated: *~~I went~~ I've **been** to Hollywood.*
- with the word *just* for actions that happened very recently: *I've **just finished** a fantastic book.*
- with time expressions like *How long, for* and *since,* especially with state verbs ▶ File 4: *How long have you **known** him?*
- with time expressions that mean 'any time up to now', e.g. *ever, never, already, yet, before, recently, lately, so far*: *Have you **finished** your homework **yet**?*
- after phrases such as *It's the first/last time … : **It's the first time** I've **eaten** Indian food.*
- after superlatives: *That's **the best** film I've **ever seen**.*

2 Present perfect continuous: *has/have* + *been* + *-ing*

We use the present perfect continuous:

- for actions that began in the past and are still continuing: *I've **been learning** to play the guitar since I was 12.*
- for recent activities when we can see the result: *You're covered in mud! **Have** you **been gardening**?*
- to emphasise the duration of an activity or situation: *We've **been walking** for hours!*

3 Present perfect or past simple?

- We use the present perfect for an action that began in the past and continues in the present. We use the past simple for an action that began and ended in the past. Compare:
  1 *I've **been** an actor for five years.* (= I'm still an actor now.)
  2 *I **was** an actor for five years.* (= I'm not an actor now.)
- We use the present perfect when the result of a past action continues in the present. We use the past simple when a past action has no result in the present. Compare:
  1 *I've **broken** my leg.* (= it's still healing now)
  2 *I **broke** my leg but it's fine now.* (= past event)
- We use the present perfect to refer to indefinite time, especially with time expressions like *already, recently, ever.* We use the past simple to refer to definite time, especially with time expressions like *yesterday, last week, (six months) ago.* Compare:
  1 *I've **started** a new job recently.*
  2 *I **started** a new job two months ago.*
- We use the present perfect for a period of unfinished time and the past simple for a period of finished time. Compare:
  1 ***Have** you **seen** John **this afternoon**?* (= still the afternoon)
  2 ***Did** you **see** John **this afternoon**?* (= now the evening)

File 9: Tenses in time clauses

We use the present simple (not *will*) to refer to the future after time indicators like *when, before, until,* etc. We can use the present perfect to indicate that the second action will be completed before the first.

- ***when** + present simple/present perfect*: *I'll buy a car **when** I ~~will~~ **pass/have passed** my driving test.*
- ***until** + present simple/present perfect*: *Wait here **until** the taxi ~~will arrive~~ **arrives/has arrived**.*
- ***whenever** + present simple*: *Come **whenever** you ~~will be~~ **are** ready.*
- ***while** + present simple*: *I'll go to London **while** I ~~will be~~ **am** in England next month.*
- ***after/before** + present simple/present perfect*: *I'll meet you **after** the show ~~will finish~~ **finishes/has finished**. / Don't leave **before** I ~~will phone~~ **phone/I've phoned** you.*
- ***as soon as** + present simple/present perfect*: *Phone me **as soon as** your plane ~~will land~~ **lands/has landed**.*
- ***by the time (that)** + present simple/present perfect*: ***By the time (that)** you ~~will get~~ **get/have got** home, I will have left.*
- ***immediately** + present simple/present perfect*: *Call me **immediately** you ~~will arrive~~ **arrive/you've arrived**.*
- ***once** + present simple/present perfect*: *I'll enjoy the job **once** I ~~will get used~~ **get used/have got used to** it.*

File 10: *-ing* forms

1 *-ing* forms

We use the *-ing* form:

- sometimes as a noun: ***Dancing** is my favourite hobby.*
- after all prepositions including particles of phrasal verbs: *I learned to play the guitar **by practising**. / I've **given up smoking**.*
- after certain expressions/prepositional phrases: *I'm **fed up with doing** exams.*
- as the second part of a compound adjective: *He's very **good-looking**.*

2 Verb + -ing

We use the -ing form after certain verbs and phrases: *I **avoid going** to crowded places. / It's **worth trying**.*

Similar verbs and phrases: *admit, adore, appreciate, can't help, consider, delay, deny, detest, dislike, enjoy, fancy, feel like, finish, imagine, involve, keep* (= continue)*, loathe, mention, mind, miss, postpone, practise, resent, risk, suggest*
! There are other verbs that can be followed by -ing or to-infinitive. ▶ File 12

3 Verb + object + -ing

We use object + -ing after *hear, see, feel* and *watch* to show that the action after the verb continued/was unfinished: *I **saw the boy** ~~drown~~ **drowning**, but luckily he was rescued just in time.* ▶ File 11.5

4 Adjectives ending in -ing

We use adjectives ending in -ing to talk about the effect someone or something has on us/our feelings: *The talk was rather ~~bored~~ **boring**.*

File 11: Infinitive forms

1 Adjective + to-infinitive

We can use the to-infinitive after certain adjectives: *It's **hard to learn** a language well.*

2 Verb + to-infinitive

We use the to-infinitive after certain verbs/phrases: *I can't **afford to go** on holiday. / I **would like to retire**.*

Similar verbs and phrases: *agree, appear, arrange, ask, attempt, care, choose, decide, expect, fail, help, hesitate, hope, intend, learn, manage, offer, plan, prepare, pretend, promise, propose, refuse, seem, threaten, want, wish, would hate, would love, would prefer*
! There are other verbs that can be followed by to-infinitive or -ing. ▶ File 12

3 Verb + bare infinitive

We use the bare infinitive:
- after most modals verbs: *I **might see** you later.*
  ! Be careful of *ought to*: *We **ought to leave** now.*
  ▶ Files 16 and 17
- after certain phrases: *I**'d rather stay** at home this evening.*
  ▶ File 20. / *You**'d better get** some fresh air.*

4 Verb + object + to-infinitive

We use object + to-infinitive after certain verbs:
*The doctor **advised me to take** more exercise.*
Similar verbs: *allow, ask, cause, command, encourage, expect, forbid, force, get, help, instruct, intend, invite, leave, like, mean, need, oblige, order, permit, persuade, prefer, recommend, request, remind, teach, tell, tempt, trouble, want, warn, wish*

5 Verb + object + bare infinitive

We use object + bare infinitive:
- after *let* and *make*: *My Dad **let us stay up** late last night. / The teacher **didn't make us do** any homework last night.*
  ! In the passive, we use *to* after *make*: *I **was made to do** sport at school.*

- after *hear, see, feel* and *watch* to show that the action after the verb was brief/finished: *I **heard a man shout**.*
  ▶ File 10.3

File 12: Verb + -ing form or to-infinitive

We can use the -ing form or to-infinitive:
- after *begin, continue* and *start* without a change in meaning:
  *I started **learning/to learn** English a year ago.*
- after *can't bear/stand, hate, like, love* and *prefer* with a very small change in meaning:
  *I **like swimming** in the sea.* (= in general)
  *I **like to swim** in the sea when I'm abroad.* (= specific situation)
- after *forget, go on, mean, regret, remember, stop* and *try* with a complete change in meaning. Compare:

1 *I'll never **forget meeting** you!* (= I'll always remember it.)
2 *Oh no! I've **forgotten to do** my homework!* (= I haven't done something I should have.)

1 *The assistant **went on talking** even though I was waiting.* (= continued talking)
2 *We discussed the problems and then **went on to talk** about possible solutions.* (= a change from one thing to another)

1 *Being a tennis champion **means practising** every day.* (= involves)
2 *I didn't **mean to worry** you.* (= it wasn't my intention)

1 *He **regrets being** rude.* (= He's sorry for what he's done.)
2 *I **regret to inform** you that you have not got the job.* (= I'm sorry to tell you this.)

1 *Do you **remember starting** school?* (= have a memory of sth)
2 *Don't worry. I **remembered to post** your letter.* (= not forget to do sth)

1 *You must **stop worrying**.* (= no longer do sth)
2 *I'll **stop to get** a newspaper on my way home.* (= stop in order to do sth)

1 *If you're worried about your exams, why don't you **try studying** harder?* (= try and see what happens)
2 *I **tried to call** you last night but there was no answer.* (= make an effort)

File 13: Indirect speech

We use indirect speech when we report what someone says, writes or thinks. When we begin with a reporting verb in the past tense, e.g. *said, admitted, claimed*, etc., we normally change tenses one step back in time. We may also need to change pronouns, and place and time indicators like *here* and *today*.

1 Reported statements

- present simple ⟶ past simple
  'He's tired,' she said. ⟶ *She said (that) he **was** tired.*

- present continuous ⟶ past continuous
  'I'm leaving soon,' he reminded her. ⟶ *He reminded her (that) he **was leaving** soon.*

- past simple ⟶ past perfect
  *'I **broke** the glass,' she admitted.* ⟶ *She admitted (that) she **had broken** the glass.*

- past continuous ➝ past perfect continuous
  *'I **was trying** to help,'* he explained. ➝ *He explained (that) he **had been trying** to help.*

- present perfect ➝ past perfect
  *'We **have won** the match,'* they announced. ➝ *They announced (that) they **had won** the match.*

- present perfect continuous ➝ past perfect continuous
  *'I've **been working** hard,'* he claimed. ➝ *He claimed (that) he **had been working** hard.*

- will ➝ would
  *'I **will** always love you,'* he promised. ➝ *He promised (that) he **would** always love her.*

- can ➝ could
  *'We **can** solve the problem,'* they insisted. ➝ *They insisted (that) they **could** solve the problem.*

- may ➝ might
  *'I **may** be late,'* he warned us. ➝ *He warned us (that) he **might** be late.*

- must ➝ had to
  *'We **must** leave,'* she said. ➝ *She said that they **had to** leave.*

2 Verb forms that do not change
We do not need to change the verb form:
- when the thing reported is still true:
  *'The currency in Argentina **is** the peso,'* the teacher told us. ➝ *The teacher told us that the currency in Argentina **is** the peso.*
- when the sentence we are reporting contains the modals *would, could, might, ought to, should,* or *must* when it used for deduction:
  *'I **could come** tomorrow,'* he said. ➝ *He said that he **could come** the next day.*
  *'He **must be** mad!'* she said. ➝ *She said he **must be** mad.*

3 Other changes in indirect speech

Direct speech	Indirect speech
here	*there*
now	*then*
this/that	*the*
today	*that day*
tomorrow	*the next day/the following day*
yesterday	*the day before/the previous day*
last (week)	*(the week) before/the previous (week)*
next (month)	*the following (month)/the (month) after*
this (morning)	*that (morning)*
ago	*before*

File 14: Indirect questions, requests and orders

1 Indirect questions
When we form indirect questions we:
- use the same word order as in statements. There is no question mark unless the introductory phrase is a question:
  'Are you going to the disco?' ➝ *My friend asked me ~~was I going~~ if I **was going** to the disco.*

- use the *wh*-question word in *wh*-questions:
  'When does the film start?' ➝ *He wanted to know **when ~~did the film start~~ the film started**.*
- use *if/whether* for *yes/no* questions:
  'Have you done your homework or not?' ➝ *The teacher asked **whether** we **had done** our homework or not.*
- must use *whether* (not *if*) when we are asking someone to make a choice:
  'Do you want tea or coffee?' ➝ *She asked me **whether I** wanted tea or coffee.*
- may use polite introductory phrases like *I wonder if you could tell me …* :
  'What's the time?' ➝ *'**I wonder if you could tell me** what the time is?*

2 Requests and orders
When we report requests and orders:
- we often use verbs like *ask, tell* + object + *to*-infinitive:
  'Will you be quiet, please?' ➝ *The teacher **asked/told me to be** quiet.* ▶ File 15
- we use *not* before the *to*-infinitive to report negative requests or orders:
  'Please don't interrupt the meeting.' ➝ *The manager asked/ told me **not to interrupt** the meeting.*

File 15: Structures after reporting and thinking verbs

1 Verb + *that*
We use the following patterns with *that* after certain verbs:
- **Verb + *that*-clause:** *The Prime Minister **announced (that)** there would be an election.*
  Similar verbs: *admit, claim, complain, explain, imagine, realise, remember, reply, say, state, think*
- **Verb + object + *that*-clause:** *He **told me (that)** he was an engineer.*
  Similar verbs: *remind, warn*
  I These verbs can also be followed by object + *to*-infinitive. ▶ File 11.4
- **Verb + *that* + *should*:** *I **agreed (that)** we **should** tell the truth.*
  Similar verbs: *advise, demand, insist, recommend, suggest*

2 Verb + *to*-infinitive
We use the following patterns with *to*-infinitive after certain verbs:
- **Verb + *to*-infinitive:** *She **agreed* to marry** him.*
  Similar verbs: *decide, offer, promise*, refuse, threaten**
- **Verb + object + *to*-infinitive:** *His parents **advised* him to study** Science.*
  Similar verbs: *ask, beg, encourage, forbid, invite, order, persuade*, remind* tell*, warn*

3 Verb + *-ing*
We use the following patterns with *-ing* after certain verbs:
- **Verb + *-ing*:** *My friends **suggested* ~~to go~~ going** out.*
  Similar verbs: *admit*, deny*, recommend**
- **Verb + preposition + *-ing*:** *They **accused** him **of stealing**.*
  Similar verbs: *apologise (for), blame sb (for), congratulate sb (on), discourage sb (from), insist (on)*

4 -ing/infinitive or that-clause?

- We can also use a *that*-clause with the verbs marked * on page 181: *She promised **to love** him. / She promised **that she would love** him.*
- If the subject of the *that*-clause is different to the object of the reporting verb, we must use a *that*-clause, not *to*-infinitive or *-ing* with the verbs marked * on page 181: *'Let's go to the cinema.'*

  ⟶ *He suggested that we (**he + I**) go to the cinema.* OR *He **suggested going** to the cinema. 'Why don't you and your friends go to the cinema?' = Dad suggested ~~me and my friends going~~ that **my friends and I (should) go** to the cinema.*

File 16: Modal verbs: ability, permission, advice, obligation, necessity

1 Ability

We use:
- *can/be able to* for present/future ability: ***Can** you **drive**? / **I'll be able to visit** you next week.*
- *could/be able to* for past ability:
  *I **could swim** when I was six. (= general ability)*
  *I **was able to swim** to safety. (= ability in a particular situation)*

2 Permission

We use:
- *can, be allowed to* and *may* (formal) to ask for and give permission: *You **can go** to the disco tonight. / **May I be** excused class this afternoon, please?*
- *could* to ask for permission when we are not sure what the answer will be: ***Could I ask** you a favour?*
- *can't/not allowed to* and *may not* (formal) for lack of permission: *I **can't**/I'm **not allowed to go** out tonight. / You **may not park** here.*

3 Advice, obligation, necessity

We use:
- *should* and *ought to* for advice: *You **should/ought to wear** a helmet when you ride your bike.* ▶ File 17.3
- *must* for strong obligation or necessity imposed by the speaker: *You **must pass** your test before you drive this car. / I **must revise** for the exams.*
- *mustn't* for strong obligation when the speaker is a person in authority: *You **mustn't eat** or **drink** in class.*
- *have to/have got to* (British English), or *need to* for strong obligations imposed by someone other than the speaker: ***Do** we **have to fill in** this form? / You **need to have** a passport to travel abroad.*
- *had to* for past obligation: *We **had to stay** in after school as a punishment.*

4 Lack of obligation/necessity

We use:
- *don't have to, don't need to* and *needn't* for lack of obligation in the present/future: *We **don't have to / don't need to / needn't pay** for the trip. It's free!*
- *didn't need to* for actions that were not necessary. We do not say if these actions were done or not: *I **didn't need to phone** my friend after all.*
- *needn't have* + past participle for actions which were done but were not necessary: *You **needn't have come** to meet me. I could have got the bus.*

File 17: Modal verbs: possibility, deduction, criticism

1 Possibility

We use:
- *could / may / might* to say that something is possibly true now: *They aren't at home – they **could/may/might be** on holiday.*
- *could / may / might* to say there is a chance something will happen in the future: *Take an umbrella – it **could / may / might rain** later.*
- *may not* and *might not/mightn't* (but not *could not/couldn't*) to say that something is possibly not true now or in the future: *He **may not/might not want** to come with us.*
- *could / may / might* + *have* + past participle to say that a past event possibly happened: *I'm not sure where she is. She **could / may / might have gone** out.*
- *could/might* (but not *may*) + *have* + past participle to say that a past event was possible but didn't happen: *Why did you drive so fast? You **could/might have had** an accident.*

2 Assumption/deduction

We use:
- *must* to express certainty about the present in the affirmative: *You **must be** tired after that long journey. / You **must be** joking!*
- *can't* (not *mustn't*) to express certainty about the present in the negative: *You **can't be** serious! / He **can't be swimming**. The pool is closed.*
- *must have* + past participle to express certainty about the past in the affirmative: *She's late. She **must have missed** her train. / I **must have been sleeping**. I didn't hear the bell.*
- *can't have/couldn't have* + past participle to express certainty about the past in the negative: *He **can't have won** the match. He looks depressed. / That man **couldn't have committed** the crime. He has an alibi. / They **couldn't have been paying** attention. They didn't see what happened.*

3 Criticism

We use:
- *should/ought (not) to* to criticise present actions: *We **should take care** of our planet. / We **ought not to leave** rubbish.*
- *should (not) have/ought (not) to have* + past participle to criticise past actions: *You **should have done** your homework./ You **ought not to have stayed** out so late.*
- *could have* + past participle to describe missed opportunities: *I **could have studied** harder for my exams but I didn't.*

File 18: Conditionals 1

1 Conditional linking words

- Some common conditional linking words are: *if, when, unless, as/so long as, provided/providing (that), until, on condition that, even if*. When the *if*-clause starts the sentence, we use a comma: ***As long as** you **don't panic**, you'll do well in the exam.*
- When the main clause starts the sentence, we don't use a comma: *You'll be better **provided** you **take** the doctor's advice.*
- We can use *unless* to replace *if … not*: *You'll miss the bus **unless** you **rush**. (= if you don't rush)*
- We can use *in case* to mean 'to avoid some future problem'. *In case* usually comes after the main clause: *Bring an umbrella **in case** ~~it will rain~~ it rains.*

- We can use *even if* for emphasis or to suggest a contradiction: **Even if** we **go** now, we **won't arrive** in time.

2 *Supposing …/Imagine …*

We can sometimes replace *if* in conditional sentences with *supposing* or *imagine*: **Supposing** you **won** the lottery next week, what **would** you **do** with the money? / **Imagine** the buses **had been** on strike yesterday. How **would** you **have got** to school?

3 Real and likely conditions

- We use *If*, etc. + present + present / modal / imperative for general truths and for instructions: **If** you **heat** snow, it **melts**. / Tigers **don't kill** humans **unless** they **are** sick or injured. / **Shout if** you **want** me to help you!
- We use *If*, etc. + present simple / present continuous / present perfect + *will*/modal for things that are likely to happen in the present or future: **If** I ~~will pass~~ **pass** my exams, I**'ll be** very pleased. / **Unless** I **study**, I **won't pass**. / **If** you**'re** still **waiting** at the bus stop when I come out, I**'ll give** you a lift. / I**'ll be able** to go / to university **if** I**'ve gained** good enough grades. / I **may work** abroad **if** my parents **agree**.

File 19: Conditionals 2

1 Unlikely and unreal conditions

- We use *If*, etc. + past simple + *would*/modal for unreal/ hypothetical situations in the present/future, and for giving advice: What **would** you **do if** you **won** the lottery? / We **could go** abroad for a holiday next year **if** we **saved** every month. / **If** I **were** you, I **would tell** your parents what's happened.
- We use *If*, etc. + past perfect + *would / could / might have* + past participle for imagining situations/events in the past which are contrary to what actually happened: I **wouldn't have got** sunburnt **if** I **hadn't stayed** in the sun too long. / Just think. **If** I **hadn't gone** to the disco last night, I **might not have met** you.

2 Replacing *if*

We can replace *if* with *were* and with *had* to make sentences more formal:
Were I **qualified**, I **would apply** for the job. (= If I were …)
Had I **known** how much the course cost, I **would never have applied**. (= If I had known …)

3 Mixed conditionals

It is possible to have sentences that mix conditionals, especially when a past event has an effect in the present. Compare:
1 **If** I **hadn't received** the invitation, I **wouldn't have gone** to the wedding. (= I did go to the wedding.)
2 **If** I **hadn't received** the invitation, I **wouldn't be** at the wedding. (= I'm at the wedding now.)

File 20: Unreal tenses

1 wish/if only + past simple / past continuous / could + bare infinitive

We use *wish/if only* + past simple / past continuous / *could* + bare infinitive:
- to express regrets about a present situation which we cannot change: I **wish** I **were** taller. / **If only** we **didn't have to** go now!

2 *wish/if only* + past perfect

We use *wish/if only* + past perfect:
- to express regrets about things that happened or didn't happen in the past. It is impossible to change them now: I **wish** I **could have gone** abroad last year, but I didn't have the money.

3 *wish/if only* + would + bare infinitive

We use *wish/if only* + *would* + bare infinitive:
- to express a desire for a change in the future which will probably never happen: I **wish** someone ~~to give~~ **would give** me a million dollars!
  ! We cannot say **I wish/If only I/we would** … We must say: **I wish** I ~~would~~ **could stop** biting my nails.
- to criticise or express irritation about present events: I **wish** you **wouldn't whistle** all the time! / **If only** you **would listen**!

4 *wish/if only* + could + bare infinitive

We use *wish/if only* + *could* + bare infinitive to express a regret about a lack of ability: My brother wishes he ~~would~~ **could drive** but he can't.

5 *It's time* + person + past simple/past continuous

We use *It's time* + person + past simple/past continuous:
- when we want to say that something should have been done before now. We are often expressing some kind of criticism. We can also use *It's about/high time* … : **It's about time** your friends **went** home! They've been here all day.
  ! We use *It's time* + *to*-infinitive to say we should do something now. In this case, no criticism is implied: **It's time to go** now.

6 *would rather*

- **would rather** + bare infinitive
  We use *would rather* + bare infinitive to express our own or other people's preferences: I**'d rather go** to the disco than the cinema. / My friends **would rather meet** in town than come to my house.
- **would rather** + person + past simple
  We use *would rather* + person + past simple to say what we would like someone or something else to do in the present or future: I**'d rather you didn't borrow** my car.
- **would rather** + person + past perfect
  We use *would rather* + person + past perfect to say what we would have preferred someone to do (or not do) in the past: I**'d rather we hadn't seen** that film. It's given me nightmares!

7 *Suppose*

We use *suppose* to mean 'What if … ?' in these forms:
- **Suppose** + **present simple** for things that may happen in the future: We shouldn't have come here. **Suppose** someone **locks** us in! How will we get out?
- **Suppose** + **past simple** for things that we are just imagining/are unlikely to happen in the future: **Suppose** you **won** a lot of money. Would you give up work?
- **Suppose** + **past perfect** for imagining what could have happened in the past but didn't: **Suppose** you **hadn't been born** in this country. Where would you have liked to be born?

File 21: The passive

1 Uses of the passive

We use the passive:

- when we are more interested in the action (what happened) than the agent (who did it).
- when we don't know who the agent is or think it's not important to say.
- when we want to avoid saying who was responsible for something.
- when we are describing processes or writing reports and want to avoid vague subjects like *they*.
- to make information more formal, e.g. in signs and notices.

2 Mentioning the agent

In passive sentences:

- we only mention the agent if it is important to know who or what was responsible for the action: *Smoking is strictly forbidden* ~~by them~~.
- we use *by* to say who or what was responsible, or *with* when we mention the instrument used: *Hamlet was written* **by Shakespeare**. / *He was killed* **with a knife**.

3 Verbs with two objects

- when there are two subjects, a person and a thing, we usually make the person the subject:
  My brother *was given* **an award**. ✓
  An award *was given to* **my brother**. ✗ = clumsy

4 Forms of the passive

- **present simple:** *English* **is spoken** *here.*
- **present continuous:** *Dinner* **is being served**.
- **past simple:** *America* **was discovered** *by Columbus.*
- **present perfect:** *The world cup* **has been stolen**.
- **past continuous:** *The bird* **was being fed** *when it escaped.*
- **past perfect:** *When we heard the football match* **had been cancelled**, *we were furious.*
- **future simple:** *The decision* **will be made** *next week.*
- **going to:** *The President* **is going to be interviewed** *on TV.*
- **future perfect:** *My sister* **will have been given** *her exam results by now.*
- **infinitive:** *Teenagers* **should be given** *less homework!*
- **perfect infinitive:** *You* **should have been warned** *not to swim here. It's dangerous.*

! Intransitive verbs (verbs that do not take an object) can't be used in the passive: *We were* ~~sat~~ **seated** *quickly.*

! We can sometimes use *get* + past participle instead of *be* + past participle in informal English: *My cat* **got run over** *by a car.*

5 Reporting verbs in the passive

We can use the passive with verbs like *allege, believe, claim, expect, fear, know, report, say, think,* and *understand* in the following patterns:

- **expect, etc. + *to*-infinitive/*that***
  Temperatures **are expected to rise** *in the next 50 years.* /
  It is expected that *temperatures* **will rise** *in the next 50 years.*
- **say, etc. + *to be* + *-ing*/*that***
  Rainforests **are said to be disappearing** *at an alarming rate.* /
  It is said that *rainforests* **are disappearing** *at an alarming rate.*

- **fear, etc. + *to* + perfect infinitive/*that***
  Many people **are feared to have been killed** *in the hurricane.* / **It is feared that** *many people* **have been killed** *in the hurricane.*

File 22: *Have/get something done*

- We use *have* + object + past participle or *get* + object + past participle (usually more informal) when we arrange for someone else to do things for us: *We've just* **had our car serviced**.
- We use *have* + object + past participle to talk about unpleasant things which are done to people without their permission: *They* **had their house broken into** *last night.*

File 23: Relative clauses

1 Relative pronouns

- *who, whom* to refer to people
- *which* to refer to things
- *that* to refer to people or things
- *whose* to express possession
- *when* to refer to time
- *where* to refer to place
- *why* to refer to reasons

2 Defining relative clauses

We use defining relative clauses:

- with relative pronouns *who/whom, which, that, whose, when, where, why* to define a person, thing, time, place or reason. No commas are used before and after the clause:
  That's the street **where I live**.
  I've just met the girl **who/that has moved in next door**.
  The boy **whose father has won the lottery** *came to school in a Ferrari!*
  ! We can leave out the relative pronoun if it is the object of the verb: *The car* **(which/that) we hired** *broke down.*

3 Non-defining relative clauses

We use non-defining relative clauses:

- to give extra information about a person or thing. The sentence would make sense without the extra information. We put this information between commas: *Our teacher,* **who has been at this school for 20 years**, *is leaving next week.*
- to refer to the whole previous clause: *I have passed my exams,* **which is a huge relief**.
  ! We cannot leave out the relative pronoun if it is the object of the verb.

4 Prepositions in relative clauses

We can put prepositions either at the end of the relative clause (informal) or before the relative pronoun (formal):
John, **who I borrowed the money from**, *is a really good friend.* (= informal)
The assistant **to whom I spoke** *advised me to complain to the manager.* (= formal)

File 24: Purpose clauses

We can express purpose:

- with *for* + *noun/-ing*: *I went to Paris **for the meeting**. / This penknife is useful **for opening** bottles.*
- with *to-infinitive* or *in order to/so as to* + infinitive (more formal) when the subject is the same in both parts of the sentence: *We went to the café **to meet** our friends. / We are sending a letter **in order to inform** students of their results.*
- with *so as not to/in order not to* + infinitive (but not *not to*) when the subject is the same in both parts of the sentence: *We took a taxi **so as not to be** late for the meeting.*
- *so that* or *in order that* (very formal) when the subject of each verb is different: *My Dad is buying me a guitar **so that I can learn to play**. / The school will be closed for a week **in order that** the painters **can redecorate**.*
- *in case* + present simple to talk about avoiding a possible problem in the future: *Take a sweater **in case it gets** cold later.*
- *in case* + past simple to talk about precautions that were taken in the past: *He took sandwiches **in case he got** hungry later.*

File 25: Participle clauses

1 Present and perfect participles

We can use present and perfect participles:

- to replace clauses that begin with *since, as, because*:
  ***Since he was scared/Being scared**, he hid in the attic.*
  ***As he didn't realise/Not realising** how sharp the knife was, he cut his finger.*
  ***Because I had never been/Never having been** on the stage before, I was really nervous.*
- for actions that happen simultaneously or in sequence:
  *He **looked** through the window and **saw** the burglar walk into the living room. = **Looking** through the window, he **saw** the burglar walk into the living room.*
  *After **he had finished speaking**, he **waited** for the applause.*
  *= **Having finished speaking**, he waited for the applause.*
- after time conjunctions and prepositions like *after, before, despite, on, when, while*: ***After I had read/After reading** the book, I went to see the film.*

! The participle you use must agree with the subject of both verbs:
~~Standing at the door, the woman's face turned white.~~
***Standing** at the door, **I saw** the woman's face turn white.* ✓

2 Present participles

We can use present participles to shorten relative clauses:
*I think the man (who is) **waiting** in the lounge is a thief.*

3 Past participles

We sometimes use past participles instead of the passive:
***Seen** in daylight, the haunted house looks quite normal.*
(= When it is seen ...)

File 26: Clauses of reason and result

1 *so much/so many, so little/so few (that)*

- We use *so many/so few (that)* with countable nouns: *There were **so many** people at the party **(that)** I couldn't get in the front door. / **So few** fans bought tickets **(that)** they cancelled the concert.*
- We use *so much/so little (that)* with uncountable nouns: *They won **so much** money **(that)** they didn't know what to spend it on. / We made **so little** progress **(that)** we had to work all night to catch up.*

2 *so/such (that)*

- We use *so ... (that)* with adjectives and adverbs: *I'm **so happy (that)** I could cry! / He drove **so fast (that)** I was scared we'd have an accident.*
- We use *such a ... (that)* with singular countable nouns and *such ... (that)* with plural countable nouns and uncountable nouns: *It was **such a lovely day (that)** we decided to have a barbecue. / He tells **such scary stories (that)** I can't bear to listen to them! / They gave us **such disgusting food (that)** we couldn't eat it.*

3 *too/enough* + clause

- We use *too* + adjective (+ *for* + sb) + *to*-infinitive for things that are difficult, and therefore impossible to do: *The hotel was **too far (for us) to walk** to so we got a taxi.*

! Compare:
1 *The homework was **too difficult (for me) to do**. (= I could not do it at all.)
2 *The homework was **very difficult to do**. (= It was difficult but not impossible.)

- We use *not* + adjective/adverb + *enough* (+ *for* + sb) + *to*-infinitive to describe things that are insufficient in some way: *You're **not old enough to drive**. You're only 14.*

! Compare:
1 *The sea was **too cold (for us) to swim in**.*
2 *The sea wasn't **warm enough (for us) to swim in**.*

- We can use *not* + *enough* + noun, *too many/too much* + noun, and *too little/too few* + noun to suggest a result, without actually saying what the result is: *He didn't have **enough money**. (= so he couldn't buy anything) / There was **too little time**. (= so we couldn't do what we wanted to)*

Writing file

1 Transactional letter
Question

You are studying at Thames College in Britain. The students on your course recently had an end-of-term party at the Star Hotel, which you helped to organise. Unfortunately, the party was not a success.

You received the booking details opposite from Mrs Jones, the manager of the Star Hotel, before the party. Read the booking details, on which you have made some notes, then write a letter to Mrs Jones, including all your complaints and asking for some money back.

Write a **letter** of between **120** and **180** words in an appropriate style. Do not write any postal addresses.

STAR HOTEL
Booking Details

To: Organiser of Thames College Party

Reservation for Friday 18th December

hot and stuffy

Pine Room – dinner for 20 at 19.00 (Waiter service) — *table not ready until 8 o'clock!*

Four-course menu to include choice of vegetarian dishes — *only one vegetarian dish*

Disco: 21.00 – 23.30 — *didn't start until 22.00*

£20.00 per person — *ask for refund*

Model answer

Always begin your letter with *Dear ...*

Start your letter by saying why you are writing.

Dear Mrs Jones,

I am writing to you about the party we held at your hotel on Friday 18th December. I have a number of complaints.

First of all, although we booked dinner for 7 p.m., our table was not ready until 8 p.m. Then, when we did sit down for the meal, we discovered that there was only one vegetarian dish available, although you had promised there would be a choice. To make matters worse, the room was hot and stuffy.

As for the disco, we had to wait until 10 p.m. for it to start because the disc jockey was late. Most of us had to leave at 11 p.m. to catch the last bus, which meant we had hardly any time for dancing.

Use the correct degree of formality or informality for the exam question.

State clearly and politely what action you want the person or company to take.

I hope you will agree that it was a very disappointing evening. I would be grateful if you could send our students an apology, and refund at least part of the cost of the meal.

I look forward to hearing from you.

Yours sincerely,

Sandra Perez
Sandra Perez

Make sure that your letter contains the information asked for in the question. Don't copy whole phrases from the question.

End a formal letter like this if you begin with a name. If you don't know the name, begin *Dear Sir/Madam*, and finish with *Yours faithfully*.

Useful language

Requesting information/an item
I am writing in response to ...
I am writing for information about ...
I would like to know more about ...
I wonder if you could possibly tell/send me ...
I am writing to ask whether ...
I would be grateful if you could ...

Making a complaint
I am writing to complain about ...
I am sorry to say that I was very disappointed with ...
I am afraid to say I have number of complaints about ...

2 Informal letter

Question

> You are spending a month abroad, learning English, with a group of people you have never met before but with whom you have a lot in common. Half way through the course, you decide to write a letter to your English-speaking pen friend, telling him/her about what you have been doing so far and what you plan to do later. Write your letter in 120–180 words in an appropriate style.

Useful language

Introductions

Thanks for your letter. It was lovely to hear from you.
Sorry I haven't written for so long but ...
I was really pleased to hear that ...
I thought I'd better write and tell you about ...

Conclusions

Well, that's all for now. Do write back soon.
Looking forward to hearing from you.
Thanks for all your help.
Good luck with the ... !
Give my love/regards to ...

Model answer

Invent a name if one is not provided in the exam question. Never begin *Dear Friend/ Pen friend.*

Divide your letter into paragraphs and include two or three points in each paragraph.

Try to use a good range of vocabulary which is relevant to the question.

Use an informal phrase like *Best wishes, Regards,* or *Love* to finish your letter.

Begin your letter with some general comments, or by apologising for a delay in writing, or by referring to a letter you have just received.

Don't begin each sentence in the same way.

End your letter by asking about the reader, thanking him/her, sending greetings to his/her family, referring to when you will next meet, etc.

Dear Antonio,

I can't believe I've been here in England for two weeks already. I'm having a fantastic time.

When I arrived, I was worried because I didn't know any of the people on my course. However, I've made lots of friends now. Most of the other students are the same age as me and although we come from different countries (South America, Greece, Poland and Spain), we have the same sort of interests and hobbies.

So far, I've been to visit lots of places of interest here, including London and Cambridge, and I have learned a lot about English history and culture. I'm planning an excursion to Scotland next weekend with people from my class. We're going to spend a night in Edinburgh and then drive across to see the islands off the west coast. It should be really beautiful – and we'll have good fun together too, I think.

I've taken lots of photos here so I can tell you all about it when I get back. Hope you are enjoying your holiday. Write soon and tell me all about what you've been doing.

Love,

Simone

3 Article
Question

You have seen this advertisement in an international magazine.

HOLIDAY COMPETITION

Write an article about the most exciting holiday you have ever had, explaining to our readers why the holiday was so special.

The best article will win a weekend for two in London.

Write your **article** for the competition in **120–180** words in an appropriate style.

Useful language

Involving your reader
Would you like to ... ?
I'm sure you can imagine ...
I'm sure you'd agree that ...
Let's ...

Conclusions
I hope ...
I suppose ...
All in all, ...

Model answer

Set your article out like this. Don't use letter format.

You can include one or two questions to get your reader's interest.

Finish your article with a conclusion that summarises your opinion.

A holiday amongst the stars

Would you like to spend two weeks' holiday in the film capital of the world? Do you fancy meeting some of the biggest stars in Hollywood? This was the dream holiday I won last year.

As the winner of a film competition, I was given a plane ticket for Hollywood where I stayed in a top-class hotel. I'm sure you can imagine how exciting it was! Every day a car came to take me to the studios and I watched performers rehearsing and shooting scenes for films.

I learned so much about the film industry, but the highlight of my holiday was when I was asked to be an extra in an adventure film. Not only did I meet one of my all-time favourite stars, but I actually acted with him too! I couldn't believe my luck!

I'm sure I will have exciting holidays in the future, but somehow I don't think there'll ever be such a special one as Hollywood. All in all, it was the holiday of a lifetime.

Think of an interesting title.

Don't use very formal language.

Make your article lively and interesting.

4 Story
Question

You have decided to enter a short story competition. The competition rules say that the story must begin or end with the words:

Tom woke up when he heard voices. He looked at the clock and saw that it was 11 p.m.

Write your story in 120–180 words in an appropriate style.

Useful language

Start of the story
At first, ...
In the beginning, ...
The first thing that
  happened was ...

Sequencing events in the story
Then, ...
(Minutes) later, ...
After some time, ...
After that, ...

Things that happen fast/slowly
Suddenly, ...
All at once, ...
Gradually, ...
Slowly, ...

The end of the story
In the end, ...
Eventually, ...
At last, ...

Model answer

Use the words supplied in the exam question in the correct place in the story. Be careful to use the names and pronouns supplied. Do not change anything.

Use a variety of narrative tenses like past simple, past continuous, past perfect.

In crime or adventure stories, you can end on a moment of suspense and let your reader imagine what happens next. Alternatively, you can show how a problem was resolved.

Tom woke up when he heard voices. He looked at the clock and saw that it was 11 p.m. Yawning, he looked out of the window, expecting to see his parents arriving home.

But there was no car outside. Deciding he must have imagined the noise, Tom went back to the book he had been reading. As he turned the page, he heard the noise again. This time however, it was louder. It sounded like a window breaking. He turned and looked at the living room door. The handle was turning!

What should he do? 'Keep cool!' he told himself. 'Think!' Quick as a flash, he jumped behind the curtains just as two men entered the room. Were they kidnappers? Had they come to burgle the house? Whatever they had come for, Tom was not going to let them succeed.

The telephone was just next to the window. Holding his breath, Tom crept towards it. The men were busy. Nobody would hear him. He was nearly there when, suddenly, the phone rang. Tom froze in horror. 'My parents must be calling me,' Tom thought. 'What am I going to do now?'

Vary the way you start your sentences.

Use a range of time phrases to sequence events in the story.

Try to make your story interesting/ exciting. Where appropriate, use short sentences to create suspense.

Choose vivid, colourful words rather than very simple vocabulary.

5 Report
Question

A group of foreign students is going to stay in your town for a month. You have been asked to write a report for their group leader, Sara Chiesa, about eating out in your town. Describe the best places for the students to eat and drink in the area and explain why you think these places would be suitable.

Write your **report** in 120–180 words in an appropriate style.

Useful language

Introductions
The purpose/aim of this report is to ...
This report is intended to ...
In order to write this report, I have interviewed/visited ..., etc.

Presenting a list
Here are some of the advantages/disadvantages:
This would provide the following (benefits):

Making recommendations
I have no hesitation in recommending ...
I can recommend ... because ...

Conclusions
In conclusion, I think that ...
In my opinion, the best ... would be ...

Model answer

Start your report in the way shown here. Invent names if necessary.

State the purpose of your report clearly in the introduction.

Use formal language.

Give a clear conclusion, stating your own opinion or evaluation, and making a recommendation if appropriate.

Make your report easy to read. Divide it into sections under clear headings and list points where appropriate.

To: Sara Chiesa
From: Daniel Agassi
Date: 5 August 20—
Subject: Places to eat and drink for your group visit

Introduction
The purpose of this report is to describe the best places for your group to eat and drink in this area. I have visited a number of cafés and restaurants to check their suitability.

Places to eat and drink
There are many restaurants in the High Street but they are expensive and very formal. Your group might prefer the restaurants in the Old Quarter. Here, you can eat outside while admiring the buildings and enjoying the atmosphere. Two places are particularly good:

1 'The Fountain' is an extremely popular restaurant. The food is excellent and the menu includes typical dishes of this country as well as a variety of international dishes to suit everyone.

2 'The Metro' also serves very high-quality food and has a lively atmosphere. There is a band every night and customers can dance and join in the singing.

Conclusion
I can recommend both 'The Fountain' and 'The Metro'. They are highly suitable for your group and they are in the Old Quarter, which is well worth visiting too.

6 Discursive composition

Question

The following comment was printed recently in a local magazine:

A great deal of what students learn in schools these days is a waste of time.

Your teacher has asked you to write a composition on this subject, with reference to your own learning experiences.

Write your composition in 120–180 words in an appropriate style.

Useful language

Expressing opinions
I agree/disagree with the statement that ...
I think/believe that ...
It seems to me that ...
In my opinion, ...
I am in favour of ...
I am against the idea that ...

Sequencing ideas
Firstly, ...
Secondly, ...
Finally, ...

Expressing contrast
but
even though
although
in spite of/despite + noun/-ing
in spite of/despite the fact that + clause
on the other hand
however
nevertheless
while

Conclusions
On the whole, I would say that, ...
In conclusion, ...
To sum up, I think that ...
All in all, I believe that ...

Model answer

Start your answer with a sentence that links to the problem/question you are discussing. Don't just begin with 'I agree with this statement'.

Use linking words and phrases.

Summarise your opinion in the final paragraph and add some further comments.

Talk about your own experience if the question asks you to do this.

Set out your opinion clearly. Separate positive and negative points and put them in separate paragraphs.

I think that most of what we learn at school is useful. The problem is that we do not always realise this fact in the beginning.

Take Science, for example. I hated Chemistry lessons when I was younger. I couldn't see the point in doing boring experiments and learning tables. Now I want to be a doctor, I appreciate how important Chemistry is. I realise that we had to learn the basics first. I used to think learning Latin was pointless too, but now it really helps me understand my medical textbooks.

On the other hand, there were some lessons that really were useless. At my school we all did Cookery – I'm sure we could learn that much better at home! We had to attend Drama classes, too. I couldn't see the point of this unless someone wanted to be an actor.

In conclusion, I would say that most of what we learn at school is quite useful. I just wish all teachers would make it clear how the subjects we study can really help us later on in life.

Vocabulary file

Unit 1

Types of film
action movie
documentary
horror film
love story
musical
romantic comedy
science fiction
thriller

Jobs and people
actor
audience
camera operator
director
film crew
hero/heroine
musician
producer
scriptwriter
technician
villain

Money
charity
finance
funding
low-budget
raise money

Art
abstract painting
art exhibition
art gallery
landscape
portrait
sculpture
still life
work of art

Other forms of entertainment
dance
football match
museum
novel
pop concert
talent show
theatre
video game

Adjectives for feelings/reactions
calm
disturbing
exciting
fantastic
frightening
intriguing
mysterious
off-putting
strange
tranquil
upsetting
violent

Adjectives for people
extrovert
hard-working
reliable
talented

Adjective + preposition
interested in
responsible for

Verb collocations
be about
be set in
book (a ticket)
have an influence on
perform (a play)
play (a role)
show (a film)
tell jokes
tell the story of

Phrasal/prepositional verbs
belong to
enrol in (a class)
give up
go to (the theatre)
look round (a place)
pay sb back

put on (a play)
set out (for)
star in (a film)

Phrases
in advance
in trouble
on stage

Other related words
contestant
episode (of a series)
film premiere
film studio
interval (in the ~)
location
performance
production
refreshments
scene
scenery
series (TV ~)
set
show

Unit 2

Challenge and adventure
achieve a goal
crew
crossing
endure
expedition
exploration
explorer
glide
injure
inspire
instructor
landing
lose (your) nerve
lose (your) way
motivate
navigator
protection
put sb's life at risk
rescue
save sb's life
sense of achievement
set sail for
shipmate
sink
stay alive
supplies
survival
survive
take risks
trek

Activities
abseiling
archery
assault course
canoeing
caving
hillwalking
map-reading
mountaineering
orienteering
rock-climbing

Equipment
harness
helmet
rope (safety ~)
target
torch
walking boots

Feelings
depression
despair
excitement
exhaustion
sadness
sleepiness

Personal qualities
ability
admiration
ambition
courage
determination
experience
ingenuity
leadership
respect

Adjectives for people
active
admirable
adventurous
ambitious
confident
courageous
determined
dishonest
experienced
fit
good-looking
impatient
inflexible
irresponsible
optimistic
patient
qualified
reckless
romantic
selfish

sensible
sensitive
skilful
strong-willed
unconventional
unfit

Adjectives for activities
addictive
challenging
demanding
frightening
messy
muddy
stimulating
sweaty
thrilling
tiring

Adjective + preposition
available to
full of
included in
ready for

Verb collocations
catch fire
drag (equipment)
get (worse)
get ready for
have (a lot of) fun
hold (your) breath
keep sb occupied

lose (your) grip
make (your) way to
make a mistake
make a plan
make an effort
make friends
make sure
pay attention to
take part in
take sth seriously

Phrasal/prepositional verbs
carry out (an inspection)
fall out of (an aircraft)
get round to (an activity)
hold on to
join in (the fun)
run out of (water)
step on (land)
suffer from (frostbite)
take back to (a place)
take off
try out (an activity)

Phrases
in danger
in (poor) condition
in good spirits
in working order
on display
on foot

Unit 3

Education and success
achieve an ambition
apply for (a grant)
attend (a school)
career (option)
college
competitive
demonstrate
develop a skill
diploma
follow a career
get (good) marks/
    qualifications
get into university
grade ('A' ~)
half-term break
hand in (your)
    homework
headmaster
high-earning
interview
laboratory
learn (practical) skills
leave school
library
'life skill'
playgroup
practical

primary school
profession
professor
pursue a career
qualifications
register
registration
revise
school rule
self-study
set (your) sights on (a
    career)
study hard
take an exam
take notes
take time off (school)
term

School and university subjects
Architectural Design
Art
Biology
Business Studies
Chemistry
Design Technology
Economics
English
Geography

History
Information Technology
Latin
Maths
Music
Philosophy
Physical Education
Physics
Politics
Religious Studies
Technical Drawing

The Internet
access the Internet
e-mail
Internet café
keyboard
mobile phone
webpage
Word Wide Web

Adjective + preposition
capable of
designed for
fed up with
good at
hopeless at
open to

proud of
relevant to
tired of
worried about

Verb collocations
catch sb's attention
do (your) best
do (your) homework
do a course (in sth)
do a test
do an experiment
do project work
do research
gain confidence
get into trouble
give a presentation
have an opportunity
make a mess
make a mistake
make a noise
make an attempt
make an effort
make friends
make progress
pay (your) way
run a business
use technology

Phrasal/prepositional verbs
blame sb for
blow up (a building)
build up (a business)
catch up on
    (coursework)
cope with
draw up (a plan)
get through (homework)
insist on
look forward to
object to
prevent from
put sb off
set up (a business)
show through
sign sb up
tell sb off
think of
turn sth down

Phrases
at (your) own pace
by heart
on (your) own

Unit 4

Amenities and attractions
bus station
castle
department store
leisure centre
leisure facilities
market
parks and gardens
pedestrian precinct
public transport
shopping mall
skating rink
subway
tourist office

Parts of a city
apartment block
district
industrial estate
office block
residential area
ring road
skyscraper
suburb(s)
the old quarter

Problems of city life
crime rate
crowd (of people)
housing
litter
pace of life
pollution
traffic congestion/jam

Culture and customs
carnival
celebration
ethnic community
festival
immigrant
immigration
lifestyle
multiculturalism
national dress
parade
sense of tradition
street party
traditional costume

Adjectives for places
bustling
colourful
cultural
densely populated
elegant
exciting
fascinating
frightening
hectic
historic
isolated
lively
overdeveloped
peaceful
picturesque
polluted
quaint
relaxing
restless
shabby
stimulating
stressful
striking
stunning
unattractive
unspoiled

up-to-date
vibrant
welcoming
well looked-after

Adjective + preposition
associated with
enthusiastic about
mad about

Verb collocations
demolish (a building)
drop litter
have an effect on
impose a fine
sweep the streets

Phrasal/prepositional verbs
act out (a story)
bring up (a child)
consist of
do up (an area)
get away from (the city)
get run over
give in
give sth away

go off
go on
grow up
hold on to (your culture)
keep up (traditions)
look after (your)self
make up (a story)
move in
pull down (a building)
put sth down to
put up (a building)
save up for
settle in
take off
take place
wear off

Phrases
at (your) fingertips
by (New York) standards
in a mess
in a rush
in origin
on (your) doorstep
on a budget
out of control
to a(n) (large) extent

Vocabulary file

Unit 5

Shopping and advertising
assistant
attract customers
bargain
brand (of shampoo)
carry out research
cashier
consumer
delivery
free sample
goods
groceries
mail-order catalogue
make (of mobile phone)
make a purchase
model (of car)
queue
range
receipt
return
sale
self-service
serve (your)self
shopaholic
shoplift
shopper
shopping spree
voucher
window-shopping

Types/Parts of shops
basket

beauty salon
bookseller
car park
check-out till
counter
fitting room
gift shop
parking facilities
rail
shelf

Money
afford
bank account/loan
bill
coin
debt
e-commerce
exchange
leave a deposit
lend
offer a (20%) discount
pay in cash / by cheque
   / by credit card
pocket money
rebate
refund
spend money on

Clothes and image
achieve an image
casual
choosy

designer labels/clothing
fabric
fashion statement
fashion conscious
fussy
jacket
jeans
jumper
material
outfit
pattern
piece of clothing/
   jewellery
pride (your)self on (your)
   appearance
scarf
scruffy
size
smart
sophisticated
sporty
style
suit
sweater
trainers
trendy
trousers
T-shirt
wardrobe
zip

Adjectives for rooms
airy
bare
cluttered
contemporary
cosy
functional
homely
impersonal
inviting
orderly
personal
plain
simple
spacious
sparse
stylish
uncluttered

Adjectives for objects
clay
full-length
handmade
iron
leather
ornate
painted
plastic
round
silk
stiff
thick

wide
wooden

Verb collocations
follow sb's lead
make a choice
make a complaint
resist the temptation
set a trend
solve a problem
take control of

Phrasal/prepositional verbs
get hold of (information)
get rid of
go off sth
keep up with (the latest
   fashions)
wear out

Phrases
at a glance
by day
face to face
free of charge
in stock
on impulse
on offer
on sale
under one roof
value for money

Unit 6

Household chores
be a tip
clean up after (your)self
do the washing-up
put (your things) away
tidy up

Weddings and family members
best man
bride
bridegroom
bridesmaid
celebrate
get married (to)
grandchild
marriage
mother-/father-in-law
nephew/niece
propose a toast
wedding reception /
   dress

Celebrations
birthday party
engagement
party hat
public holiday
social event/occasion

Personal qualities
confidence
generosity
honesty
intelligence
loyalty
originality
patience
politeness
sense of humour
sensitivity
sincerity
sociability
understanding

Adjectives for people
argumentative
arrogant
bad-tempered
communicative
easy-going
funny
generous
grateful
guilty
honest
independent
intelligent
jealous

lazy
loyal
mean
original
outgoing
polite
rebellious
rude
sincere
sociable
stubborn
unreasonable

Adjective + preposition
committed to
similar to

Verb collocations
come to an agreement
come to terms with
feel anxiety about sth
find a solution
follow in sb's footsteps
form a relationship
give an/the impression
   that
have a row
have an argument
insist on doing sth

lay down the law
lose (your) temper
make a decision
make a success of sth
make sth (worse)
play a part
reach an agreement
reach the stage where
respect sb's privacy
take the example of
tell sb a secret

Phrasal/prepositional verbs
approve of sb
ask sb out
blame sb for
bother about sth
disapprove of sb
fall for/in love with sb
fall out
get to know sb
go on at sb
go out with sb
keep sth from sb
live up to (a parent)
make up
pick on sb

pick sb up
split up
talk sth over
tell sb off
trust in sb
turn into
work through (feelings)

Phrases
on no account
the centre of attention

Other related words
adolescence
behaviour
character
disturb
friendship
identity
interfere
issue
nag
personal space
personality
point of view
quarrel
romance
share
social life
support

Unit 7

Sporting venues

basketball/tennis court
fitness centre
football pitch
gymnasium
running track
sports hall
swimming pool

People in sport

agent
athlete
boxer
coach
cyclist
fan
footballer
hockey player
referee
runner
spectator
sponsor
swimmer
the press

Sports equipment

cycling machine
flippers
gloves
goggles
helmet
net
punchbag
racquet
rowing machine
running machine
stick
trainers
weight-lifting equipment
whistle

Qualities of sportspeople

agility
courage
dedication
fast reflexes

good sense of balance
hand–eye coordination
motivation
speed
stamina
strength

Food and diet

beef
bread
butter
carbohydrate
cereal
cheese
chocolate
cream
crisps
eggs
fat
fibre
fish
French fries
green vegetables
lentils
meat
milk
nuts
orange juice
pasta
porridge
potatoes
protein
rice
root vegetables
salad
salt
sausages
shellfish
snack
steak
toast
vegetables
vitamins

Ways of cooking food

bake
barbecue

boil
grill
microwave
roast
steam
stew

Parts of the body

ankle
arm
calf
chest
elbow
finger
forehead
heart
hip
joint
knee
leg
lung
muscle
shoulder
stomach
thigh
thumb
toe
tongue
vein
wrist

Medical problems and stress

backache
be sick
boredom
cause stress
competition
cough
eating disorder
feel sick
flu
headache
heart disease
infection (chest ~)
injury
pain

peer pressure
sore throat
sprained (ankle)
stiff neck
stomach pains
stress factor
swelling
symptom
temperature
workload
wound

Dealing with medical problems and stress

antibiotic
aromatherapy
bandage
crutches
cure
go on a diet
heal
increase (your) sense of well-being
massage
medicine
meditation
operation
pill
plaster
recover
relaxation therapy
relieve stress
remedy
sling
specialist
therapist
treat
treatment
yoga

Verb collocations

blow out of proportion
do athletics/ weight-lifting
get fit
go jogging
impose restrictions

improve (your) performance/fitness
keep a diary
kick a ball
lose weight
make a demand on
make an appointment
play football/basketball
satisfy hunger
stand a chance
suffer in silence
take up (pottery)
tone (your) muscles
toss a coin
train hard

Phrasal/prepositional verbs

beat off (anxiety)
build (your)self up
calm (you) down
come down to
come up
cope with
deal with
end up
face up to
look forward to
look into
put sb off sth
put up with

Phrases

a matter of life or death
under pressure

Other related words

club
fitness
moody
panic
score
sponsorship
transfer deal

Vocabulary file

Unit 8

Holidays and activities
activity holiday
beach holiday
cruise
cultural holiday
educational holiday
hiking
horse-riding
safari
scuba diving
sightseeing holiday
skiing
sunbathing
two-centre holiday
walking and trekking
  holiday
weekend break
wildlife holiday
working holiday

Travel and tourism
apply for a passport/visa
arrange travel insurance
board a coach / plane /
  train
cancel a flight
charter
coach trip
delay a flight
destination
fare
go abroad
guided tour

holidaymaker
journey
luggage
miss a train / plane / bus
nightlife
place of interest
reach
resort
sightseeing excursion
souvenir
take photos
terminal
tour operator
travel light

Accommodation
balcony
bed and breakfast
high season
vacancy
youth hostel

Scenery
border
coast
hillside
jungle
mountainside
national park
nature reserve
path
shore
valley

view
volcano

Things to pack
easy-to-pack clothing
first aid kit
insect repellent
sun hat
sunglasses
suntan lotion
travel sickness tablets
walking shoes
wrinkle-free clothing

Adjectives for holidays, resorts and activities
action-packed
disappointing
exhausting
sensational
taxing
undemanding

Adjectives for scenery
breathtaking
coastal
dense
deserted
dramatic
open-air
rocky
rural
sandy
spotless

Adjective + preposition
associated with
aware of
blessed with
built for
crowded with
designed by
famous for
good for
included in
lined with
linked to
located off
satisfied with
set on
situated in
surrounded by
twinned with
visited by

Verb collocations
confirm a booking
get an upset stomach
get sunburnt/sunstroke
get vaccinations
make a (hotel) reservation
pose a threat to

Phrasal/prepositional verbs
break down
check in

drop sb off
get off (the plane)
get to (a place)
hold sb up
make for (a place)
pick sb up
set out
sign up for
slow down
speed up
take off
turn back

Ecotourism
benefit wildlife
bring in revenue
cause pollution
destroy habitats
disturb wildlife
endangered species
environment
improve facilities
mass tourism
protect species
regulate development
rubbish

Phrases
off the beaten track
peace and quiet
up to standard

Unit 9

Life on other planets
alien civilisation
alien creature
astronomer
decode
detect
extra-terrestrial
galaxy
human race
intelligent life
life form
orbit (the Earth/Sun)
outer space
radio telescope
scan
sighting
signal
solar system
space colony
space exploration
spacecraft (unmanned ~)
travel at the speed of
  light

UFO (unidentified
  flying object)
universe

Mysteries and discoveries
concoct
fake
genuine
hoax
hoaxer
invention
legend
nonsense
prove
rational
rumour
sceptic
theory
trick photography
unconvincing

Discovering the past
ancestor
ancient
archaeological dig
archaeologist
artefact
bone
buried treasure
dig
excavate
find sth by chance
formerly
generation
heritage
metal detector
predecessor
prehistoric
preserve
ruin
skeleton
tomb
tool
tribe

Adjective + preposition
unsuitable for

Verb collocations
accept a dare
come to a conclusion
come to light
crack a code
hold (your) breath
make an impression
pin (your) hopes on
point a finger
shine a torch
sustain life
take (your) breath away
take for granted
take long
tell the truth
trap heat
turn (pale)

Phrasal/prepositional verbs
bring about (a change)
come across

come up with
cover up (evidence)
hand over
let out (a cry)
link up
make of
make sth up
turn out
wipe out (a civilisation)
work out (an equation)

Other related words
analyst
clue
coincidence
deny
evolve
ghost
haunted
likelihood
likely
reveal
search
top-secret
unlikely

Unit 10

Parts of a computer
CD drive
computer display
disk drive
floppy disk
hard disk
microchip
monitor
mouse
printer
screen
software

Gadgets and services
CD player
desktop computer
hand-held positioning
    device
labour-saving devices
lap-top computer
pocket calculator
voice mail

Using gadgets and services
check (your)
    message box
play back
plug sth in
press the 'send' button
press the right key
run on electricity/
    batteries
speak after the tone
store a document
surf the Internet

switch on/off
tap the right numbers
type a document

Verb collocations
become a reality
follow a
    recommendation
get in touch with
give feedback
install a system
lack confidence
launch an initiative
make use of
prolong life
take a lot of care
take advantage of
take the trouble

Phrasal/prepositional verbs
carry out (an operation)
find out
give out (a signal)
go through (records)

Crimes
arson
burglary
drink-driving
forgery
fraud
graffiti
hijacking
joyriding
mugging
murder

pickpocketing
robbery
shoplifting
smuggling
speeding
theft

Criminals and trials
accuse
appeal
court
death penalty
hijacker
imprison
jury
justice system
law court
mugger
offender
pardon
prison cell
punishment
sentence
shoplifter
thief
trial
try
witness

Fighting crime
arrest
charge
closed circuit television
crime scene
database
DNA analysis
fingerprint

handcuff
improve security
monitor the public
patrol an area
patrol car
police force
police officer
police records
question
scan a crowd
security camera
suspect
video camera

Verb collocations: crime
burgle a (house)
catch a (thief)
commit a crime
find sb guilty (of)
hold sb hostage
pay a fine
pay a ransom
rob a (bank)
send sb for trial
send sb to prison
set sb free
steal a (wallet)
take sb into custody
take sb's fingerprints

Phrasal/prepositional verbs: crimes
break into (a car)
get away
get off with (a warning)

get up to (mischief)
give (your)self away
give (your)self up
let sb off with (a caution)
make off with (an
    amount of money)

Phrases
in favour of
on duty
on patrol
on the beat
on the market

Other related words
advance
civil rights
crime-proof
design
detect
detection
device
electronic
escape
form of communication
hand-held
headset
online
operator
pocket-sized
receiver
revolutionise
scientist
sensor

Unit 11

Birds and animals
alligator
ant
chicken
chimpanzee
dolphin
eagle
insect
monkey
rat
sea otter
seal
shark
squirrel
whale
wolf

Environmental problems
acid rain
air pollution
burn fossil fuels
burn tropical forests
CFCs
chemical residues in food
cut down rainforests
deforestation

dump oil
emissions from factories
exhaust fumes
fumes from power stations
greenhouse gases
health risk
hole in the ozone layer
landfill dumps
over-farming
packaging
pesticides
poisonous gases
population growth
rubbish dump
soil erosion
toxic waste
waste resources/water
water pollution

Environmental solutions
ban pesticides
ban vehicles
biodegradable cleaning materials
collect rainwater

organic farming
protect wildlife
recycling facilities
reduce traffic congestion
renewable energy sources
solar power
use less packaging
water conservation
wildlife reserves
wind power

Weather conditions and natural disasters
air pressure
avalanche
breeze
cloud
cyclone
drought
famine
flood
fog
forecast
freezing cold
heatwave
humidity

hurricane
rainfall
rainstorm
shower
snowfall
temperature
thunder and lightning
thunderstorm
tornado
wind speed

Verb collocations
become extinct
draw a conclusion
give rise to
grow crops
play (your) part
raise the alarm
take shelter

Phrasal/prepositional verbs
carry on (a tradition)
cope with (a change)
cut down on
cut off (a source of energy)
die out

dispose of
face up to (a challenge)
give off (heat/a gas)
heat up
lead to
pass on (behaviour)
result from
turn up
use up (resources)

Phrases
at a distance
in captivity
in the wild

Other related words
aerosol
atmosphere
conservation
contaminate
extinction
hunt
ice cap
melt
poison
sea level
vegetarian

Unit 12

Jobs
accountant
army officer
DJ
education officer
lawyer
marketing manager
model
soldier

The world of work
application form
career prospects
colleague
commute
do voluntary work
earn
employer
employment
flexitime
freelance
full-time (worker)
gap year
get work experience
go on strike

graduation
holiday job
job agency
job market
job satisfaction
job security
open-plan office
overtime
part-time (worker)
pension
perk
promote
promotion
reference
retirement
salary
self-employed
temporary contract
vacancy
work from home
workforce
workplace
workstation

Personal qualities
commitment
drive
expertise
flexibility
focus
imagination
independence
initiative
maturity
personality
resourcefulness
self-discipline

Careers in the arts
concert hall
concert tour
perform
play the violin / cello / drums / flute / trumpet / saxophone / keyboards
recording
rehearse

Adjective + preposition
impatient with
jealous of
satisfied with
successful at
suitable for
tired of
worried about

Verb collocations
get to the top
have a change of heart
join the army
keep sb company
keep up to date with
perform a miracle
take responsibility for
take sb by surprise

Phrasal/ prepositional verbs
branch out
build up
end up

face up to (a demand)
feel about
fill in (a form)
fill up (a basket)
focus on
fool around
let (your)self in for
meet up with (a person)
miss out on
resign from (a job)
set up (a course)
take sb on
track down (a person)

Phrases
in (your) own way
in charge of
in the (computing) field
out of practice
out of work

Communication tasks and answers

Unit 2, Reading 1, Exercise 3, page 17

1 What makes Shackleton's story so special for the writer?

  A the fact that Shackleton wrote it himself
  B the way that people react to it
  C the fact that it was not a success
  D the way that it is still remembered

2 What did Shackleton see as the greatest threat to his crew on the ice?

  A having nothing to do
  B lack of food
  C the weather conditions
  D loss of hope

3 What does the word 'dragging' in line 38 tell us about the small boats?

  A They were difficult to move.
  B They were easily damaged.
  C They were in poor condition.
  D They were very uncomfortable.

4 How did the men feel when they reached Elephant Island?

  A too tired to care about anything
  B thrilled by the adventure they'd had
  C too ill to travel any further
  D relieved to have completed the journey

5 Why did Shackleton decide to leave Elephant Island?

  A The weather was getting worse.
  B Nobody would find them there.
  C The crew was getting depressed.
  D There was no food for them there.

6 What does 'It' in line 55 refer to?

  A the plan
  B the boat
  C the whaling station
  D the navigator

7 How did the writer feel when she saw the small boat in London?

  A disappointed
  B shocked
  C puzzled
  D upset

8 Which phrase best summarises the writer's opinion of Shackleton?

  A He deserves to be better remembered.
  B He was lucky to have survived.
  C He commands our great respect.
  D He took unnecessary risks.

Unit 7, Lead-in, Exercise 2, page 78

TOP CAUSES OF STRESS
Boys and girls in two UK schools were asked to list their top five stress factors.

Boys	Girls
[3] **girls**: looking good and acting cool in front of girls	[2] **parents**: imposing restrictions
[5] **competition**: exams, sport	[5] **being organised**
[2] **image**: pressure to look good/wear the right clothes	[4] **peer pressure**: what to wear/look like
[1] **toughness**: trying to be tough and mature	[1] **exams**: coursework and homework
[4] **classmates**: peer pressure	[3] **friendships**: arguments and problems

Unit 10, Grammar, Exercise 2.1, page 118

Q.1 The results imply that most of you think there are aliens out there. Not all the no answers were from disbelievers, however – they just reckoned that 'even by 2050 extra-terrestrials would still find us too stupid'.

Q.2 A close result, but not all the women answered yes, nor all the men no. Many of the men reckoned 'women already are the dominant sex' and many of the women vowed that 'they would never want to be dominant anyway'. Work that one out for yourself!

Q.3 You've been watching too much science fiction. 'It's already accepted,' some readers reckon, 'the police use psychics to find kidnap victims.' An interestingly strong yes vote, but then we knew that's what the result would be ... thanks to ESP!

Q.4 This was seen as an almost unpreventable aspect of the future, although most of you hoped 'it would not be morally allowed. Your child might "go out of fashion" – what an awful thought.'

Q.5 You were horrified at the prospect, and even more horrified about who would program the computer.

Functions file

1 Comparing and contrasting

- Well, there are people doing (dangerous activities) in both photos.
- Both (activities) look (hard/exciting).
- Both photos show (very different climates).
- Well, I can see (two very different places).
- In the first photo/this picture, I can see (a man with a bike) but in the second/that one (the people are climbing a mountain).

2 Paraphrasing

- I don't know the word in English. It's something/a thing you use to (help you climb in the ice).
- I'm not sure of the word in English. It's something you use for (protecting your eyes).

3 Speculating

- (This person/The person in the background) looks as if he/she (is feeling tired).
- One person seems to be (leading).
- In this photo, I think (the man) is probably (in Australia).
- I get the impression that (the main is in a race).
- Perhaps (he's working)./Maybe (they're trying to break a record).
- He/she/it might be …
- He/she/it might have been …

4 Starting a discussion

- Shall I start?
- Would you like to start?
- OK, let's talk/shall we talk about this one?
- Well, I think (working in groups) is very (effective), because (you can learn from other people).

5 Expressing and justifying opinions

- Well, I think (using a computer) can be (dull), because (you can't really communicate with a computer).
- In my opinion, (practical lessons are very effective, because you remember the information more clearly).
- What I mean is (it's difficult to get help if you are working on your own).
- I'm thinking about (people who don't pay attention in a big class).

6 Expressing preferences

- I like (working in small groups) better than (working on my own).
- I (would) prefer (a smaller group) to (a very big group).
- I prefer (using a computer) to (studying from books).
- I'd rather (work on my own) than (be in a class of 40 students).
- If I had to choose, I would (do practical lessons all the time).
- It depends. Sometimes (I like working in small groups) but other times (I like the teacher to explain everything).

7 Involving the other person

- What do you think?
- What's your opinion?
- What about you?
- Do you agree?
- Would you agree with that?
- We haven't talked about this one. What do you think of it?
- Do you think …?
- Which (way of studying) do you think …?
- (This way of studying is boring), don't you think?
- Tell me what you think about (doing experiments in class).
- You've got a different opinion, haven't you?
- And what else?

8 Discussing advantages and disadvantages

- (Using a computer) has a lot of advantages, such as/like (being able to save and revise your work).
- Another advantage is that (you can surf the Internet for information).
- One advantage of (using a library) is that (you have a lot of references to use). On the other hand, (it can sometimes be difficult to find what you want).
- There are some disadvantages to (working in small groups). For example, (one student might talk all the time and dominate the others).
- I think the benefits of (working in groups) outweigh the disadvantages. I mean, (you can get more ideas and learn at your own pace).

9 Agreeing and disagreeing

- Yes, I agree, and … / but …
- I think you're right, but …
- I'm not sure about that. Don't you think …?
- Actually, in my opinion …
- That's a good idea but I prefer …
- I think those are interesting choices but don't you think …
- Y-e-s, but what about …?
- People might like to (have) that but on the other hand …
- It could be (interesting) but I think that … would be even more (fascinating).
- I like that too but I think that I would rather (have) …

10 Reacting to your partner's ideas

- Do you?
- Yes, and … / but …
- But don't you think …?
- Yes, that's a good point. I agree with that.

11 Suggesting

- We could (choose one indoor and one outdoor facility).
- What about (the track)? That would be a good choice for (young people).
- How about (having the theatre and the park)? That way, we could (appeal to lots of different people).

12 Coming to a conclusion

- OK, so which (two) are the best?
- So, have we decided which (two) are best?
- So, are we agreed, (the theatre and the leisure centre would be the most useful)?
- So, we've decided (to choose the park and the fountain).

13 Summarising and reporting a decision

- Well, I chose (the theatre) and (the fountain).
- We both agreed that (the fountain and the leisure centre) would (be the best options).
- We decided on (the track and the theatre).
- We couldn't agree.
- X was in favour of (the fountain) but I thought (the theatre would be more fun).
- Neither of us liked (the fountain).
- So that was the conclusion we reached: (to build the leisure centre and the park).

14 Asking for clarification

- I didn't quite catch that. Could you say it again, please?
- I'm not quite sure what we have to do. Could you repeat that, please?
- Sorry, I don't understand what I have to do. Could you repeat it, please?

15 Checking you have understood

- So you want us to (choose the best options)?
- Do we have to (talk about these pictures)?

16 Giving yourself time to think

- Well, …
- Let me think, …
- So, I think …

17 Interrupting politely

- If I could just add something to that: …
- Could I say something here? …

Unit 2, Speaking (individual long turn) page 21

Candidate B photos, Exercise 5

to make an effort   to climb a mountain   to run uphill
to look hard / exciting / dangerous   to be ambitious
to enjoy a challenge   to like adventure/excitement
a sense of achievement

Unit 5, Speaking (individual long turn) page 59

Candidate B photos, Exercise 4

counter   assistant   cashier
basket   trolley
convenient   self-service
personal/friendly service
to wait until you are served
limited choice of goods/brands
(check-out) tills
a wide range of goods
to queue/stand in line (for service)
to serve yourself
fast/slow service
low/competitive prices
to offer a (20%) discount
out-of-town location
to pay in cash / by cheque /
    by credit card
parking facilities

Examiner's script for Candidate A photos, page 59, Exercise 3

To Candidates A and B:
'I'm going to show each of you two different photographs and I'd like you to talk about them.'

To Candidate A:
'[*Give name*], here are your two photographs [*point to the photos on page 59*]. They show people wearing different styles of clothing. Please let Candidate B have a look at them. I'd like you to compare and contrast these photographs, saying which style of clothing you find more attractive, and why. You have only about a minute for this so don't worry if I interrupt you.'

To Candidate B:
'[*Give name*], which of these styles of clothing do you prefer?'

Unit 6, Speaking (individual long turn) page 70

Candidate B photos, Exercise 3

to pose for a photograph   to record a moment
to smile at the camera   to remind you of a happy time
to be sitting/standing
a/an formal/informal setting   an indoor/outdoor setting
a group of friends   students of a school
to have your arm round sb's shoulder

Examiner's script for Candidate A photos, page 70, Exercise 2

To Candidates A and B:

'I'm going to show each of you two different photographs and I'd like you to talk about them.'

To Candidate A:

'[*Give name*], here are your two photographs [*point to the photos on page 70*]. They show two family events. Please let Candidate B have a look at them. I'd like you to compare and contrast these photographs, saying who you think these people are and why they are celebrating. You have only about a minute for this so don't worry if I interrupt you.'

To Candidate B:

'[*Give name*], do you enjoy family events like these?'

Unit 9, Speaking (individual long turn) page 109

Candidate B photos, Exercise 2

> a UFO   to hover   a flight of stairs   a candlestick
> to be genuine / unconvincing / a hoax / a fake   to use trick photography
> to concoct something in a studio   to have no hard evidence
> to make people believe something   to make things up

Examiner's script for Candidate A photos, page 109, Exercise 1

To Candidates A and B:
'I'm going to show each of you two different photographs and I'd like you to talk about them.'

To Candidate A:
'[*Give name*], here are your two photographs [*point to the photos on page 109*]. They show people who have just found something. Please let Candidate B have a look at them. I'd like you to compare and contrast these photographs, saying where the people are, what you think they have found and how they are feeling. You have only about a minute for this so don't worry if I interrupt you.'

To Candidate B:
'[*Give name*], how would you feel if you found something like this?'

Unit 12, Speaking (individual long turn) page 145

Candidate B photos, Exercise 2

an open-plan office   a workstation
to work in a team
to separate work and home life
support   contact   job security
to work from home   independence
to be freelance/self-employed   flexibility
self-discipline   to be interrupted
to be able to concentrate

Examiner's script for Candidate A photos, page 145, Exercise 1

To Candidates A and B:

'I'm going to show each of you two different photographs and I'd like you to talk about them.'

To Candidate A:

'[*Give name*], here are your two photographs [*point to the photos on page 145*]. They show young people doing work experience. Please let Candidate B have a look at them. I'd like you to compare and contrast these photographs, saying which of these temporary jobs you think offers better preparation for the world of full-time work, and why. You have only about a minute for this so don't worry if I interrupt you.'

To Candidate B:

Examiner's scripts for Candidate B photos and Part 3 tasks

Unit 5, page 59, Exercise 4

To Candidate B:

'[*Give name*], here are your two photographs [*point to the photos on page 203*]. They show two different places to shop. Please let Candidate A have a look at them. I'd like you to compare and contrast these photographs, saying what are the advantages and disadvantages of shopping in the different places. You have only about a minute for this so don't worry if I interrupt you.'

To Candidate A:

'[*Give name*], in which of these places would you rather shop?'

Unit 6, page 70, Exercise 3

To Candidate B:

'[*Give name*], here are your two photographs [*point to the photos on page 204*]. They show different types of group photograph. Please let Candidate A have a look at them. I'd like you to compare and contrast these photographs, saying who you think the people are and why they are posing for these photographs. You have only about a minute for this so don't worry if I interrupt you.'

To Candidate A:

'[*Give name*], do you prefer formal or informal photographs?'

Unit 7, page 82, Exercise 2

'I'd like you to talk about something together for about three minutes. Imagine your local leisure centre is running a programme called "Health matters" to promote regular exercise and improve people's physical and mental health. The programme offers a wide range of activities. These are shown in the photographs [*point to the photos on page 82*]. First, talk to each other and discuss the benefits of each activity. Then choose two activities you would like to sign up for. You have only about three minutes for this, so don't worry if I stop you. Please speak so that I can hear you.'

Unit 8, page 94, Exercise 1

'I'd like you to talk about something together for about three minutes. Two-centre holidays are becoming very popular these days. I'd like you to imagine that you are planning a two-centre holiday. The photographs show some suggested destinations [*point to the photos on page 95*]. First, talk to each other and decide which of these suggestions would provide an interesting and varied holiday. Then decide which two places you would like to visit on your holiday. You have only about three minutes for this, so don't worry if I stop you. Please speak so that I can hear you.'

Unit 9, page 109, Exercise 2

To Candidate B:

'[*Give name*], here are your two photographs [*point to the photos on page 205*]. They show two strange events. Please let Candidate A have a look at them. I'd like you to compare and contrast these photographs, saying who might have taken them and how genuine you think they are. You have only about a minute for this so don't worry if I interrupt you.'

To Candidate A:

'[*Give name*], which photo do you think is most likely to be a fake?'

Unit 10, page 121, Exercise 1

'I'd like you to talk about something together for about three minutes. Imagine that you have been asked to choose the two most important inventions of the 19th and 20th centuries. The photographs show some suggestions [*point to the photos on page 121*]. First, talk to each other about the importance of each invention. Then decide which two have had the greatest influence on our everyday lives. You have only about three minutes for this, so don't worry if I stop you. Please speak so that I can hear you.'

Unit 11, page 133, Exercise 2

'I'd like you to talk about something together for about three minutes. Imagine you have been reading this leaflet entitled "A bright new future for people, animals and the environment" [*point to the leaflet on page 133*]. It contains several suggestions for things you can do to improve the environment for people and animals. First, talk to each other about the different suggestions. Then choose the two which you think are the most practical and effective. You have only about three minutes for this, so don't worry if I stop you. Please speak so that I can hear you.'

Unit 12, page 145, Exercise 2

To Candidate B:

'[*Give name*], here are your two photographs [*point to the photos on page 206*]. They show two different working environments. Please let Candidate A have a look at them. I'd like you to compare and contrast these photographs, saying what are the advantages and disadvantages of working in the environments shown in the photographs. You have only about a minute for this so don't worry if I interrupt you.'

To Candidate A:

'[*Give name*], would you prefer to work in an office or from home?'

Pearson Education Limited
Edinburgh Gate
Harlow
Essex CM20 2JE
England
And Associated Companies throughout the World

www.longman.com

First published 2001
Eleventh impression 2007

ISBN 978-0-582-40575-2

Set in Optima 9.75/11.5 pt

Printed in China GCC/11

Publisher Acknowledgments

The publisher wishes to express thanks and appreciation to the following reporters: Cristina Djivanian, Nora Krichmar (Argentina); Georgia Pappas school, Helen Koumatou school, Kriakos Petropuleas school, Stamatis Papadimitriou school, Zozetta Androulaki, Anna Leventeris, Georgia Zographou (Greece). Arek Tkacz, Agnieszka Tyszkiewicz—Zora (Poland); Tom Fernandez, Lisa Girling, (Spain); Aycil Akalin, Çidem Oral, Nur Sahin (Turkey)

Authors' Acknowledgments

The authors would like to thank Mike Gutteridge and Lucrecia Luque-Mortimer for their invaluable comments and advice. With grateful thanks to Heather Jones and all the team at Harlow, and to Amanda Maris for her helpful suggestions and sheer hard work.

We are grateful to the following for permission to reproduce copyright material: APA Publications UK Limited for an adapted extract from INSIGHT GUIDE TO SARDINIA 1996; Artists & Illustrators Magazine for an extract from the article 'Building light and shade with watercolour washes' by Liz Butler first published in ARTISTS & ILLUSTRATORS MAGAZINE March 2000; Atlantic Syndication Partners for adapted extracts from the articles 'Minimalist' by Natalie Clark from DAILY MAIL 13.10.98, 'Found in the ice after 5,000 years, a hunter (and his hat)' by Ivor Key in DAILY MAIL 26.8.99. 'Enter the lost world of the Ancient Pharoahs' by Rebecca Levene in DAILY MAIL 29.2.00, 'We're following in father's footlights' by Gauanndra Hodge in DAILY MAIL 29.2.00 and 'Where the rich are always ahead' by Barbara McMahon in EVENING STANDARD 23.3.99;H. Bauer Publishing for an adapted extract from 'Open season on the stars, by Andy Coombes in BELLA 27.6.00; Best of British for an adapted extract from 'Rocking all over the world' by Angela Clay in BEST OF BRITISH 10/99; the BBC for an extract adapted from 'Tales from the Bush' by Andy Rouse, published in BBC WILDLIFE Magazine, September 1999; the author Marcus Binney for an adapted extract from the article 'The great wall of England' in HERITAGE Magazine Apr/May 1999; The author, Kathryn Brown for an adapted extract from the article 'Smart Stuff' from 'Your New Look' in SCIENTIFIC AMERICAN Autumn 1999 Vol 3; Cassell Publishers for a simplified extract from 'The Coiled Serpent' by P. Whitfield from OUR MYSTERIOUS PLANET 1990; Classic FM for an adapted extract from the article on 'Hilary Hahn' from CLASSIC FM website; Express Newspapers Plc for adapted extracts from the articles 'My Sporting Life – Tim Vincent' by Anna Wright in SUNDAY EXPRESS 23.4.00 and 'Go upstairs and tidy your room' from SUNDAY EXPRESS MAGAZINE 19.3.00 (c) Express Newspapers; the author, Christine Fagg, for an adapted extract from the article 'Fairest Land' from MONARCH AIRLINES magazine Summer 2000; Financial Times Limited for an adapted extract from the article 'The social life of chimps' by Clive Cookson, published in FINANCIAL TIMES WEEKEND 19th-20th June 1999; Gruner & Jahr Ltd for adapted extract from 'Wright Brothers' in FOCUS March 2000; Guardian Newspapers Ltd. for adapted extracts from the articles 'How to get through your first day in the job' by Hilary Freeman in THE GUARDIAN 17.6.00. 'Putting Classroom Before Catwalk' by Clare Longrigg in THE OBSERVER 3.1.97, 'Bones of crocodile-like creature confirm that arctic was once a hot spot' by Tim Radford from THE GUARDIAN 18.12.98, 'FT phone home' by John Grace from GUARDIAN EDUCATION 1.6.99 and 'Shoppers upset by being spoilt for choice' by Graham Diggines in THE GUARDIAN 24.4.00; the author, Greg Hadfield, for an adapted extract from the article 'My son's just a normal healthy computer genius' in SUNDAY TIMES 25.4.99 www.schoolsnet.com; The Independent Syndication for an adapted extract from the article '3 Careers' by Anna Melville-James in THE INDEPENDENT; 'Wish you were here...? The fantasy builder' by Helen Foster in INDEPENDENT ON SUNDAY 1.8.99 the author, Patrick Joseph, for an adapted extract from the article 'Living in Technology' SCIENTIFIC AMERICAN PRESENTS; KnightRidder.com for adapted extracts from the articles 'Parent-teen relationships suffer from lack of communication', 'Affordable ways to spice up your life' by Sierra Santos, 'Are video games a negative influence on children' by Sumir Kataria and 'The good, bad and ugly of relationships' by Sandy Chang (c) 2000 All Rights Reserved. www.Bay.Area.com; the authors Jerome Boyd Maunsell and Alain de Botton for an extract based the article 'How I write' Alain de Botton/Jerome Boyd Maunsell in THE CONSOLATIONS OF PHILOSOPHY published by Hamish Hamilton; National Geographic Society for an extract adapted from the article 'Epic of Survival of Shackleton' by Caroline Alexander, published in NATIONAL GEOGRAPHIC, November 1998; National Magazine Company for adapted text from the article 'Fitness of purpose' from FOCUS; News International Syndications for adapted extracts from 'Superwoofers' by Flynn Sarler in THE SUNDAY TIMES MAGAZINE 19.7.98, 'Tree Tops' in THE TIMES 15.4.00, 'How kids can get their kicks' by Arabella Warner in THE

TIMES WEEKEND 22.4.00, and 'Muzak' by Candida Crewe in THE TIMES 27.5.00; Telegraph Group Limited for an adapted extract from an article by Lesley Graner in The Daily Telegraph 9.12.95, adapted extracts from the articles 'Someone to watch over you' by Matthew Day in DAILY TELEGRAPH 21.5.96,'The way it was' in DAILY TELEGRAPH 21.5.96. 'Is it a shop?' by Jacqui Swift in DAILY TELEGRAPH 6.11.99; extract from a case history interview conducted by Clare Thomson in the travel section of THE SUNDAY TELEGRAPH 4.6.00; and 'Stressed out' by Victoria Stanley in DAILY TELEGRAPH 25.9.00, (c) Telegraph Group Ltd; Travellerseye Ltd. for an extract adapted from 'Frigid Women' by Sue and Victoria Riches (www.travellerseye.com); Wanderlust Magazine for an adapted extract from 'Gateway to the global village' by Matt Rudd, published in WANDERLUST August/September 1999; YHA (England and Wales) Lid for an adapted extract from the article 'Hanging out with the wild ones' by Stuart Morris in TRIANGLE No.32 Spring/Summer 1995.

In some instances we have been unable to trace the owners of copyright material and would appreciate any information which would enable us to do so.

We are grateful to the following for permission to reproduce copyright photos:
Ace Photo Agency for 28 middle(Mugshots), 33 top right(John Guidi), 37(Kevin Phillips), 43(Ian McKinnell), 45 middle(Gabe Palmer), 45 top right(Richard Walker), 46 right(Roger Howard), 46 left(Roger Howard), 60 bottom(Aitch), 70 top(Roger Howard), 82 top right(OMG), 84-85 background(Steel Photography), 91 background(Megasnaps), 95 UK(Pawel Libera), 95 Europe(bottom)(Roger Howard), 95 Middle East(Mauritius), 96-97 background(Peter Adams), 121 bottom middle left(Chris Middlebrook), 121 bottom left(PLI), 140 bottom right(Mauritus), 141 top(Kevin Phillips), 175 top right(Dave Moore), 204 top(John Guidi), 206 bottom(Mugshots); Action Plus for 25 bottom right(David Davies), 82 bottom right, 83 left(Glyn Kirk), 83 bottom right(Steve Bardens), 84 bottom(Mike Hewitt); Adams Picture Library for 82 bottom left, 141 middle right; Carlos Reyes-Manzo/Andes Press Agency for 47; Heather Angel/Natural Visions for 128 bottom; Art Directors & TRIP Photo Library for 21 bottom(Eric Smith), 34 top(F Good), 41(S Grant), 54 middle(P Kwan), 55(P Kwan), 55 background(P Kwan), 82 middle right(B Gibbs), 91 bottom right(J Ringland); Barnabys Picture Library for 28 right(H K Maitland), 82top right(Brian Gibbs), 141 background(H K Maitland), 147; Gareth Boden for 63 top, 63 bottom, 67, 87, 116 bottom, 116 top left, 119, 121 middle left, 121 bottom right, 121 top right, 133 middle left, 175 bottom right; John Birdsall for 31 bottom; Bridgeman Art Library for 10 bottom right (©Ex-Edward James Foundation, Sussex, UK, 10 bottom left(Southampton City Art Gallery, Hampshire); Britain on View for 26 right(Brian Boyd), 26 left; Britstock-IFA for 133 bottom right(Comnet); Bubbles Photolibrary for 70 bottom(Jennie Woodcock); BUNAC for 144; Camera Press for 22 bottom(Stewart Mark), 91 top right(Cyril Delettre), 107(Henry Gris), 111 background(Vienna Report); Trevor Clifford for 174 top; Collections for 173 left(Anthea Sieveking); Colorsport for 83 top right; Corbis for 141 bottom right(Neil Rabinowitz); The Daily Telegraph for 54 top right; Dyson for 121 top left; English Heritage Photo Library for 113 top, 113 bottom; Greg Evans International for 25 bottom middle, 45 top left, 82 middle left, 90 bottom, 97, 143; Mary Evans Picture Library for 125, 205 right; Format Photographers for 28 left(Ulrike Preuss), 133 middle right(Melanie Friend); Fortean Picture Library for 205 left; Friends of the Earth for 133 top right(Tim O'Leary); GeoScience Features Picture Library for 112 bottom, 112 top; Ronald Grant Archive for 4, 5 below, 118; Sally & Richard Greenhill for 145 top; Robert Harding Picture Library for 22 top(Explorer), 25 bottom left(Jay Thomas), 48(I Talby), 91 bottom left(Philippe Brylak), 141 bottom left; Holt Studios International for 175 top middle; David Hoffman Photolibrary for124 right; Image Bank for 5 background(Thierry Dosogne), 56(Jason Homa), 128 top left(William Lombardo), 134 top right(A T Willett), 175 top left, 203 top; The Kobal Collection for 5 top(Universal); Frank Lane Picture Agency for 133 middle(R P Lawrence), 133 top left(David Hosking), 175 middle (Dembinski/Mike Barlow); Lebrecht Collection/NL for 146 bottom; Lucas Film Ltd for 104 middle right(Ronald Grant Archive); Metropolitan Police Museum for 122 top right, 122 bottom right, 122 top left; Moviestore Collection for 32 right, 104 middle left, 104 bottom right; NHPA for 96 bottom(B & C Alexander), 114(Yves Lanceau); Natural History Museum, London for 106 top right; Newham Leisure Services for 45 bottom right; News Team International for 18 top(Mick Scott); Oxford Scientific Films for 21 top(Ben Osborne), 129(Martyn Colbeck), 130 top(Konrad Wothe), 131(Animals Animals); PA Photos for 29, 57 bottom(Matthew Fearn), 111(EPA), 121 middle right(EPA), 134 bottom right(EPA), 137; Photofusion for 31 middle right(Liam Bailey), 123 bottom left(Bob Watkins), 122 background(Ray Roberts); Pictor International for 31 top, 33 top middle, 33 bottom middle, 54 top left, 69, 79 background, 85 top, 95 USA, 102 left, 104 top, 117 background, 121 bottom middle right, 140 bottom left, 140 top right, 175 bottom left; Pictures Colour Library for 92; Planet Earth Pictures for 128 top right; Popperfoto for 8 left, 18 bottom, 32 left; 47 background(Paul Hackett); PowerStock/Zefa for 25 top left; PYMCA for 13(Darren Regnier); Quadrant Picture Library for 19; Rex Features for 6, 71 left, 106 bottom right, 109 top(Sipa-Press/Hegazy-Benami-Media), 109 bottom(Peter Kemp); Royal Geographical Society for 17(F Hurley); St Edmund's College, Ware for 173 right; Science Photo Library for 124 left(Astrid & Hanns-Frieder); Scott Polar Research Institute for 16; Snow + Rock for 116 top right; Frank Spooner Pictures for 72 left(King-Liaison), 72 top right, 72 bottom right; Sporting Pictures (UK) for 23 top, 84 top, 85 middle, 85 bottom; Stockfile for 132(Steven Behr), 202 top(Steven Behr); Stock Market Photo Agency for 34 bottom, 133 bottom middle, 140 top left, 141 middle left(Peter Beck), 204 bottom(John Henley); Stone for 20(Ted Wood), 25 middle(Ted Wood), 25 top right(Paul Harris), 40 middle(Bob Krist), 42 top(David Young-Wolff), 44(Oliver Benn), 54 bottom(Tony Arruza), 59 right(Dave Nagel), 59 left(Philip Lee Harvey), 71 right(William S Helsel), 73 background(Wayne Eastep), 78(Lori Adamski Peek), 86(Gregg Adams), 90 top(Chris Harvey), 91 top left(Bob Thomas), 93(Alan Smith), 95 Europe (top)(Jess Stock), 95 Africa(Chris Harvey), 95 S.America(Stuart Westmorland), 96 top(Renee Lynn), 99(Frank Herholdt), 104 bottom(Peter Pearson), 106 top left(Hugh Sitton), 106 bottom left(Richard Elliott), 120 middle(Marc Dolphin), 121 middle(Paul Dance), 129 background(Renee Lynn), 134 top left(Ralph H Wetmore II), 134 bottom left(Jeremy Walker), 135 background(World Perspectives), 175 bottom middle(Robert A Mitchell), 202 bottom(Jess Stock), 206 top(Bruce Ayres); Tate Gallery for 10 top; Telegraph Colour Library for 5 background(Robert Clare), 8 bottom(Benelux Press), 16-17 background(Jeri Gleiter), 33 top left(Doug Corrance), 35 background(L Lefkowitz), 40 top (Peter Adams), 41 background(Mike Yamashita), 42 bottom(F.P.G ©R Chapple), 58(Rob Brimson), 61 background(FF), 74(V.C.L), 79(Antonio Mo), 95 Australia(Gary Bell), 105 background(B & M Productions), 112 middle(Planet Earth/Ken Lucas), 130 bottom(F.P.G ©C Roessler), 203 bottom(Ian McKinnell); Topham Picturepoint for 40 bottom, 45 bottom left, 57 top(Matthew Fearn), 133 bottom left, 146 middle; UCLES EFL for 9; John Walmsley for 23 bottom, 31 middle left, 33 bottom left, 33 bottom right, 35, 81; Wanderlust for 174 bottom(Paul Morrison); Elizabeth Whiting Associates for 60 top; Janine Wiedel for 145 background, 146 top.

Picture research by Louise Edgeworth.

Illustrations by Clive Goodyer, Peter Massey (c/o Zantium), Stephen May, Richard Morris, Mike Phillips (c/o Beehive Illustration, Jeremy Sancha (c/o Central Illustration Agency)
Cover photo (c) Telegraph Colour Library
Designed by Pentacor plc, High Wycombe, Bucks
Project Managed by Amanda Maris